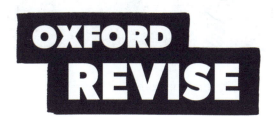

Oxford Revise

AQA GCSE

ENGLISH LANGUAGE

COMPLETE REVISION AND PRACTICE

Series Editor: Jennifer Webb

Steve Eddy

Graham Elsdon

Jennifer Webb

OXFORD
UNIVERSITY PRESS

Contents

 Shade in each level of the circle as you feel more confident and ready for your exam.

Exam Knowledge 64-175

The key requirements of the exam and revision guidance for each question.

How to use this book

Oxford Revise AQA GCSE English Language is divided into two parts:

1 Concept Knowledge
2 Exam Knowledge

 Part 1: Concept Knowledge

This section covers the key concepts and devices that you need to revise going into your exams.

Each topic includes Knowledge Organisers and Retrieval questions to support you to revise effectively.

The topics covered in this section include: texts and their meaning, figurative language, rhetorical language, character, setting, and mood, attitudes and perspectives, sentence forms, narrative structure, and structuring an argument.

Part 2: Exam Knowledge

This section takes you through all the questions you will encounter in Paper 1 and Paper 2 of your AQA GCSE English Language exam, following the Knowledge, Retrieval, Practice approach. It includes an overview of each paper, with guidance on each question and sample questions and answers. You will then check your knowledge through the Retrieval questions before moving onto the Practice exam-style questions.

The exam will measure how you have achieved against assessment objectives (AOs). In the Paper overview spreads in the Exam Knowledge section, you will see which AOs are tested in each question. Go to the back of the book (page 200) for a list of the Assessment objectives.

A Source Bank at the end of the book provides the source texts in the style of the exam and they are explored in questions in the Practice section.

On the following page, you will learn more about the Oxford Revise three-step approach to revision: Knowledge, Retrieval and Practice.

How to use this book

This book uses a three-step approach to revision: **Knowledge**, **Retrieval**, and **Practice**. It is important that you do all three; they work together to make your revision effective.

 **Knowledge**

Knowledge comes first. Each chapter starts with a **Knowledge Organiser**. These are clear, easy-to-understand, concise summaries of the content that you need to know for your exam. The information is organised to show how one idea flows into the next so you can learn how everything is tied together.

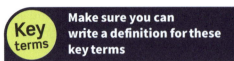
Key terms — Make sure you can write a definition for these key terms

The **Key terms** box highlights the key words and phrases you need to know, remember, and be able to use confidently.

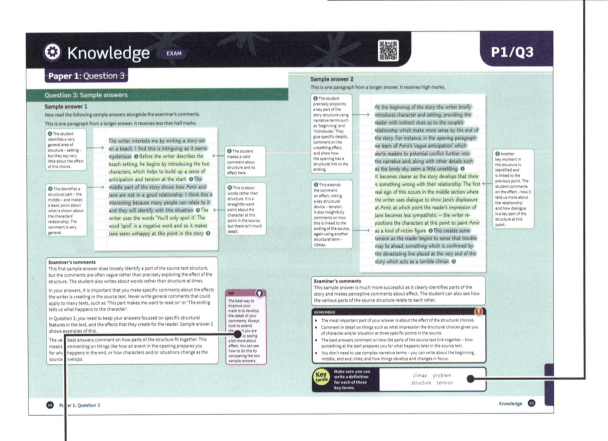

TIP

The **Tip** box offers you helpful advice and guidance to aid your revision and help you to understand key concepts and question requirements.

Additional features

QUESTION CONNECTION

The **Question Connection** box offers a reference to a related exam question where you could practise or include that piece of knowledge.

LINK

The **Link** box offers a reference to a related topic or piece of knowledge that you could refer to for an exam question.

REMEMBER

The **Remember** box offers useful guidance and a summary of the key points and guidance covered in each exam unit.

Retrieval

The **Retrieval questions** help you learn and quickly recall the information you've acquired. These are short questions and answers about the content in the Knowledge Organiser you have just revised. Cover up the answers with some paper and write down as many answers as you can from memory. Check back to the Knowledge Organiser for any you got wrong, then cover the answers and attempt all the questions again until you can answer *all* the questions correctly.

Make sure you revisit the Retrieval questions on different days to help them stick in your memory. You need to write down the answers each time, or say them out loud, for your revision to be effective.

Previous questions

Each chapter also has some **Retrieval questions** from **previous chapters**. Answer these to see if you can remember the content from the earlier chapters. If you get the answers wrong, go back and do the Retrieval questions for the earlier chapters again.

Practice

Once you are confident with the Knowledge Organiser and Retrieval questions, you can move on to the final stage: **Practice**.

Each chapter has **exam-style questions** to help you apply all the knowledge you have learnt.

Answers and Glossary

You can scan the QR code at any time to access sample answers and mark schemes for the exam-style questions, a glossary containing definitions of the key terms, as well as further revision support at go.oup.com/OR/GCSE/A/EngLang

EXAM TIP

Exam tips show you how to interpret the questions, provide guidance on how to answer them, and give advice on how to secure as many marks as possible. Guidance is also offered on how to approach different command words.

 # Knowledge   CONCEPT

1 Texts and their meaning

What are texts and how do they create meaning?

It is important to establish the text form, **audience** and **purpose** of any text, as these will influence the language, style, and structure.

Text forms

All texts are either **fiction** or **non-fiction** and they can be further divided into different forms of text. The text form refers to the style or type of text, such as a short story or speech. You will be asked to comment on and write a range of text forms in your English Language exam.

QUESTION CONNECTION

You could comment on text form in Paper 2 Questions 3 and 4.

- In Paper 1, the source text to comment on will be prose fiction (a story written from a writer's imagination). The text you will write will be fiction (either a description or narrative).

- In Paper 2, there will be two source texts to comment on and both will be non-fiction. They might include one or more of the following forms:

| articles | reports | essays | accounts |

| letters | diaries | speeches | travel writing |

The text you will write in Paper 2 will be one of the following forms:

| letter | speech | article | essay |

Audience

The audience is the intended reader of a text or listener of a speech. Who the audience is will shape the text's language, content, and the way it is presented to the reader. Look at the examples below.

Text form: A personal letter
Audience: One person
← This will likely have a relaxed tone, mentioning details known only to the writer and the reader.

Text form: A speech
Audience: Multiple people
← This is likely to be more formal and well presented. However, the language used in a speech for children would be different to the language used in a speech for MPs, so it is important to establish the specific audience.

Purpose

The purpose of a text is the reason it is written, based on what the writer wants to achieve. It will also influence its content and how it is presented and written. One of the primary purposes of fiction is to engage readers in the characters and their story. Some of the purposes of non-fiction are below.

> **QUESTION CONNECTION**
>
> When writing a response to Paper 2 Question 5, you will need to give careful thought to the purpose of the text, as this will shape the language, content, and structure of your writing.

| to inform | to instruct | to argue a case | to persuade | to advise | to entertain |

Explicit meaning

This refers to information that is openly and clearly stated. The reader does not have to work it out or interpret it in any way.

> Toby was frightened of the dark.

> **QUESTION CONNECTION**
>
> The exam section explains how you will need to find explicit meaning for Paper 1 Question 1 (see pages 66-71) and both *explicit* and *implicit* meaning for Paper 2 Question 1 (see pages 120-125).

> This sentence is a clear statement. The information is **explicit**.

Implicit meaning

This refers to information that must be deduced from clues in the text. The writer could be implying, hinting, or suggesting something. The reader must pick up on those clues, make conclusions, and work out what the **inference** is.

> 'Could you leave a light on?' said Toby nervously.

> In this sentence, the reader can work out that Toby is scared of the dark, as he wants the light on and was nervous. The information is **implicit**.

Connotation

A **connotation** is a common association or link that a word or phrase might carry, in addition to its main explicit meaning.

> As they approached the house, night suddenly fell and the moon disappeared.

> The ideas of dark nights and moonlight have connotations of uncertainty and danger, because of links with gothic stories.

Knowledge CONCEPT

1 Texts and their meaning

What effects do writers create in different texts?

The text below is a non-fiction text and is a piece of travel writing, which might be included as a source text in Paper 2. Its purpose is typically to engage and entertain an audience who are curious and keen to share the writer's experiences of the place described.

Notice how the writer conveys information both explicitly and implicitly, using connotations to add subtle suggestions.

Extract 1: 'Through the Pyrenees on the little yellow train' by Gavin Bell

This extract below is one of a series of newspaper articles published in the *Telegraph* about rail journeys. The writer describes travelling through the mountains of France.

The train I board has a choice of four closed and two open-air carriages, all painted bright yellow, **1** and as the sun is beaming from clear blue skies I opt for one of the latter. With a shrill whistle we are off, **2** quickly
5 reaching our cruising **3** speed of about 15mph as we rock and roll past Vauban's battlements.

This is the way to travel through tumultuous scenery, at a gentle pace with time to gaze on fast flowing streams, deep forests, and dizzying gorges. Mountain villages are
10 etched on the skyline, clinging to impossible slopes **4**, their church towers like rockets poised to take off **5** for the heavens.

The eyes are constantly drawn upwards to forests in the sky, and convoluted valleys snaking up to barren
15 peaks, **6** a grand, sweeping symphony of nature. At times the railway seems to defy gravity, and when we halt there is no rumbling of diesel engines, only silence broken by the rushing of a river below.

1 Connotation

The colour of the train sounds happy and positive: bright yellow has connotations of sunshine or a new day to begin the journey.

3 Implicit meaning

This suggests that the journey will be at a continuous pace, *implying* that it will be easy and relaxing from this point.

5 Connotation

Rockets taking off have connotations of being otherworldly.

2 Explicit meaning

An *explicit* statement. The use of an adjective to describe the whistle as 'shrill' and the short sentence 'we are off' reflects how the train leaves the station quickly.

4 Implicit meaning

This implies that houses are built on steep slopes, but by describing them as being 'etched on the skyline', it suggests first that they look beautiful rather than being unsafe.

6 Implicit meaning

These details *imply* that there is a lot to look at in the mountains, both high and low, as eyes are being drawn to look.

Another form of text that might be included in Paper 2 is a news article. Whereas a news *report* is likely to focus mainly on explicit facts and information, the purpose of a news *article* is to convey the writer's own opinions and ideas.

In the news article below, the writer expresses an opinion about the constant updates he has to download to his new smartphone. He presents his ideas and feelings in a humorous way using vivid imagery to convey meaning and to entertain his readers. The writer also uses both implicit and explicit meaning to express his point of view.

Extract 2: 'Apple's software updates are like changing the water in a fish tank. I'd rather let the fish die' by Charlie Brooker

This extract is an article from the *Guardian* about one person's view of software updates.

❶ Explicit meaning

An *explicit* statement. It shows his opinion of updates clearly.

❸ Implicit meaning

For comic effect, this *implies* that the phone has feelings, and that the update is unnecessary.

Updates are awful. ❶ All you want to do is watch TV and rot in your own filth. ❷ Instead you spend the evening backing up your phone, downloading a gigantic file and sitting around while your phone undergoes an intense psychological makeover, ❸ at the end of which it may
5 or may not function. Often, it takes an hour or more. Fiddly, time-consuming admin – it's like having to change the water in a fish tank. … it's why I don't have an aquarium. I'd rather let the fish die. ❹

❷ A direct address encourages readers to identify with the writer. This also includes exaggeration for comic purposes.

❹ Exaggerated comic comparison and humorous confession.

TIP

When you are reading any non-fiction text, always think about what effects the writer is trying to create in order to fulfil the purpose of the text and to make it relevant and appealing to a specific audience.

Knowledge

CONCEPT

1 Texts and their meaning

How can I write about different types of text?

When writing about a fiction text, think carefully about the **genre** of the text. There are many different genres, such as: horror, romance, fantasy, science-fiction, mystery, thriller. Some stories are more than one genre. The genre of the text will help you to identify the type of effects that the writer is trying to create.

In fiction, writers often convey implicit information ('showing' the reader) rather than conveying explicit information ('telling' the reader). Look at the dialogue below from the novel: *The Unlikely Pilgrimage of Harold Fry* by Rachel Joyce.

Extract 3: *The Unlikely Pilgrimage of Harold Fry* by Rachel Joyce

> This extract is from a novel, and is about Maureen and her husband, Harold, as they eat breakfast. Harold has received a letter.

'Well?' said Maureen again.

'Good lord. It's from Queenie Hennessy.'

Maureen speared a nugget of butter with her knife and flattened it the length of her toast. 'Queenie who?'

5 'She worked at the brewery. Years ago. Don't you remember?'

Maureen shrugged. 'I don't see why I should. I don't know why I'd remember someone from years ago. Could you pass the jam?'

'She was in finances. She was very good.'

'That's the marmalade, Harold. Jam is red. If you look at things before you pick

10 them up, you'll find it helps.'

If you were asked how the writer presents the character of Maureen, a sample response might be like the one below. Notice how this focuses on implicit meaning to suggest Maureen's mood and character, rather than explicit meaning.

> Maureen speaks abruptly to her husband, indicating her impatience with him: 'Well?', 'Queenie who?' ❶ The use of the verb 'shrugged' implies her lack of interest ❷ in something that seems important to him, implied by his exclamation 'Good lord'. The description of Maureen's actions also portrays her as angry and perhaps aggressive. ❸
> She 'spears' the butter and 'flattened' it, bringing in connotations of war and weapons. ❹ This impression is strengthened by her sarcastically stating the obvious — that 'jam is red', and advising Harold ironically that 'you'll find it helps'. This creates tension between the characters, and leaves the reader unsure of what caused this. ❺

❶ Analysis of what is *implied*, followed by evidence.

❸ Statement leads on to another aspect of the dialogue.

❺ Summarises the effect.

❷ Focuses on what one word *implies*.

❹ Evidence followed by what it *implies*.

TIP

Try to keep your quotations short and embed them within your sentences, rather than copying out large chunks of text.

When writing about a non-fiction source text, think carefully about the writer's purpose and the effects they are aiming to create for the reader. Then look closely at *how* exactly the writer conveys meaning. You may wish to draw out what is explicitly stated and what the reader can **infer** (work out).

For example, for Extract 1 on page 4, if you had to explore how the writer creates a beautiful and otherworldy impression of his train travel through the mountains of France, you could focus on the details and language in the text. A sample response might be like the one below. As well as entertaining the reader, the writer is giving detailed information to convey the positive experience he felt as a traveller. This creates a powerful effect for the reader.

❶ Introduces the idea of a new day with embedded quotations.

❸ Shows how the sense of old-fashioned, traditional travel is introduced and continued through the passage.

❺ Builds up to an inference that nature is beautiful in an otherworldly way.

The author creates a cheerful impression of the train, with bright yellow 'open-air carriages' reinforced by the 'clear blue skies', suggesting the start of a new day. **❶** He explicitly states that 'with a shrill whistle, we are off', which suggests quick, easy, and exciting travel, as the sentence is short and the whistle is 'shrill'. **❷** A train whistle also implies old-fashioned train travelling, giving a sense of comfort and familiarity, which is reinforced by words such as 'cruising' and 'gentle pace' to describe the journey. **❸** The writer describes the view as a 'sweeping symphony of nature', looking up at 'barren peaks' and down at 'convoluted valleys'. This implies that the view is going up and down, and is beautiful, like different notes of music that create a symphony. **❹** This is reinforced as the railway seems to 'defy gravity' and towers are 'like rockets poised to take off', implying the beauty is otherworldly, in the same way space is. **❺**

❷ Includes a quotation and an explicit statement.

❹ The reader infers information from descriptions.

⚙ Knowledge CONCEPT

1 Texts and their meaning

How can I write in a particular text form?

In Paper 1 Question 5, you will write a fictional text of your own (a description or a narrative). In Paper 2 Question 5, you will be asked to write a non-fiction text, such as a speech, article, or letter.

Newspaper or magazine articles

You might be told about the readership of your article. It could be 'for your school magazine', in which case you would need to appeal to teenagers but without alienating parents, governors, or teachers. This means writing in a slightly informal way, with some direct address to teenagers.

> **TIP**
> Remember that an article has to be engaging and can include personal opinions.

Letters

A letter might, for example, be addressed to the head teacher and argue a case. Think carefully about how you open the letter, how you structure the paragraphs, and the most appropriate way of signing off.

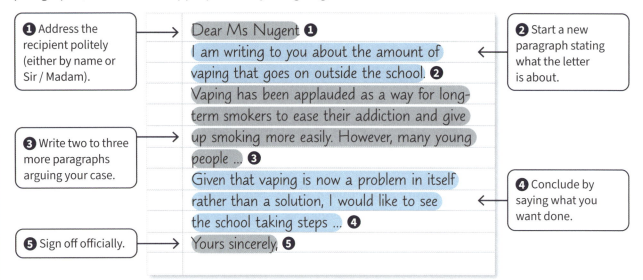

❶ Address the recipient politely (either by name or Sir / Madam).

❸ Write two to three more paragraphs arguing your case.

❺ Sign off officially.

Dear Ms Nugent **❶**

I am writing to you about the amount of vaping that goes on outside the school. **❷**

Vaping has been applauded as a way for long-term smokers to ease their addiction and give up smoking more easily. However, many young people ... **❸**

Given that vaping is now a problem in itself rather than a solution, I would like to see the school taking steps ... **❹**

Yours sincerely, **❺**

❷ Start a new paragraph stating what the letter is about.

❹ Conclude by saying what you want done.

Speeches

A speech could be aimed at a particular audience. It should be fairly formal and polite but could still include some humour and anecdotes (short stories about personal experiences). It could use personal pronouns to include the audience.

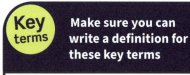

I'm delighted to see you all here. I'll be talking about a subject that affects us all, but especially young people: the environment.

> **Key terms**
> Make sure you can write a definition for these key terms
>
> audience   connotation
> explicit   fiction   genre
> implicit   infer   inference
> non-fiction
> purpose   text form

Retrieval CONCEPT 1

Use the following questions to check your understanding of the knowledge covered in this section. Then cover the answers column with a piece of paper and write down as many as you can. Check and repeat.

	Questions	Answers
1	All texts are either fiction or non-fiction. True or false?	True.
2	What type of source text will you be given to read and comment on in Paper 1?	Prose fiction – an extract from a novel or short story.
3	Name at least four different types of non-fiction text forms that you might be given to read and comment on in Paper 2.	Possible answers include: report; travel writing; biography or autobiography; diary; speech; letter; argument; article.
4	Name at least four different genres of fiction.	Possible answers include: science fiction; fantasy; romance; historical fiction; thriller; mystery; horror.
5	What are the three key features to identify in a text and why are they important?	Text form, audience, purpose. They strongly influence the structure, language, and style of a text.
6	Name at least four possible purposes of a non-fiction text.	Possible answers include: to inform; to entertain; to persuade; to instruct; to argue; to explain.
7	What is explicit information?	Information that is clearly stated. The reader does not have to infer the meaning.
8	Which of these sentences contains an implicit meaning, and what is that meaning? (a) Cricket: just when you think the game has to be nearly over, it goes on – and on, and on. (b) Rugby is a contact sport.	Sentence (a): it implies that cricket is boring.
9	What does *infer* mean?	To work out meaning that is only hinted at, rather than explicitly stated.
10	Why is it important to think about audience when writing a text?	The audience are the people you hope will read your text or listen to your speech. You need to write in a way that is appropriate and appealing to your audience.
11	What is the connotation of a word or phrase?	It is the additional meaning that it commonly carries, as well as its main, explicit meaning.
12	What might be an appropriate way of signing off a letter to a head teacher or school governor?	Yours sincerely; Kind regards; Regards.

Put paper here

⚙ Knowledge   CONCEPT

2 Figurative language

What is figurative language?

Figurative language uses descriptive words and phrases, such as **similes** and **metaphors**, to convey meaning imaginatively rather than just literally.

> **QUESTION CONNECTION**
>
> You will have to comment on the effect of language features, including figurative language in Paper 1 Question 2 and Paper 2 Question 3. You may also use figurative language in the writing tasks in Paper 1 Question 5 and Paper 2 Question 5.

Simile

Similes create an image in the reader's mind by directly comparing something with something else that it somehow resembles. They always use comparison words, such as 'like', 'as', 'as if' or 'than'.

| The child wriggled like a worm. | Her smile was as wide as the desert sky. | He ran desperately, as if pursued by a pack of wolves. |

Metaphor

Metaphors, like similes, compare two or more things. However, instead of using comparison words, such as 'like' or 'as', they describe things as if they actually *are* something else.

| The road was a ribbon of moonlight. | He barked a command and they all stood to attention. | The dark pathway snakes into the distance. |

A metaphor (or simile) may create meaning in more than one way. A 'dark pathway' that 'snakes' could be long and winding, like the body of a snake. It could also be secretive and unpredictable like a snake. Both ideas imply a sense of danger and uncertainty in where the path might be heading.

Extended metaphor

Extended metaphors takes the comparison of two ideas a step further, creating further similarities. They can use the same idea several times in a sentence, in a paragraph, or across a text.

| The company's mountain of debt proved too steep to climb. | Swept along on the tide of her enthusiasm, I found myself washed up on strange shores. | Life is a long and twisting road. Sometimes the going is rough, sometimes easy, and sometimes you get to a crossroads where you don't know which way to go. |

Symbolism

Symbolism is the use of a simple image to represent something more than its literal meaning. Symbols usually represent a complex or abstract idea. Many symbols can represent more than one idea, like the eagle example below.

> A rose with thorns is often used to symbolise love, but also the pain it can bring.

> An eagle soaring high could either symbolise freedom, as it flies free, or power and dominance, as it preys on other animals.

Personification

Personification is when something non-human or abstract is described as if it has human qualities.

> The house scowled unwelcomingly on all who approached it.

> The sun smiled through the stormy clouds.

> Love comes to your door when you've given up waiting.

Pathetic fallacy

Pathetic fallacy is when something non-human (often in the natural world) is given human emotions.

> Furious waves tossed our little boat without mercy.

> Mount Everest jealously guards its summit from the unprepared.

> The storm raged around the house, determined to do damage.

2 Figurative language

What are the effects of figurative language?

Figurative language brings writing to life by appealing to the reader's imagination. It describes something imaginatively by drawing on its similarities with something else. It is important when analysing figurative language to focus on what the imagery has in common with the thing it is describing, and what the effect of that is.

Writers often use figurative language to create an overall impression, for example, of a setting or person.

Read the extracts and annotations on these pages, which highlight the writers' use of figurative language in the texts. The first extract uses figurative language when describing how tractors are demolishing farmland.

TIP

When writing about the writer's use of figurative language in the exam, you must do more than just 'spot' examples. You need to explain how it affects the reader and how each example suggests further qualities or ideas.

❶ Metaphor and simile

'Crawlers' and 'crawled' metaphorically describe the tractors as being animal or insect-like, which is reinforced by the simile 'like insects'. This makes them seem relentless and lacking in human sympathy.

❸ Metaphor

The words 'snub-nosed' and 'sticking their snouts into it' are features and images of pigs, digging down into the earth and searching in the soil for food, which suggests the tractors are greedy, only focusing on getting the crops and making money.

Extract 1: *The Grapes of Wrath* by John Steinbeck

This extract is from a novel set in America during the Great Depression and focuses on the poverty of farmers. It describes how tractors are demolishing the farmland.

The tractors came over the roads and into the fields, great crawlers moving like insects, having the incredible strength of insects. They crawled ❶ over the ground, laying the track and rolling on it and picking it up. Diesel
5 tractors, puttering while they stood idle; they thundered when they moved, ❷ and then settled down to a droning roar. Snub-nosed monsters, raising the dust and sticking their snouts into it, ❸ straight down the country, across the country, through fences, through
10 dooryards, in and out of gullies in straight lines.

❷ Personification

The verb 'thundered' implies the tractors are loud, powerful, and threatening. The phrase 'they thundered when they moved' implies that they have minds, but still no concern for the farms and features of the landscape that they destroy.

The figurative language in the extract suggests that the tractors represent a powerful, greedy, inhuman force that does not consider the natural environment. The writer does this by comparing the movement of the mechanical tractors to the relentless, single-minded activity of insects or animals that destroy and devour the landscape as they look for food.

The next extract is from *Great Expectations* and describes the strange, unwelcoming room that Miss Havisham resides in. The writer uses figurative language to show the gloomy, desolate atmosphere of the room, focusing on the fire and tablecloth.

❶ Pathetic fallacy

The fire is 'more disposed to' (meaning more willing to) go out rather than burn up. It suggests the fire has feelings.

❸ Metaphor

The candles in the candelabra are described as 'wintry branches' (i.e. bare branches). This description contributes to the unwelcoming atmosphere of the room, as wintry branches give the impression of cold discomfort outside, rather than being inside in the warm.

❺ Simile

Describing the centrepiece as 'like a black fungus' makes it seem as if there is something rotten and unhealthy about the room.

Extract 2: *Great Expectations* by Charles Dickens

> A young boy, Pip, is visiting the unwelcoming home of the elderly Miss Havisham. He describes the visit years later from the perspective of his adult self.

A fire had been lately kindled in the damp old-fashioned grate, and it was more disposed to go out than to burn up, ❶ and the reluctant ❷ smoke which hung in the room seemed colder than the clearer air – like our own

5 marsh mist. Certain wintry branches of candles ❸ on the high chimney-piece faintly lighted the chamber; or it would be more expressive to say, faintly troubled its darkness. ❹

[*There is a table in the centre of the room.*]

10 … it was so heavily overhung with cobwebs that its form was quite undistinguishable; and, as I looked along the yellow expanse out of which I remember its seeming to grow, like a black fungus, ❺ I saw speckle-legged spiders with blotchy bodies running home to it, and

15 running out from it, as if some circumstances of the greatest public importance had just transpired in the spider community. ❻

❷ Pathetic fallacy

The 'reluctant' smoke also seems to have feelings. This builds on the idea of the fire wanting to go out.

❹ Pathetic fallacy

For the darkness to be 'troubled' it must have feelings.

❻ Simile

This suggests that the spiders are hurrying in and out, which seems a little threatening. However, the idea of a 'spider community' is comical. Dickens seems to want the reader to be both disgusted and fascinated.

The figurative language in this extract makes the room seem unwelcoming and inhospitable. The writer does this by using pathetic fallacy to show the mood of the room: the fire is reluctant to burn and gives little warmth or light to the room or any visitors. The language seems to build up to the climax of the spiders rushing in and out for comical and repulsive effect.

Knowledge CONCEPT

2 Figurative language

How can I write about figurative language?

In order to write about language in a text, including figurative language, you must identify the techniques the writer uses and analyse their effects and how these are achieved.

If writing about Extract 1 (on page 12), you could begin with a *statement*, such as:

> The writer uses metaphors, similes, and personification to portray the tractors as powerful, inhuman, and unconcerned about what they destroy …

You also need *evidence*. You could continue the first sentence:

> … describing them as crawling 'like insects', as 'monsters', and as animals 'sticking their snouts' into the dust.

> **TIP**
>
> Your evidence can be a direct quotation from the text itself, such as a word or phrase, or a reference to a specific part of the text, such as 'In the first sentence' or 'in line 10'.

Finally, you need to *analyse the effects in detail* of this evidence on the reader:

> This implies that the tractors lack any human feeling about what they are destroying. The machines are like greedy pigs, aggressively feeding on the land.

When analysing the effects of figurative language, you may find it helpful to use sentence stems such as those below.

| This implies that … | This creates a sense of … | This gives the reader the impression that … | Using this comparison suggests that … |

When writing about figurative language and its effects, try to include some subject terminology and comment in detail on the cumulative effects of the language, as well as individual examples. Develop your interpretation in as much detail as possible.

You could improve this answer by using terminology and suggesting further interpretation:

❶ Subject terminology. →

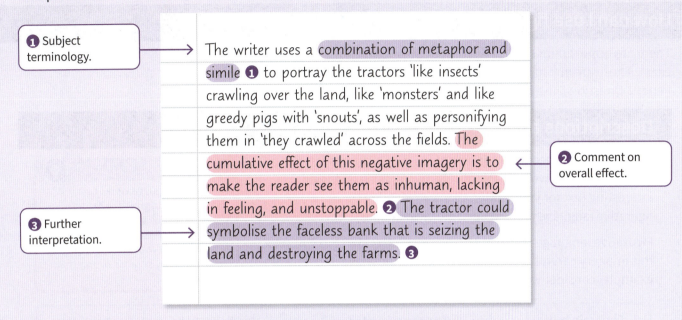

The writer uses a combination of metaphor and simile ❶ to portray the tractors 'like insects' crawling over the land, like 'monsters' and like greedy pigs with 'snouts', as well as personifying them in 'they crawled' across the fields. The cumulative effect of this negative imagery is to make the reader see them as inhuman, lacking in feeling, and unstoppable. ❷ The tractor could symbolise the faceless bank that is seizing the land and destroying the farms. ❸

← **❷ Comment on overall effect.**

❸ Further interpretation. →

For Extract 2 (on page 13), you could focus on how the figurative language creates an overall impression. The example below explores a number of different language devices to show how the author uses them to create a powerful effect for the reader.

❶ Statement that provides an overall impression of the scene. →

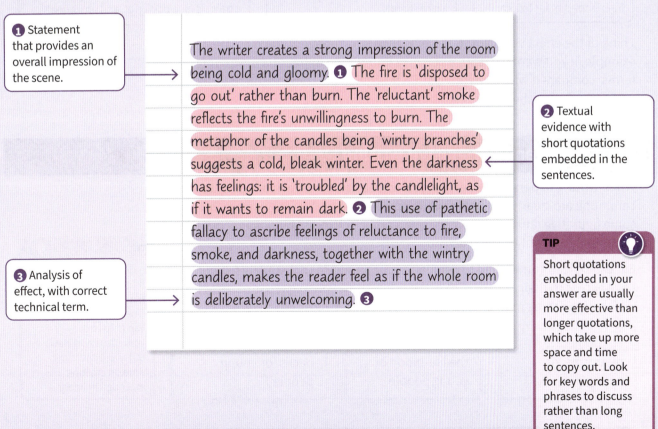

The writer creates a strong impression of the room being cold and gloomy. ❶ The fire is 'disposed to go out' rather than burn. The 'reluctant' smoke reflects the fire's unwillingness to burn. The metaphor of the candles being 'wintry branches' suggests a cold, bleak winter. Even the darkness has feelings: it is 'troubled' by the candlelight, as if it wants to remain dark. ❷ This use of pathetic fallacy to ascribe feelings of reluctance to fire, smoke, and darkness, together with the wintry candles, makes the reader feel as if the whole room is deliberately unwelcoming. ❸

← **❷ Textual evidence with short quotations embedded in the sentences.**

❸ Analysis of effect, with correct technical term. →

TIP

Short quotations embedded in your answer are usually more effective than longer quotations, which take up more space and time to copy out. Look for key words and phrases to discuss rather than long sentences.

⚙ Knowledge CONCEPT

2 Figurative language

How can I use figurative language in my own writing?

There are opportunities to use figurative language in your own writing in the exam. These are in Paper 1 Question 5 in a description or narrative text and Paper 2 Question 5 in a non-fiction text to persuade or argue.

Descriptions and narratives

When writing a description or narrative, you will be assessed on your ability to write imaginatively, to create an engaging, interesting text for your reader. One way of doing this is to use figurative language to build up some vivid images.

Figurative language compares two images, so make sure you select this imagery carefully. Try to create images that have impact. For example, consider which of these three similes works best.

> **TIP**
> Figurative language works best if the comparison gives the reader powerful, varied ideas about what is being described. Try to be imaginative in your ideas, drawing on images may surprise or entertain your reader.

1. The train hurtled past like a fast car.	2. The train hurtled past like a big bird.	3. The train hurtled past like a raging bull.
↑	↑	↑
Simile 1 is weak because a train is too similar to a car.	Simile 2 is better: a train resembles a bird slightly.	Simile 3 is best, because a raging bull, like a train, is fast, powerful, and unstoppable.

Think of the effect you want to achieve, then what imagery could create it. For example, if you want to create a negative impression of tractors destroying farms, compare it with something monstrous, like the comparison to thunder and animals that the writer selects in Extract 1 on page 12.

Arguments and persuasive writing

When writing to persuade or argue, you will be assessed on your ability to communicate clearly and put forward your viewpoint. You may wish to include some figurative language to emphasise a point or express an opinion, but use it sparingly and only when relevant.

For example, if you wanted to persuade your audience that students should have access to their phones during the school day, you might use a metaphor. Which of the three metaphors below do you think is most effective?

> **TIP**
> Avoid overusing figurative language in Paper 2 Question 5. One or two images can help to convey your ideas and views, but avoid spending time on creating extended imagery.

1. Phones are platforms for young people.	2. Phones are the life-blood of young people.	3. Phones are survival packs for young people.

> **Key terms** Make sure you can write a definition for each of these key terms.
>
> extended metaphor   figurative language   metaphor
> pathetic fallacy   personification   simile   symbolism

Use the following questions to check your understanding of the knowledge covered in this section. Then cover the answers column with a piece of paper and write down as many as you can. Check and repeat.

Questions   Answers

	Questions	Answers
1	What two words are typically used in similes?	Like, as.
2	How is a metaphor different from a simile?	It speaks of a thing as if it is something else, without using 'like' or 'as'.
3	Explain how the sentence 'The train rocketed past' is more effective than 'The train rushed past like a rocket'?	The word 'rocketed' already conveys the idea of speed, so 'rushed' is unnecessary.
4	What technique is used here, and what is its effect? *The students swarmed into the dining hall.*	Metaphor. It suggests that a crowd of students moves quickly and all at once, like swarming insects.
5	What technique is used in this sentence and what it its effect? *The pen resisted the urge to keep writing.*	Personification. It suggests that the pen has thoughts and feelings, like a person.
6	What is pathetic fallacy?	A figurative language technique that gives human emotion to something non-human (usually something in the natural world).
7	Is the following an example of pathetic fallacy or personification, and why? *Time waits for no one.*	This is personification because it makes time sound like a person but does not describe it as having any human emotion.

Put paper here

Previous questions

Now go back and use these questions to check your knowledge of previous topics.

Questions   Answers

	Questions	Answers
1	What is explicit information?	Information that is clearly stated. The reader does not have to work it out.
2	What does *infer* mean?	To work out meaning that is only hinted at, rather than explicitly stated.

Put paper here

⚙ Knowledge

3 Rhetorical language

What is rhetorical language?

Rhetorical language aims to persuade, motivate or inspire people. It uses techniques (devices) that help to impress ideas on the audience, emphasising the ideas and making them persuasive and memorable. Rhetorical language can be used in speeches or in written texts.

QUESTION CONNECTION

You may have to analyse rhetorical language features in Paper 2 Question 3. You may need to use rhetorical language when writing your response to Paper 2 Question 5.

Repetition

Writers often use **repetition** of words or phrases to emphasise them and to help secure ideas in the audience's mind.

We must fight for <u>freedom</u> to speak, <u>freedom</u> to go where we want, <u>freedom</u> to live as we want.	Exercise will help you build a <u>stronger</u> body and a <u>stronger</u> mind.	<u>We need</u> access to clean water. <u>We need</u> a market for our crops.

Emotive language

Emotive language aims to make readers respond emotionally – for example, with sympathy or outrage.

Lucy spent last Christmas shivering in a shop doorway. Will you provide her with warmth and comfort this year?	Precious rainforest is being devoured by monstrous machinery.	Our beautiful river is dying – poisoned by chemicals, choked by algae.

Rhetorical questions

Rhetorical questions are asked to challenge the listener or reader, but without expecting answers.

Should people who've worked hard all their lives be left in poverty when they retire?	Do you really expect people to put up with this?	Is it right that young people have nowhere to meet but street corners?

TIP

When writing about rhetorical features, explain why the writer has used them and what effect they create. Do not just name the feature.

Tricolons (triples)

Tricolons, or triples, are lists of three connected things. Often, the third one is the most powerful, and sometimes it is expressed in more words.

> People are tired of empty promises; they're tired of the same old lies; and they're tired of being told that everything is wonderful when clearly it isn't!

> Thousands are dying from ignorance, greed, and cynical indifference.

> There are people who don't know, people who don't care, and people who care but don't act.

Direct address

When a writer or speaker makes a **direct address** to a reader or audience, using the pronouns 'you' or 'we', it makes the audience feel personally involved and included. The use of 'we' gives a sense of unity and common purpose.

> You've worked for your exams, and now you expect a job that rewards your efforts.

> We all want our efforts to be appreciated.

> If, like me, you want our children to have a planet to live on …

Hyperbole

Hyperbole is **exaggeration** used to emphasise a point, either for humorous effect or to ensure a strong impact on the reader.

> I'm so hungry, I could eat a horse!

> When it comes to prisoner rehabilitation, we're still in the Middle Ages!

> You might as well look for a working phone box on Mars as on the streets of London.

Juxtaposition

Juxtaposition means contrasting two ideas or objects in order to highlight their differences, make a point or create a literary effect.

> We will turn the darkness of despair into the light of hope.

> Some are born into wealth and privilege, others into poverty and disadvantage.

> A good result could mean fame and fortune; a bad one will mean disappointment and relegation.

Anecdotes

Anecdotes are short, personal stories of a few lines that illustrate a point.

> I was walking up the high street the other day when a car sped past me …

> The other day I saw a group of students at a bus stop – all on their phones.

> Last summer I took my family to the seaside, hoping for a good day out …

Knowledge CONCEPT

3 Rhetorical language

What are the effects of rhetorical language?

Rhetorical language can be used in many ways, but it works particularly well in texts that aim to persuade the audience or argue a point of view, such as speeches or articles.

In the extract below, President Obama reflects on the history of the presidential oath and how it has served America well and should continue to do so, even though the country is facing many challenges. Notice how he uses rhetorical features to reinforce his argument.

TIP

A persuasive text must have a clear, strong argument running through it. Rhetorical language can help to reinforce that argument, simplifying and summarising ideas and making them memorable.

Extract 1: President Obama's Inaugural Address, calling for 'a new era of responsibility'

This extract is from President Obama's inauguration speech, the first speech he gave after becoming President.

Forty-four Americans have now taken the presidential oath. The words have been spoken during rising tides of prosperity and the still waters of peace. ❶ Yet, every so often the oath is taken amidst gathering clouds and raging storms. ❷ At these moments, America has
5 carried on not simply because of the skill or vision of those in high office, but because We the People ❸ have remained faithful to the ideals of our ❸ forebears, and true to our ❸ founding documents.

10 So it has been. So it must be ❹ with this generation of Americans.

That we are in the midst of crisis is now well understood. Our nation is at war, ❺ against a far-reaching network of violence and hatred. Our economy
15 is badly weakened, a consequence of greed and irresponsibility on the part of some, but also our collective failure to make hard choices and prepare the nation for a new age. Homes have been lost; jobs shed; businesses shuttered. ❻ Our healthcare is too costly;
20 our schools fail too many; and each day brings further evidence that the ways we use energy strengthen our adversaries and threaten our planet. ❼

❶ Juxtaposition

The two images of 'rising tides' and 'still waters' reflect positive periods in American history.

❸ Direct address

The words 'we' and 'our' create a sense of unity with the audience.

❺ Hyperbole

The 'war' is not literal, but refers to the fight against terrorism.

❼ Tricolon

Three more items in the list of challenges, building up to a climax, with the longest and most serious item last.

❷ Juxtaposition

Weather metaphors for social upheaval contrast strikingly with previous metaphors for prosperity and peace.

❹ Repetition

This reinforces a sense of continuity.

❻ Tricolon

Three items give a concise, powerful summary of the difficulties faced by many Americans.

The rhetorical language in the extract above helps to impress strong ideas and images in the audience's mind: the importance of the principles that America was founded upon; the responsibility of current Americans to uphold those principles; the extent of the challenges that they all face. The words and images conveyed through the language are powerful and memorable.

Rhetorical language can be used to make the audience think carefully about an issue and stir up an emotional response to trigger them into action, or to agree with the argument.

In the article below, the writer uses rhetorical language to reinforce her argument against trophy hunting (hunting wild animals for pleasure). Notice how she uses rhetorical language to engage the reader and provide memorable images.

Extract 2: 'The hunter who killed Cecil the lion doesn't deserve our empathy' by Rose George, 29 July 2015

> This extract is from an article in the *Guardian* and shows the writer's view of a trophy hunter killing a famous lion in Zimbabwe.

Trophy hunters like Walter J. Palmer shouldn't receive death threats – but there is no excuse for their argument that hunting serves conservation.

We love a good fight, don't we? ❶ Enter Walter J. Palmer,
5 a tanned dentist from Minnesota, with a bow and arrow. Along comes Cecil the lion, the alpha male of his pride, minding his own business being the best-known and most beloved lion in Zimbabwe if not in Africa, as well as the subject of an Oxford University study. ❷ Then Cecil
10 is shot with a bow and arrow, taking 40 hours to die, ❸ all because Palmer thought killing a magnificent animal was sporty.

I read the story of Cecil's killing and my education and intellect deserted me for a minute. I felt only
15 disgust and rage, somewhat inarticulately. I feel no calmness about big-game hunters. I am not persuaded by their justifications, which can be easily punctured with buckshot. ❹ Trophy hunting contributes to conservation, they say: when the Dallas Safari Club
20 auctioned the right to kill an endangered Namibian black rhino, it said the $350,000 winning bounty – they called it a "bid" – went towards conservation efforts in Namibia.

Elephants, leopards, polar bears and giraffes are all hunted for "sport" too. Shooting an endangered species
25 and calling it sustainable is like waving a fan and thinking you're helping to stop global warming. ❺

❶ Rhetorical question and direct address

The question challenges the reader to think about the issue. The use of 'we' creates a bond between the writer and the reader.

❸ Emotive detail

Stimulates the reader's awareness of the extent of Cecil's suffering.

❺ Hyperbole

Using a comparison to demonstrate how nonsensical this idea is.

TIP

Emotive language doesn't necessarily have to shock; it can be more subtle. Look out for any language that seems to create an emotional response in the reader.

❷ Emotive language

Empathy for the lion is created by naming him, making him sound majestic ('alpha male'), innocent, and widely loved – a celebrity.

❹ Imagery

An appropriate hunting metaphor adds colour and wit to the writing.

The rhetorical language in the extract helps to engage the reader, challenging them to think carefully about the issue and stirring up their emotions. The imagery, humour, and exaggeration help to reinforce the argument, making it powerful and memorable for the reader.

3 Rhetorical language

How can I write about rhetorical language?

In order to write about rhetorical language, you must identify the techniques the writer uses and analyse how their effects are achieved. It might be tempting to simply 'spot' devices, but you must focus on the effect of individual devices and on their cumulative effect throughout a source text.

Re-read the first paragraph of Extract 1 on page 20. In analysing this paragraph, you could write about the rhetorical language and its effects like this:

TIP

Think about the writer's or speaker's purpose. What are they trying to achieve by using rhetorical language? For example, are they trying to inspire the public or promote a viewpoint or argument?

1 Identifies the purpose and audience.

The purpose of the speech is to inspire and reassure Americans, **1** so the speaker uses a variety of rhetorical devices to help do this.

First he uses juxtaposition to establish two images of prosperity and peace: 'rising tides' and 'still waters'. **2** Then he contrasts these two positive images with two metaphors for troubled times 'gathering clouds' and 'raging storms'. As dark clouds suggest a storm is coming, this has connotations that something else negative could happen, such as national threat or economic difficulty. **3**

2 Explains how the juxtaposition works with embedded quotations.

3 Identifies connotations and how they link to the context of the speech.

These contrasts reinforce the idea that the presidency always survives change. **4** The speaker also congratulates Americans, personified collectively as 'America', for remaining 'faithful' to national ideals. This encourages a sense of national solidarity, reinforced by the inclusive use of pronouns and determiners in 'We the People', 'our forebears', and 'our founding documents'. **5**

4 Focuses on the broad effects of the contrasts.

TIP

When analysing the use of any language feature, remember to make a point, use evidence from the text, and explain the effect it creates for the audience.

5 Analyses the direct address and inclusive language.

Now re-read the first two paragraphs of Extract 2 on page 21. Here is how you could write about this paragraphs:

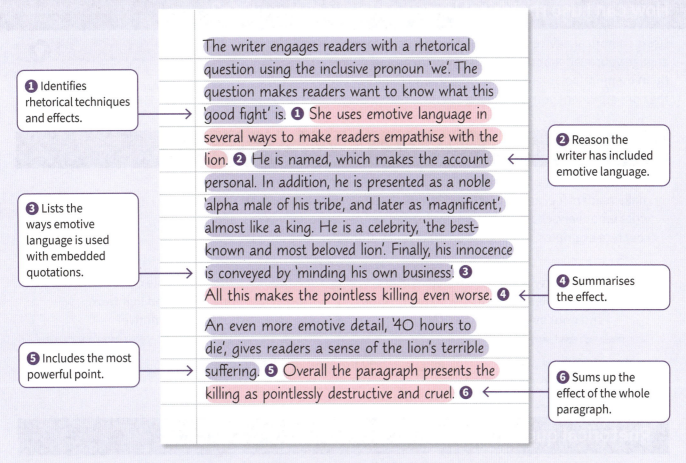

① Identifies rhetorical techniques and effects.

② Reason the writer has included emotive language.

③ Lists the ways emotive language is used with embedded quotations.

④ Summarises the effect.

⑤ Includes the most powerful point.

⑥ Sums up the effect of the whole paragraph.

The writer engages readers with a rhetorical question using the inclusive pronoun 'we'. The question makes readers want to know what this 'good fight' is. **①** She uses emotive language in several ways to make readers empathise with the lion. **②** He is named, which makes the account personal. In addition, he is presented as a noble 'alpha male of his tribe', and later as 'magnificent', almost like a king. He is a celebrity, 'the best-known and most beloved lion'. Finally, his innocence is conveyed by 'minding his own business'. **③** All this makes the pointless killing even worse. **④**

An even more emotive detail, '40 hours to die', gives readers a sense of the lion's terrible suffering. **⑤** Overall the paragraph presents the killing as pointlessly destructive and cruel. **⑥**

Notice how this student varies the way in which they identify rhetorical language and explain its effects. They use words and phrases to link their ideas together fluently. You may find some of the following useful in your own work.

The writer engages …	The writer encourages readers …	… to make readers empathise
In addition …	… is conveyed by …	The paragraph presents …
The overall effect …		

3 Rhetorical language

How can I use rhetorical language in my own writing?

Using rhetorical devices in your writing will help you to engage your reader and emphasise your ideas and make them memorable. Rhetorical devices should reinforce the core argument you are making.

> **TIP**
>
> Whichever effect you want to achieve, don't overdo it. If readers feel you are trying to manipulate them, or if what you say is too horrifying, you will just turn them off.

Emotive language

The aim of emotive language is to produce an emotional response. You might make readers feel angry, disgusted, sympathetic – even guilty or fearful. To write emotively, choose emotionally 'loaded' words, especially verbs, and concrete examples, rather than abstract ideas. Consider, for example:

> Child poverty is a serious problem in our society, often leading to inadequate nutrition and poor living conditions. (Abstract)

> A toddler, clutching a stale crust – her only breakfast – unwashed and half-frozen, will not thrive. (Emotive)

Look again at how words like 'clutching' are used (rather than just 'holding') and consider the emotive effect of this.

Rhetorical questions

Use rhetorical questions sparingly to give them maximum effect. If arguing against a ban on risky sports, you might write:

> Is it right to ban the very spirit of adventure that is at the heart of human progress?

Juxtaposition

Juxtaposing images or ideas can create contrast or balance. Think carefully about the effect you want to create. Avoid placing images or ideas next to each other without a specific purpose.

> **TIP**
>
> Check your exam response to make sure you haven't overused any one rhetorical technique.

Direct address and anecdotes

By directly addressing your audience and recounting anecdotes, you may find that you create more of a bond with your listeners or readers, as you are making your argument more personal and appealing. People are more likely to agree with someone whom they like.

 Key terms Make sure you can write a definition for each of these key terms.

anecdote   direct address   emotive language   exaggeration
juxtaposition   repetition   rhetorical questions   tricolons

Use the following questions to check your understanding of the knowledge covered in this section. Then cover the answers column with a piece of paper and write down as many as you can. Check and repeat.

Questions | Answers

#	Questions	Answers
1	What is emotive language? Choose from: • Language describing movement. • Language aiming for an emotional response. • Language with a purpose.	Language aiming for an emotional response.
2	Which of these is a rhetorical question, and what is its effect? • What is the capital of Wales? • Have you bought the train tickets? • Do you think I was born yesterday?	Do you think I was born yesterday? The speaker means he or she is not easily fooled, like a newborn baby.
3	What technique is used here, and what is the effect? *We're tired, we're hungry, and we want to go home.*	Tricolon (triple). Having three items makes the list more powerfully persuasive. Here, the final item is the most important.
4	What technique is used here, and what is the effect? *We all want to do well in our exams.*	Use of the first person plural pronoun (we) and determiner (our) makes readers feel included in the statement.
5	What is juxtaposition and what is its effect?	It is placing two ideas or images near each other to create a sense of balance or contrast.
6	Rhetorical language is only found in speeches. True or false?	False.
7	Rhetorical language can influence the way people think and what they do. True or false?	True.
8	You should aim to include as many rhetorical features in your writing as possible. True or false?	False.

Put paper here

Previous questions

Now go back and use these questions to check your knowledge of previous topics.

Questions | Answers

#	Questions	Answers
1	What two words are typically used in similes?	Like, as.
2	How is a metaphor different from a simile?	It speaks of a thing as if it is something else, without using 'like' or 'as'.

Put paper here

4 Characterisation, setting, and mood

What are characterisation, setting, and mood?

A fiction writer creates different characters, settings, and moods to convey stories to the reader. All these elements build a context for the plot to develop, taking the reader into the writer's imaginative world.

QUESTION CONNECTION

You will comment on **characterisation**, setting, and **mood** when responding to Paper 1 Questions 2, 3, and 4. You will need to use your knowledge of these aspects when writing your own text in Paper 1 Question 5.

Characterisation

A writer can portray character through explicit information, by telling the reader directly about how the character looks. This might include their features, clothes, and other aspects of their physical appearance.

> Under the brim of an immaculate top hat, her smiling eyes reflected the green of her waistcoat.

As well as direct information about the character's clothes, the 'smiling eyes' suggest a cheerful, friendly character.

LINK

See more about explicit and implicit meaning on page 3.

TIP

Remember that characters are not real people. Also, the views they express may not be the same as the views of the writer. Writers make deliberate choices about how they portray their characters in order to influence the way that readers will respond.

Writers also convey character through implicit information. The writer *shows* the reader what the character is like through:

- their actions
- what they say
- how they interact with other characters.

For example, this character's *actions* show his concern and sense of responsibility for his younger siblings, which imply he is kind and mature:

> Before they embarked on their journey, Sameer checked that his younger brothers had their warm coats and comfortable shoes.

Look at the **dialogue** below. The *speech* and *interaction* between these two characters suggests, in this situation, that Maureen is domineering, while Zoe is sensitive and trusting:

> 'I don't want to hear any more about it,' Maureen said.
>
> Zoe blinked back tears. 'But you promised,' she sobbed. 'And now everyone knows.'

When drawing conclusions about characters in your writing, it is important to consider the context of the situation and infer why characters might be acting in certain ways.

Setting

Setting gives an overall context for the story. The setting is when and where the action occurs: the time and place. Time might be:

- a historical period, such as medieval times or in the future
- a season, such as autumn or summer
- a particular month or celebration, such as Ramadan, Diwali or Christmas
- a time during the day, for example at dawn, at midday, the evening.

Setting also covers place, which could refer to a particular town or country, to a building like an oil rig, to scenery like the desert, or to a fantasy world. Writers often use setting as a device to establish the mood of the text, set the scene, and reflect the themes and characters. Look at an example below.

> The planet's third moon was just rising as Thar stepped out of the silver pod onto the dusty yellow soil. She was surrounded by a random scattering of jagged rocks, each with its own moon shadow pooling from beneath it. The faint breeze carried a distinct smell of sulphur.

Mood

A good writer will choose language to describe events, characters, and setting to create a mood. Mood is the overall emotion and atmosphere that the writer wants the reader to feel when reading a story. For example, notice how in the extract below the writer uses the setting of a 'cold and gloomy room' and a locked door to create a mood of fear and danger:

> As Marek stepped into the cold and gloomy room, a deeper darkness detached itself from the shadows and began to creep steadily towards him. He fumbled for the door behind him. It was locked.

TIP

Exam source texts often include a setting that creates a particular mood. Comment on this if it is relevant to Questions 2, 3, or 4 in Paper 1.

Mood can also be created by descriptions of weather. The weather can be used to echo the feelings of the characters or to enhance dramatic effects. For example, a hot, sultry day might echo the idleness or boredom of a character; the gathering clouds of a storm might echo tension building up between characters before an argument.

> The day of the wedding dawned unpromisingly. Dark clouds loomed, and a sharp north wind lifted and scattered the dead leaves across the road like ghostly confetti. She looked uncertainly out of her window and shivered.

4 Characterisation, setting, and mood

Characters are often established at the start of a novel or story. As you read through a source text, think about why the writer has made the choices they have.

- What effects have they tried to create for the reader?
- Why have they chosen to use certain language?

- What is being implied about the character?
- What is being suggested, beyond the direct information we are given?

Read the extract below. The annotations focus on how the writer presents the character of Mr Knoppert and the effects they create.

1 The use of his full name and title makes him sound rather formal and distant, and therefore unsympathetic.

3 The word 'repellent' strongly suggests their negative reaction. His pleasure in this makes him seem strange as a character.

5 His words make him seem mysterious, as he has not previously cared about nature but finds snails beautiful – unlike most people.

Extract 1: 'The Snail Watcher' by Patricia Highsmith

This extract from a short story is about Mr Knoppert and his hobby of snail watching.

When Mr Peter Knoppert **1** began to make a hobby of snail-watching, he had no idea that his handful of specimens would become hundreds in no time. Only two months after the original snails were carried up
5 to the Knoppert study, some thirty glass tanks and bowls, all teeming with snails, lined the walls, rested on the desk and windowsills, and were beginning even to cover the floor. **2** Mrs Knoppert disapproved strongly, and would no longer enter the room. It smelled, she
10 said, and besides she had once stepped on a snail by accident, a horrible sensation she would never forget. But the more his wife and friends deplored his unusual and vaguely repellent pastime, the more pleasure Mr Knoppert seemed to find in it. **3**
15 'I never cared for nature before in my life,' Mr Knoppert often remarked – he was a partner in a brokerage* firm, a man who had devoted all his life to the science of finance **4** – 'but snails have opened my eyes to the beauty of the animal world.' **5**
20 If his friends commented that snails were not really animals, and their slimy habitats hardly the best example of the beauty of nature, Mr Knoppert would tell them with a superior smile that they simply didn't know all that he knew about snails. **6**

brokerage: *buying and selling stocks and shares*

2 For most readers, the character's fascination with snails would make him seem unpleasant. The use of 'teeming' might make readers feel uncomfortable with this environment, and therefore with the character.

4 The use of 'science' implies that Knoppert also has a scientific interest in snails.

6 His 'superior smile' and the mysterious way he presents his knowledge suggests that he feels he is better than other people.

The writer uses language to present Mr Knoppert as a mysterious man with a strange interest in snails. The effects of this language will make the reader curious about him, therefore likely to pay attention to him when they continue to read.

Writers also use language to create a setting and a particular mood in a story. As you read a source text, ask yourself:

- What is being implied?
- What is the effect of any figurative language?
- What sort of mood do certain words and phrases create?

It is important that you can comment on the language choices a writer makes, explaining the effects they create for the reader.

Read the extract below. The annotations focus on how the writer builds up a particular sense of place and mood.

① Glass and steel are cold, hard materials, reflecting the **narrator's** experience of the setting in which she finds herself.

③ The woman is raised up and very visible, and even her desk is made of glass. This makes her seem vulnerable and visible in a way that the character herself would hate.

⑤ These statements are not literally true. They imply that this is a world of impersonal, unsympathetic corporate power.

⑦ The men are part of the setting. The phrases 'trotted briskly', 'barked', normally apply to horses and dogs, so this world seems inhuman. There is also a sense of them being on important business from which Nazneen is excluded.

Extract 2: *Brick Lane* by Monica Ali

This extract is from a novel, and is from the point of view of Nazneen, who has recently arrived in London from Bangladesh, and is walking in a business district in London.

She looked up at a building as she passed. It was constructed almost entirely of glass, with a few thin rivets of steel holding it together. The entrance was like a glass fan, **①** rotating slowly, sucking people in, wafting others out. **②** Inside, on a raised dais, a woman behind a glass desk **③** crossed and uncrossed her thin legs. She wedged a telephone receiver between her ear and shoulder and chewed on a fingernail. Nazneen craned her head back and saw that the glass above became dark as a night pond. **④** The building was without end. Above, somewhere, it crushed the clouds. **⑤** The next building and the one opposite were white stone palaces. There were steps up to the entrances and colonnades* across the front. **⑥** Men in dark suits trotted briskly up and down the steps, in pairs or in threes. They barked to each other and nodded sombrely. **⑦**

colonnades: *rows of columns, as in ancient Greek architecture*

② The entrance, personified as 'sucking people in', implies that the institution the building represents devours people, ignoring their individuality.

④ Nazneen craning her head back suggest that she is awed by the huge impersonal nature of the building. The 'night pond' simile is an image from nature, suggesting the village world that Nazneen comes from.

⑥ They are not really 'palaces', but the word implies how much wealth has gone into building them.

Overall, the writer presents Nazneen's perception of the setting as being huge, hard, and cold. This shows the reader how alienated she feels in this environment, surrounded by corporate wealth and power rather than comfort. Through the mood of these descriptions, the writer suggests that there is nothing that the narrator can relate to.

Knowledge CONCEPT

4 Characterisation, setting, and mood

How can I write about characterisation, setting, and mood?

When you are commenting on how the writer creates characterisation, setting, and mood, remember to refer to words or phrases in the text, then explain the effects that the language creates for the reader. You might find some of the words and sentence stems below helpful in your commentary.

> ...portrays...   ...conveys a sense of...   ...implies that...
>
> ...creates an impression of...   ...focuses attention on...
>
> ...emphasises...

TIP

Remember: there is not always a right answer when writing about these features. There will be variations in why the writer has made certain choices. Your own interpretations are valid if you can support them with evidence and explanation.

Writing about characterisation

When writing about characterisation, consider the explicit information that the writer gives you and also the implicit information that you can gain from the way a character acts, speaks, and interacts with others.

Imagine you have been given Extract 1 (page 28) and that the question asks:

> How does the writer convey Mr Knoppert's attitude towards his hobby?

TIP

Focus on whatever the question asks you. For example, here the focus is on *Mr Knoppert's attitude towards his hobby* – not just 'his character' or 'how the snails are presented'.

Read one student's response below, considering how the language reveals more about Mr Knoppert's character.

❶ Analyses language closely, linking word choice to information given later.

> Mr Knoppert's 'hobby of snail-watching' sounds casual, but 'specimens' implies a more scientific approach that reflects his previous devotion to the 'science of finance'. **❶** The author's language suggests Mr Knoppert's growing obsession by creating an impression of the huge number of snails that he quickly acquires. **❷** She lists the 'thirty glass tanks and bowls,' while 'teeming' suggests a crawling mass of them. A tricolon emphasises how they fill his study, on the 'walls', 'desk', and 'windowsills' and even 'the floor'. This makes him seem disturbingly eccentric. **❸**
>
> The negative verb 'deplored' and the description 'vaguely repellent' convey how his wife and friends react to his hobby. He seems to take 'pleasure' in their response, as if he enjoys their disgust. **❹**

❷ Makes a point about how the language sheds light on his obsessive character.

❸ Supports the point with precise evidence and sums up the effect.

❹ Explains, with evidence, how his attitude to their reaction reveals his own character.

Writing about setting and mood

The creation of character, setting, and mood are usually closely interlinked, but an exam question might ask you to focus on just one or two aspects of a text. Take care to focus on exactly what is asked and do not stray into more general commentary.

TIP

Focus closely and in detail on the effect of just one or two words from the source text at a time. They will give you more than enough to write about, so be selective.

Imagine you have been given Extract 2 (page 29) and the question:

> How does the writer describe the setting and create mood?

Read one student's response below. The annotations focus on how the student structures their response, keeping their focus clearly on setting and mood.

❶ A clear statement about the link between setting and character.

❷ Works out implied meaning, through the writer's word choice.

❸ Makes a point, gives evidence, and analyses it.

❹ Focuses on one important feature, analysing how the image creates mood.

❺ Comments on how the description of the setting builds, interpreting language and symbolism.

The city setting is seen through the character's eyes. **❶** The fact that she notices the construction of the buildings, even making an effort by craning her head back to see one, implies that they are strange to her. **❷** It seems extraordinary that one could be 'constructed almost entirely of glass, with a few thin rivets of steel'. It seems both hard and improbably flimsy. **❸**

Glass is everywhere. The entrance is 'like a glass fan', and the woman sits 'behind a glass desk'. Glass and steel are cold, hard materials, reflecting the character's experience of this world and creating a mood of unsympathetic alienation. The glass becomes 'dark as a night pond'. This simile from the natural world, applied to this very unnatural world, creates a tense mood with the frightening suggestion of falling into a pond at night. **❹**

The skyscraper is seen as 'without end'. This, together with its violent 'crushing' of the clouds — a part of nature, creates a setting which seems unnatural and overwhelming. **❺**

If a question asks you to focus on particular aspects of a text, you should make explicit reference to these aspects at least once in your response. Note that the student response above mentions 'setting' in the first sentence and the final paragraph, and 'mood' in the second paragraph.

4 Characterisation, setting, and mood

How can I use characterisation, setting, and mood in my own writing?

Characterisation

If you are writing a story in the exam, it is best to focus on just two or three characters, so that you have time to develop them properly. The diagram below shows what to consider for each character.

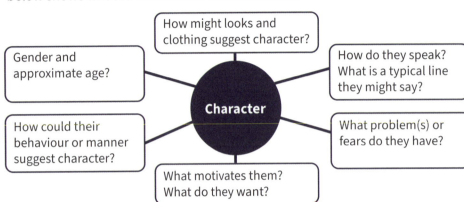

> **TIP**
>
> Remember, as a writer, you can portray characters through explicit information, *telling* the reader directly about the character, or through implicit information, through their actions.

In your writing, consider:

- the reason for including that particular character
- how that links to the impact you want your text to have
- what are characters' intentions
- how they are feeling in the context they are in.

Setting and mood

A story or description works best if it has a clear sense of where and when it takes place. This provides a background for the action in a story or a clear context for more detailed description.

Think about what mood you want to create. What type of emotional world will you take your reader into? It might be one of the following:

| joyful | sinister | melancholy |
| relaxed | tense | romantic |

You can create mood by the details and language you use to describe the setting. For example:

> Summer is truly over. The swallows have abandoned us. Bees no longer buzz through the flowers and a moaning wind has swept upon us.

Notice how this student has conveyed a depressed mood through careful, vivid description of the setting. A moaning wind has replaced the buzz of bees, suggesting a change to a more unpleasant environment.

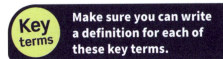

Key terms Make sure you can write a definition for each of these key terms.

characterisation dialogue mood narrator

Use the following questions to check your understanding of the knowledge covered in this section. Then cover the answers column with a piece of paper and write down as many as you can. Check and repeat.

Questions | Answers

	Questions	Answers
1	Writers create characters only by describing their appearance. True or false?	False.
2	How else can writers convey information about their characters?	Through a character's actions, words, and relationships with other characters.
3	Setting just refers to time. True or false?	False: it also includes place.
4	What sort of timing could be included in a setting?	Historical time, time of day or night, season, yearly or monthly festival or celebration.
5	What is the 'mood' of a text?	The atmosphere created in the text and the emotional response in the reader, created by the writer.
6	What mood is created by the following description? *It was a warm spring morning and the garden was beginning to come into bloom. Early birds sang brightly, and cherry blossom waved in a kindly breeze.*	Happy, optimistic.
7	How can a description of weather help to create mood?	It can reflect the feelings of a character, or the situation they are in.

Put paper here

Previous questions

Now go back and use these questions to check your knowledge of previous topics.

Questions | Answers

	Questions	Answers
1	What is emotive language?	Language aiming for an emotional response.
2	What is juxtaposition and what is its effect?	It is placing two ideas or images near each other to create a sense of balance or contrast.

Put paper here

⚙ Knowledge CONCEPT

5 Attitudes and perspectives

What are attitudes and perspectives?

Perspective

The **perspective** in a text is the view that the writer has taken on a topic. The writer will consciously decide their perspective at the beginning of the text, based on what they want to convey and the purpose they want to achieve.

A perspective is revealed through what the writer says - their attitude, opinions, thoughts and feelings. It's conveyed in what they say, but also how they say it. It's revealed through voice, **tone**, **register** and various other methods, including:

- narrative viewpoint, and mood
- word classes, such as verbs, adjectives, and adverbs
- figurative, emotive, or sensory language
- structural elements, such as repetition of key ideas or a very short sentence in its own paragraph to emphasise an idea.

> **QUESTION CONNECTION**
>
> You should comment on attitudes and perspectives in Paper 2 Question 4 when comparing how writers express their views in two source texts.

Tone

The tone of a text reveals a writer's attitude towards a topic and also the type of relationship they want to establish with their reader. They might create a serious, angry tone to shock and engage the reader:

> We are frustrated by the same old excuses!

Or a light-hearted, friendly tone to bond with the reader:

> If you're like me, you probably like to put your feet up at the end of the day.

> **TIP** 💡
>
> A tone can vary throughout a text, varying in intensity from mildly annoyed, for example, to furious ranting.

There are a variety of tones that writers might choose to create, for example:

| irritated | thoughtful | humorous | sarcastic | encouraging |

| sympathetic | detached | comic | judgemental |

Register

Register is the way a writer, or speaker, uses language differently in different circumstances and for different audiences. For example, think of the differences between the way you might speak to your friends and the way you might speak to your head teacher and older members of your family.

Register can refer to the level of formality in a text or speech. For a formal register, a writer will choose serious language, as well as longer and more complex sentences. A formal register is appropriate for texts such as legal reports, NHS health leaflets or letters to your MP. An informal register uses simpler, more **colloquial language**.

> Temperatures are predicted to be high today. (formal register)
> I reckon it's gonna be a right scorcher. (informal register)

Standard and non-standard English

Standard English is a widely recognised formal version of English not linked to any region, but used in schools, books, official publications, and public announcements. Standard English uses standard grammar and vocabulary. It can be spoken in any accent.

Non-Standard English is a more informal version of English, and can include **dialect** (words and grammar used only in one region), colloquial words and expressions, and slang.

> The potatoes were delicious. (Standard English)
> Them tatties were yummy. (non-Standard English)

TIP

You should use Standard English in your exam question responses (unless you choose not to for a purpose in the writing questions).

Viewpoint

The viewpoint is the point of view from which a text is written or narrated.

An article in a magazine might use a **first-person viewpoint**, using the pronouns 'I' and 'we' as they offer an opinion on a current event or issue.

> I've always loved watching films, so the controversy about film ratings has made me think about the influence films can have on young people.

A news report is likely to be written with a **third-person viewpoint**, giving facts and recounting events using the pronouns 'he', 'she', 'it', and 'they'.

> A great storm caused damage to towns on the coast. It also swept a man into the sea as he walked along a beach.

⚙ Knowledge CONCEPT

5 Attitudes and perspectives

How do writer's methods convey attitudes and perspectives?

You would expect certain types of text to be in a very formal register, so that their meaning is clear and they are taken seriously. One such text type is a presidential speech. Look at the attitude of the speaker: he is critical of what has come before him and motivated for a new beginning. These are conveyed through methods in the speech.

LINK

The context of this speech and the rhetorical devices included are explored in more detail on page 20.

❶ Formal wording conveys a serious tone. The first-person plural perspective ('we') includes himself with all Americans.

❸ Three examples convey a regretful tone that people have suffered these losses.

Extract 1: President Obama's Inaugural Address, calling for 'a new era of responsibility'

> This extract is from President Obama's inauguration speech, the first speech he gave after becoming President.

That we are in the midst of crisis is now well understood. **❶** Our nation is at war, against a far-reaching network of violence and hatred. Our economy is badly weakened, a consequence of greed and
5 irresponsibility on the part of some, but also our collective failure to make hard choices and prepare the nation for a new age. **❷** Homes have been lost; jobs shed; businesses shuttered. **❸** Our healthcare
10 is too costly; our schools fail too many; and each day brings further evidence that the ways we use energy strengthen our adversaries and threaten our planet. **❹**

---

❷ Long, complex sentence with the formal 'on the part of some' showing he wants to indicate that some people have been greedy, but without naming any particular group. First-person plural perspective ('Our') has been included to be as one with the audience.

❹ Formal register expresses his deep concern. The words 'adversaries' and 'threaten', together with the use of 'we' and 'our', imply a caring attitude and a sense of unity.

The overall effect is to command respect, and to convey his attitude of concern for the serious problems all Americans face, without apportioning blame. He also expresses a sympathetic tone for people's personal losses and implies a sense of unity in that he and all Americans are facing these problems together.

To understand the formality of this language, consider what Obama says above alongside possible informal versions.

Formal	Informal
That we are in the midst of crisis is now well understood.	Everyone knows we're in a mess
a consequence of greed and irresponsibility on the part of some	because of a few greedy, irresponsible people
Homes have been lost	People have got nowhere to go / are on the streets
brings further evidence that the ways we use energy strengthen our adversaries	shows more and more that our energy use helps our enemies

The formal language conveys a more serious tone, reflecting the concern and determination in the speaker's attitude towards the country's situation.

A magazine or newspaper article may seek to convey a humorous tone if the purpose is to entertain the reader.

Look again at this extract from an article in the *Guardian* by Charlie Brooker, in which he shares his perspective on updating his smartphone. Notice how it differs from the President Obama speech. The writer knows that exaggerating his attitude for comic effect, while still making a point about the modern world, will be successful with his audience.

LINK

The context of this article is explored in more detail on page 5.

❶ Simple sentence, showing a negative attitude.

❸ Casual expression implying an impatient attitude: the update is a waste of his time. The register is informal and annoyed.

❺ Colloquial word 'fiddly' reveals his attitude: the update is not hugely important, but it's annoying – and probably pointless.

Extract 2: 'Apple's software updates are like changing the water in a fish tank. I'd rather let the fish die' by Charlie Brooker

> This extract is an article from the *Guardian* about one person's view of software updates.

Updates are awful. **❶** All you want to do is watch TV and rot in your own filth. **❷** Instead you spend the evening backing up your phone, downloading a gigantic file and sitting around **❸** while your phone undergoes
5 an intense psychological makeover, **❹** at the end of which it may or may not function. Often, it takes an hour or more. Fiddly, time-consuming admin **❺** – it's like having to change the water in a fish tank. … it's why I don't have an aquarium. I'd rather let the fish die. **❻**

❷ Direct address 'you' and a casual, humorous expression reflect his attitude that he would rather waste time in his own chosen way.

❹ Humorous exaggeration shows an exasperated attitude to what he thinks is an unnecessary procedure.

❻ Exaggerated humour shows his quirky view that both things are equally tedious.

The overall effect of this informal register and humorous tone is to make readers identify with the writer. It also entertains them, as the writer comically expresses his negative, critical attitude towards wasting time updating his phone.

5 Attitudes and perspectives

How can I write about attitudes and perspectives?

Identifying the writer's perspective and attitude is key, so make sure you explicitly state this in your answer. You can then explore the reason that this attitude or perspective is taken, and through what language or structural devices.

You should now be able to identify:

- ways in which writers reveal their attitude towards a subject
- typical differences between a formal and an informal register
- what types of text are more likely to use a formal or informal register
- Standard and non-Standard English – an important element of register
- how writers create tone to help express their attitude
- the different perspectives that writers can use, depending on the type of text they are writing, its purpose and audience.

To comment on the attitudes in Extract 1 (page 36), you could write:

> **QUESTION CONNECTION** 🔗
>
> It is essential that you identify perspectives and attitudes that relate to the focus in the question in Paper 2 Question 4 and compare corresponding perspectives from both sources.

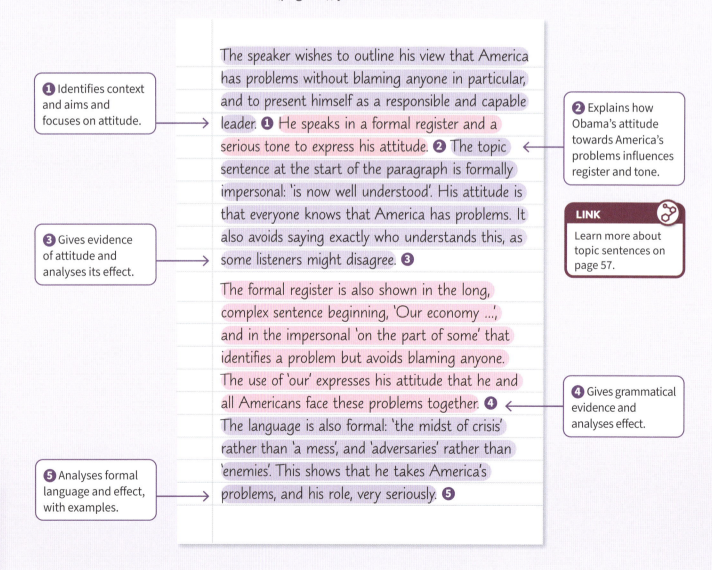

① Identifies context and aims and focuses on attitude.

The speaker wishes to outline his view that America has problems without blaming anyone in particular, and to present himself as a responsible and capable leader. **①** He speaks in a formal register and a serious tone to express his attitude. **②** The topic sentence at the start of the paragraph is formally impersonal: 'is now well understood'. His attitude is that everyone knows that America has problems. It also avoids saying exactly who understands this, as some listeners might disagree. **③**

② Explains how Obama's attitude towards America's problems influences register and tone.

> **LINK** 🔗
>
> Learn more about topic sentences on page 57.

③ Gives evidence of attitude and analyses its effect.

The formal register is also shown in the long, complex sentence beginning, 'Our economy …', and in the impersonal 'on the part of some' that identifies a problem but avoids blaming anyone. The use of 'our' expresses his attitude that he and all Americans face these problems together. **④** The language is also formal: 'the midst of crisis' rather than 'a mess', and 'adversaries' rather than 'enemies'. This shows that he takes America's problems, and his role, very seriously. **⑤**

④ Gives grammatical evidence and analyses effect.

⑤ Analyses formal language and effect, with examples.

To comment on the attitudes and perspectives in Extract 2 (page 37), you could write:

❶ States writer's aim and gives an example.

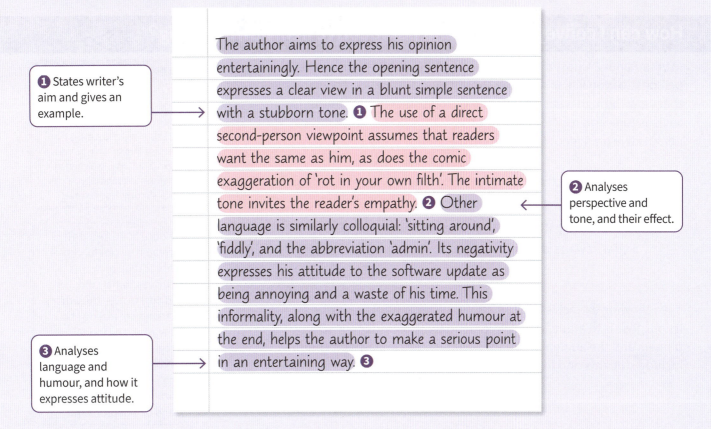

The author aims to express his opinion entertainingly. Hence the opening sentence expresses a clear view in a blunt simple sentence with a stubborn tone. **❶** The use of a direct second-person viewpoint assumes that readers want the same as him, as does the comic exaggeration of 'rot in your own filth'. The intimate tone invites the reader's empathy. **❷** Other language is similarly colloquial: 'sitting around', 'fiddly', and the abbreviation 'admin'. Its negativity expresses his attitude to the software update as being annoying and a waste of his time. This informality, along with the exaggerated humour at the end, helps the author to make a serious point in an entertaining way. **❸**

❷ Analyses perspective and tone, and their effect.

❸ Analyses language and humour, and how it expresses attitude.

The student identifies how register and tone combine to express the writer's attitude towards the update as being an annoying waste of his time – a view with which he assumes his readers will empathise.

TIP

When commenting on a source text, you should always write in Standard English. You should also use Standard English when writing your own text, unless you are writing dialogue between characters.

⚙ Knowledge CONCEPT

5 Attitudes and perspectives

How can I convey attitude and perspective in my own writing?

In your Paper 2 Question 5 writing task, you should decide on the perspective you will take on the subject, and ensure you convey that view through what you say and the relevant writer's methods, such as tone and register. For example, a letter conveying a critical perspective on river pollution might use a firm, angry tone:

> Environmental authorities whose responsibility it is to protect the river and how clean it is have consistently failed to do so. The river is dying from a lethal cocktail of agricultural phosphates, illegal sewage discharge, and chicken manure.

The following extract is from an article for the school magazine. Its purpose is to argue for healthier food to be provided for school dinners and the audience is readers of the magazine, which could include students and teachers.

> Of course, in an ideal world, teenagers should eat what's good for them, which means lots of fresh veg and salad, and dishes that are low-fat, low-sugar, and low-salt. This would probably improve their brain function (pass that maths test!) and their all-round health. It would also set up good habits which would stop them being prone to heart disease or diabetes later in life. However, the reality is that teenagers want tasty snacks, which wipes all that low-fat and low-sugar off the menu.

Notice how the register here is a little more informal ('lots of fresh veg', 'off the menu'). The tone is informative and helpful, but it aims to appeal to teenagers, as in the humour of 'pass that maths test!'. The writer's attitude is realistic, aware of health issues, but resigned to the fact of teenagers often liking unhealthy food.

TIP

As a general rule, you should use a formal register in your exam responses. However, if an exam question asks you to write an article aimed at fellow teenagers, you can be slightly less formal.

Notice how the tone is created by careful choice of vocabulary: words such as 'lethal' and 'dying' convey the writer's strength of feeling about the river. The formal register and serious tone ('consistently failed to do so') convey the writer's attitude towards a serious and urgent problem.

Key terms

Make sure you can write a definition for each of these key terms.

attitude   colloquial language   dialect
first-person viewpoint   non-Standard English
perspective   register   second-person viewpoint
Standard English   third-person viewpoint   tone

Use the following questions to check your understanding of the knowledge covered in this section. Then cover the answers column with a piece of paper and write down as many as you can. Check and repeat.

Questions | Answers

#	Question	Answer
1	A text that is written from a first-person viewpoint will use the pronouns 'I' and 'we'. True or false?	True.
2	A text that is written from a third-person viewpoint uses the pronoun 'you'. True or false?	False. A text written from a third-person perspective would use the pronouns 'he', 'she', 'it', and 'they'.
3	A text that is written from a second-person viewpoint speaks directly to a reader or audience, addressing them as 'you'. True or false?	True.
4	What is meant by the writer's attitude?	Their thoughts and feelings about the topic they are writing about.
5	How would you describe the tone of this sentence? *'Go home; I'm not going to listen to another word you say.'*	Possible answers include: assertive; aggressive; angry; decisive; determined; exasperated.
6	What is Standard English?	English that is widely accepted as appropriate formal English, following standard grammar rules, and used in schools and official publications.
7	What is colloquial language?	Conversational, casual language.
8	What is dialect?	A type of language that is spoken just in one area, rather than nationwide.
9	The register of your language will vary depending on who you are talking to and where. True or false?	True.

Put paper here

Previous questions

Now go back and use these questions to check your knowledge of previous topics.

Questions | Answers

#	Question	Answer
1	What sort of timing could be included in a setting?	Historical time, time of day or night, season, yearly or monthly festival or celebration.
2	What is the 'mood' of a text?	The atmosphere created in the text and the emotional response in the reader, created by the writer.

Put paper here

6 Sentence forms

What are sentence forms?

Writers organise words into sentences to convey meaning. Understanding different sentence forms will help you in your own writing.

QUESTION CONNECTION

You will use your knowledge of sentence forms in your own writing for Paper 1 Question 5 and Paper 2 Question 5.

Single-clause (simple) sentences

A single-clause sentence is a sentence that contains just one main clause. A main clause is a group of words that has a verb as its headword and a subject (either a noun, noun phrase, or pronoun).

It is important not to overuse simple sentences, and include a variety of sentence types in your writing.

TIP

A single-clause sentence can stand alone as a paragraph, if the writer wants to make a sentence stand out for the reader.

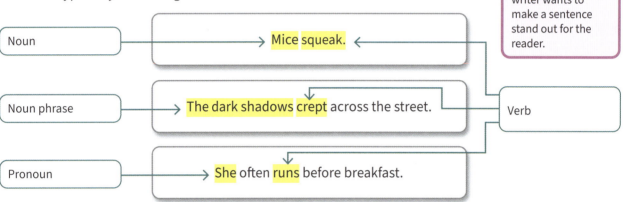

Minor sentences

These are short sentences. They might not contain a subject or a verb. A writer might use a **minor sentence** to emphasise a point. Note that the term 'minor sentence' does not mean they are unimportant. They can be used to express strong emotion or to draw attention to something.

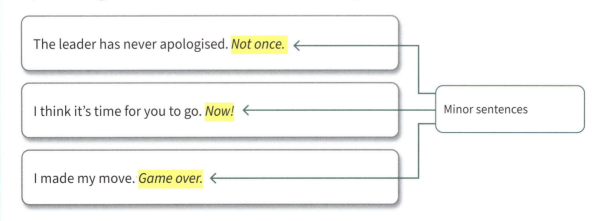

Multi-clause (compound) sentences

These combine two or more clauses, using a **coordinating conjunction**, such as 'and', 'but', or 'yet'.

> Fish have to swim **and** bats have to fly.

> Cats are independent, **but** some enjoy being stroked.

Coordinating conjunctions. There are other examples you can use in your writing; these are just the most common.

> I looked through the window every day, **yet** I never saw the fox again.

Multi-clause (complex) sentences

These combine at least two clauses using a **subordinating conjunction**, such as 'despite', 'which' or 'because'. Complex sentences contain one main clause and one or more subordinate clauses (subordinate clauses can add detail to a main clause but can't work as a sentence on their own).

> Aaron, despite being a poor swimmer, jumped in immediately to save his friend.

Subordinate clause adding information in mid-sentence, with a comma before and after.

> Hamid apologised, which is more than could be said for Elena.

Subordinate clause adding information at the end of the sentence, preceded by a comma.

Subordinate clauses can be found at the beginning of a sentence, in the middle or at the end, and are usually separated from the main clause by a comma, or commas. Writers often decide where to position the subordinate clause depending on what they want to draw the reader's attention to first.

Sentence types

There are four main types of sentences, each with a different purpose:

- **Statements** – state a fact: 'You're my best friend.'
- **Questions** – seek information: 'What's that?'
- **Imperatives** – give an order or instruction: 'Replace the lid.'
- **Exclamations** – express an emotion, such as surprise or disapproval: 'You've got to be kidding!'

TIP

Remember to check the punctuation of your sentences. This includes the correct use of commas, full stops, question marks, exclamation marks, apostrophes, and speech marks.

⚙ Knowledge   CONCEPT

6 Sentence forms

What are the effects of varying sentence forms?

Understanding how writers use different sentence forms can help you to use them effectively in your own writing. Look at how the writer uses sentence structures in the extract below to help build up an argument. Note that the full text is on page 21.

Extract 1: 'The hunter who killed Cecil the lion doesn't deserve our empathy' by Rose George

This extract is from an article in the *Guardian* and shows the writer's views on a trophy hunter killing a famous lion in Zimbabwe.

❶ Single-clause sentence to set out the writer's point of view clearly.

I feel no calmness about big-game hunters. **❶**
I am not persuaded by their justifications, which can be easily punctured with buckshot. **❷** Trophy hunting contributes to conservation, they say: when the Dallas Safari Club auctioned the right to kill an endangered Namibian black rhino, it said the $350,000 winning bounty – they called it a 'bid' – went towards conservation efforts in Namibia. **❸** There are only 5,000 black rhinos left. **❹**

5

❷ Multi-clause sentence to provide additional detail.

❹ Single-clause sentence simply to defeat the counter-argument and confirm the writer is correct.

❸ Long multi-clause sentence to explain the counter-argument.

Notice how the writer varies the sentence forms to introduce, explain, and then build up her argument. The final short sentence is an effective statement of fact that proves how hollow and misguided the big-game hunters' claims are.

How can I write about sentence forms?

It is not necessary to comment on sentence forms in your exam, as it is quite simple analysis and will receive few marks. The only time you might comment on sentences would be when they are used for specific effect. The answer below will help you understand how the writer uses sentence structure to convey their argument.

LINK

You can read more about using discourse markers to build an argument on page 57.

❶ Opening statement about technique.

The author uses increasing sentence length and complexity to build a case. **❶** She begins with a simple sentence clearly stating her viewpoint and proceeds with a longer complex sentence about how hunters attempt to justify themselves, then builds to a climax with an even longer complex sentence putting forward the hunters' argument. **❷** Finally, this puffed up argument is punctured with the short simple statement that only 5,000 black rhinos are left. **❸**

❷ Demonstrates how the climax is reached.

❸ Uses discourse marker ('Finally') to introduce dismissal of the hunters' argument.

How can I vary sentence forms in my own writing?

In the Writing questions of the exam, you must vary your sentence structures effectively. This means knowing how to use different sentence structures to keep your reader engaged and following your narrative or argument closely.

QUESTION CONNECTION

In Paper 1 Question 5 and Paper 2 Question 5, you will be assessed on AO5 and AO6. AO6 states that you must use a range of sentence structures for clarity, purpose, and effect.

Sentence forms in fiction

In fiction, different sentence forms can help to convey the pace of action and the mood of a scene.

Look at how the sentence forms vary in the narrative extract below, reflecting the content of the narrative and breaking it up into logical snippets.

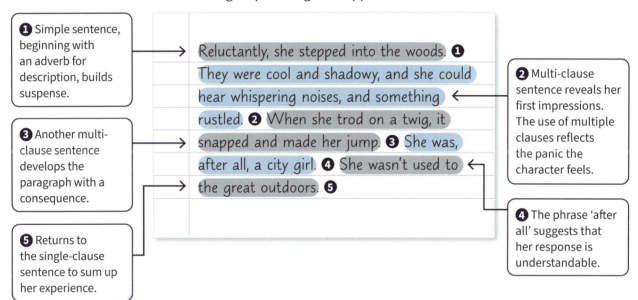

❶ Simple sentence, beginning with an adverb for description, builds suspense.

❸ Another multi-clause sentence develops the paragraph with a consequence.

❺ Returns to the single-clause sentence to sum up her experience.

> Reluctantly, she stepped into the woods. ❶ They were cool and shadowy, and she could hear whispering noises, and something rustled. ❷ When she trod on a twig, it snapped and made her jump. ❸ She was, after all, a city girl. ❹ She wasn't used to the great outdoors. ❺

❷ Multi-clause sentence reveals her first impressions. The use of multiple clauses reflects the panic the character feels.

❹ The phrase 'after all' suggests that her response is understandable.

Sparing use of simple and minor sentences can be effective when writing fiction.

Here the sentence variations are used to control the mood of the text and the effects on the reader.

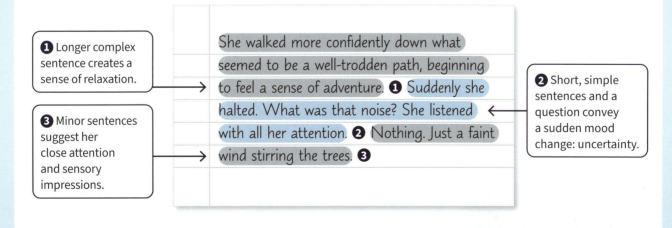

❶ Longer complex sentence creates a sense of relaxation.

❸ Minor sentences suggest her close attention and sensory impressions.

> She walked more confidently down what seemed to be a well-trodden path, beginning to feel a sense of adventure. ❶ Suddenly she halted. What was that noise? She listened with all her attention. ❷ Nothing. Just a faint wind stirring the trees. ❸

❷ Short, simple sentences and a question convey a sudden mood change: uncertainty.

6 Sentence forms

Sentence forms in non-fiction

When writing a non-fiction text, such as presenting a viewpoint or argument, you will need to vary the sentence forms you use. This variety can be used to:

- emphasise important points
- add detailed information
- challenge your audience to consider issues and make memorable points
- generally strengthen the power of what you are saying.

See the writing below uses a range of sentence forms to present an argument effectively.

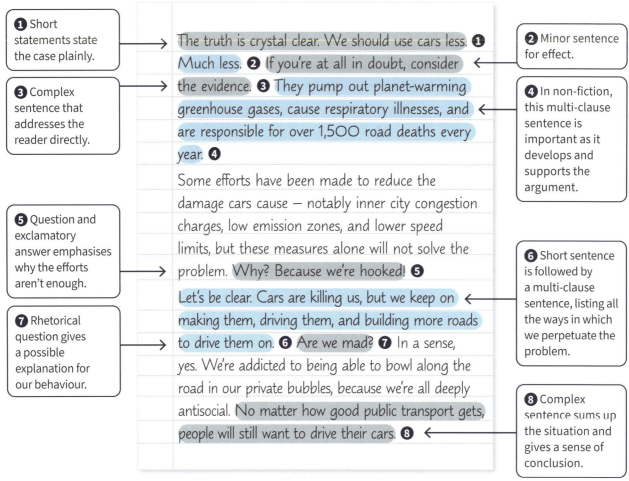

❶ Short statements state the case plainly.

❸ Complex sentence that addresses the reader directly.

❺ Question and exclamatory answer emphasises why the efforts aren't enough.

❼ Rhetorical question gives a possible explanation for our behaviour.

The truth is crystal clear. We should use cars less. **❶** Much less. **❷** If you're at all in doubt, consider the evidence. **❸** They pump out planet-warming greenhouse gases, cause respiratory illnesses, and are responsible for over 1,500 road deaths every year. **❹**

Some efforts have been made to reduce the damage cars cause — notably inner city congestion charges, low emission zones, and lower speed limits, but these measures alone will not solve the problem. Why? Because we're hooked! **❺**

Let's be clear. Cars are killing us, but we keep on making them, driving them, and building more roads to drive them on. **❻** Are we mad? **❼** In a sense, yes. We're addicted to being able to bowl along the road in our private bubbles, because we're all deeply antisocial. No matter how good public transport gets, people will still want to drive their cars. **❽**

❷ Minor sentence for effect.

❹ In non-fiction, this multi-clause sentence is important as it develops and supports the argument.

❻ Short sentence is followed by a multi-clause sentence, listing all the ways in which we perpetuate the problem.

❽ Complex sentence sums up the situation and gives a sense of conclusion.

Overall, this student uses a variety of sentence forms to state the case clearly, create dramatic emphasis, and draw the reader into the issue. The sentences build up to state the problem, explain efforts to solve it, and analyse why these efforts may never work.

Key terms Make sure you can write a definition for each of these key terms.

coordinating conjunction   exclamation   imperative
minor sentence   multi-clause sentence
single-clause sentence   statement   subordinating conjunction

Use the following questions to check your understanding of the knowledge covered in this section. Then cover the answers column with a piece of paper and write down as many as you can. Check and repeat

Questions | Answers

	Questions	Answers
1	What is a clause?	A sentence or part of a sentence that includes a subject (noun, noun phrase, or pronoun) and a verb.
2	A multi-clause sentence can have more than two clauses in it. True or false?	True.
3	A single-clause sentence is always very short. True or false?	False. For example: The young boy on the drums gave an incredible performance last night.
4	What kind of sentence is in italics below, and what is its effect? 'You mean everything to me. *Everything*.'	A minor sentence. Here it is used for emphasis and focus.
5	Turn the following into a multi-clause sentence. (You can add or take away words.) Abshir comes from Somalia. It is in Africa. Many African countries experience drought.	Answers may vary. For example: Abshir comes from Somalia, which is in Africa, where many countries experience drought.
6	You will gain marks by simply identifying sentence structures in a text. True or false?	False. Only identify sentence structures if there is a significant reason the writer has chosen them and explain the effect they create.
7	What is a statement?	A sentence that states a fact, such as: *Birds have wings*.
8	What are *imperative* sentences and in what kind of text might you find them?	Sentences giving orders or instructions. You might find them in persuasive, advisory, or instructional texts.
9	What kind of sentence is this, and what is its effect? '*Don't tell me you forgot the marmalade!*'	Exclamative. It expresses an emotion such as shock, dismay, disbelief, or anger.

Put paper here

Previous questions

Now go back and use these questions to check your knowledge of previous topics.

Questions | Answers

	Questions	Answers
1	What is meant by the writer's attitude?	Their thoughts and feelings about the topic they are writing about.
2	What is colloquial language?	Informal language, as if in conversation.

Put paper here

⚙ Knowledge   CONCEPT

7 Narrative structure

What is narrative structure?

Narrative structure is the way in which a writer organises the sequence of events. It can be a fiction story or a sequence of events in a non-fiction text, such as a narrative which describes a journey in travel writing. Some of the key features of narrative structure can be found below.

> **QUESTION CONNECTION**
>
> You will have to comment on narrative structure in Paper 1 Questions 3, and possibly in Paper 1 Question 4 and Paper 2 Question 4. You will have to create your own narrative structure in your writing when responding to Paper 1 Question 5.

Openings

Here are some of the ways a story may begin:

- In the middle of the action (this is known as *in media res*):

> It was only half a mile to school. He'd probably make it if he pedalled fast.

- Describing a scene or setting:

> It was a hot, cloudless, and almost windless day, and there was hardly an inch of bare sand left on Saltash Beach.

- Introducing a character:

> Aisha viewed herself in the bathroom mirror: dark, thoughtful eyes in a rounded face.

Inciting incident

Near the start of a story, there is usually an **inciting incident** – a problem or event that sets off a sequence of events that drive the narrative of the story.

> Jamila was just checking her phone as she stepped off the kerb into the path of the pizza delivery bike.

Endings

Here are some of the ways a story may end:

- A resolution to a problem, bringing reconciliation between characters.
- A **cliffhanger** – a dramatic point in the story, leaving the reader wondering what will happen next.
- A return to the beginning of the story, or mirroring the start of the story in some way (a circular narrative).

Shifts in focus

The **focus** of a narrative is whatever the writer is concentrating on at any particular time. This focus will shift as the narrative develops. It may:

- move from one character to another
- move from one location to another
- shift between description and action or dialogue and internal thoughts
- zoom in or zoom out on aspects of the setting or character.

Writers often signal a change of focus with structural features, such as a **discourse marker** or new paragraph:

> Georgia steadied her feet as she walked out of the tube station.
>
> With a step forward, she became just one person in a sea of thousands. The buildings soared high, piercing the skyline.

This example begins with a zoom in on Georgia's emotions. A new paragraph then begins with a discourse marker to zoom out and shift the reader's focus on aspects of the setting.

Sequencing

A narrative may tell a story in **chronological** order, with a straightforward sequence of events each following on from each other, linked by cause and effect. It could also involve a shift backwards or forwards in time. The narrative could shift forwards to later that day, include a **flashback** (shifting backwards to the previous day or five years earlier) or **foreshadowing** (shifting forwards to a moment in the future).

> **TIP**
>
> It can work well to begin a story with an exciting problem and then flash back to what led up to it: 'Just a few hours earlier …'.

> She swung the axe until the tree was felled. The crash rippled through the forest. (A chronological sequence of events)
>
> Gazing at the river, all at once she was a child again, with her brother playing near the water – much too near the edge. (Flashback)
>
> If he had known then what he knew later, he might have paid more attention. (Foreshadowing)

Tension and suspense

A good writer considers how to create **tension** and **suspense** by making structural choices about their story, such as including flashbacks and foreshadowing. Structural features, such as withholding information and dropping hints will build suspense and tension with the reader. Tension builds up the reader's anticipation, and suspense creates a sense of danger or uncertainty.

Climax

The **climax** is the peak of excitement in a whole text; for example, when the superhero confronts the villain and is in the greatest danger. The climax normally comes towards the end of the story structure, before the resolution. Some stories include a small **crisis** (before the main climax), but they usually build towards the main climax.

⚙ Knowledge CONCEPT

7 Narrative structure

What are the effects of different narrative structural devices?

A writer organises the narrative structure to lead the reader through the story, shifting focus to keep the reader entertained and interested, revealing more details about setting and characters as the plot unfolds.

Writers control levels of tension and suspense through their narrative structure. Sometimes information is withheld and only gradually revealed. Readers may enjoy picking up hints and clues from the writer, guessing what the outcome may be.

In Extract 1 below, the writer creates a shift in focus by beginning with a description of a busy street scene and then zooming in on a hesitant, nervous character. The effect of this contrast is to concentrate the reader's attention on the character's emotional state. This builds up a sense of suspense before Arjun finally enters the building.

> **TIP**
>
> When reading a text, think about the story visually as it would be shown in a film. This will help you notice any shifts in the narrative focus, time or perspective.

❶ Topic sentence

This sums up what the writer is about to describe.

❸ Focus shift

Contrasting Arjun with the crowd in his momentary stillness. Writer withholds why Arjun is 'consumed by hesitation', to keep the reader guessing.

❺ Hint

Indicating the character's anxiety.

❻ Focus shift

New paragraph marks focus shift. The discourse marker ('Finally') signals a shift in focus.

Extract 1: *Transmission* by Hari Kunzru

> This extract is from a novel and is about a man trying to make a success in his career as a computer programmer.

Around him Connaught Place seethed with life. ❶ Office workers, foreign backpackers, messengers and lunching ladies all elbowed past the beggars, dodging traffic and running in and out of Palika Bazaar like
5 contestants in a game. ❷ For a moment Arjun Mehta, consumed by hesitation, was the only stationary figure in the crowd. He was visible from a distance, a skinny flagpole of a boy, hunching himself up to lose a few conspicuous inches before making his entrance. ❸
10 The face fluttering on top wore an expression of mild confusion, partly obscured by metal-framed glasses whose lenses were blurred with fingerprints. Attempting to assert its authority over his top lip was a downy moustache. ❹ As he fiddled with his collar, it twitched
15 nervously, a small mammal startled in a clearing. ❺

Finally, ❻ feeling himself as small as he would ever get, he clutched his folder of diplomas to his chest, stated his business to the chowkidar [watchman], and was waved up the steps into the air-conditioned cool of the
20 office lobby. ❼

---

❷ Description of setting

Emphasis on the confusing, frenzied activity.

❹ Zoom in

On Arjun's face as a way of conveying character.

❼ Focus shift

Arjun clutching folder, announcing himself, and his being 'waved up', prepare for a scene change. His 'diplomas' hint that he is going for a job.

In the extract below, the writer organises the narrative structure to build up tension and suspense, vividly conveying the sense of danger and desperation felt by the protagonist.

❶ Opening

Launches into the action (*'in media res'*) but provides key information: a lone man at night is in danger from some young men.

❸ Raises tension

He is now in a 'sea' of danger, with no help at hand.

❺ Foreshadowing

Foreshadows (anticipates) the probable attack and his possible death.

❼ Tension

Extreme tension in his intense physical fear response. Beginning of climax.

❾ Focus shift

New paragraph signals focus shift and creates sense of drama for the moment of greatest suspense: will the young men look under the lorry?

Extract 2: 'The Waste Land' by Alan Paton

In this short story, a man gets off a bus at night with his week's wages.

The moment that the bus moved on he knew he was in danger, for by the lights of it he saw the figures of the young men waiting under the tree. ❶ That was the thing feared by all, to be waited for by young men. It
5 was a thing he had talked about, now he was to see it for himself. ❷

It was too late to run after the bus; it went down the dark street like an island of safety in a sea of perils. ❸ Though he had known of his danger only for a second,
10 his mouth was already dry, his heart was pounding in his breast, ❹ something within him was crying out in protest against the coming event. ❺

[*He is chased through a dark wasteland. He knocks one man down with his stick.*]

15 Then he turned and began to run again, but ran first into the side of an old lorry, which sent him reeling. He lay there for a moment expecting the blow that would end him, but even then his wits came back to him, and he turned over twice and was under the lorry. ❻ His
20 very entrails seemed to be coming into his mouth, and his lips could taste sweat and blood. His heart was like a wild thing in his breast, and seemed to lift his whole body each time that it beat. ❼ He tried to calm it down, thinking it might be heard, and tried to control the noise
25 of his gasping breath, but he could not do either of these things. ❽

Then suddenly against the dark sky he saw two of the young men. ❾

❷ Foreshadowing

He is about to experience his fear becoming reality.

❹ Tension

His physical response raises tension even more.

❻ Tension

Tension pauses as he finds a hiding place.

❽ Suspense

He is doomed if they hear him.

TIP

In the exam, there will be an introduction at the top of the extract, which will give you a greater understanding of the extract and enable you to write about it with more insight.

7 Narrative structure

How can I write about narrative structure?

When writing about the structure of a story, think carefully about what aspects of the narrative you are going to focus on and also how the writer takes the reader from one focus point to the next.

For example, if writing about the structure of Extract 1 (on page 50), you might start like this:

TIP

In the exam, you may find it helpful to highlight and label sections of the source text that you want to focus on and identify the shifts to a different time, place, or character.

1 Introduces extract, with a link to place and character.

3 Notices how the pronoun shifts the focus.

5 Technical term correctly used, with note of effect ('intrigues').

> The text begins with a sentence that sets the scene, and introduces a place and a main character. **1** It then shifts to lots of people who make up the 'seething' mass, and what they are doing: elbowing past beggars, 'dodging traffic', 'running in and out' of the bazaar. By describing the place as busy, 'seething', and zooming out to show multiple people 'around him', it highlights that the main character is feeling out of place. **2** The focus then shifts back to the 'him' in the first line, as if zooming in. **3** His being a 'stationary figure', reinforces the idea of him standing out, anxious and not knowing where he is or what to do. **4** The author intrigues the reader by withholding information **5** about why Arjun is 'consumed by hesitation' and what 'entrance' he is about to make. The wording foreshadows the fact that he is about to do something important. **6**

2 Neatly leads on from the previous sentence to explain the focus shift.

4 Awareness of interplay between character and setting.

6 Comments on how wording relates to structure.

Structurally, Extract 2 (on page 51) is all about tension and suspense building to a climax. You could analyse the **opening** like this:

1 Identifies the function and impact of the opening.

> The author engages the reader's interest immediately by launching straight into the action with the story's problem — a lone man getting off a bus at night to find menacing young men waiting for him. **1** The author heightens the reader's anticipation by ensuring the reader is

with the main character as he gets off the bus, seeing the young men waiting in the distance at the same time. Therefore, the reader will empathise more with his situation. The writer also uses foreshadowing: 'now he was about to see it for himself'. This reveals that the story will be about whether the man survives. ❷ The reader sees, as the man does, the lights of the bus disappearing into the darkness, moving away from him and leaving him alone. The structural choice to position the reader with the character creates a more vivid or intense experience of the emotions of the character. ❸ The man's rapid physical fear reaction reinforces this tension. ❹ The author almost makes the man's fate seem inevitable in the foreshadowing of his 'protest against the coming event'. This makes the reader even more anxious for him, ❺ as the 'event' will be his being attacked, perhaps killed.

❷ Comments on the effect of the reader's position, time, and foreshadowing, with evidence.

❸ Explains the importance of the reader position and bus in raising tension and suspense.

❹ Comments on another means by which tension is increased.

❺ Explains what is foreshadowed.

A further paragraph could analyse how the author builds to a climax:

The passage develops towards a frightening climax with the man hiding under the lorry. ❶ The physicality of his fear is intense, with his guts seeming to fill his mouth, the taste of his own 'sweat and blood', and his hammering heart. This shift in focus to zoom in on his body makes the emotion much more believable to the reader. ❷ The sense of tension and crisis is perhaps strongest ❸ when he is unable to calm his heart or breathing and fears that his pursuers will hear. The suspense, however, reaches a peak with him seeing 'two of the young men'. ❹ The new paragraph, consisting of a single sentence, underlines what a moment of crisis this is. ❺

❶ Identifies structural development: the character's fear reaching its peak.

❷ Well-chosen evidence: reference and direct quotation.

❸ Gives an opinion on how a key detail creates a sense of crisis.

❹ Identifies a structural climax.

❺ Explains how two structural features contribute to this.

CONCEPT

7 Narrative structure

How can I create narrative structure in my own writing?

To use narrative structure effectively, you need to plan your writing carefully. Consider the whole story or description that you intend to write, even if you're not sure of the details. Focus on the progression – how you will take the reader on a journey, start to finish.

QUESTION CONNECTION

In Paper 1 Question 5, you will be asked to write a narrative or a description. Whichever form you write, plan the structure before you start.

Planning a story

Consider:

- How will you begin? For example, you could begin in mid-flow, like Extract 2 in this unit. You could also begin with dialogue or a rhetorical question.
- Plan how you will move the story on stage by stage, through conflict to resolution. Begin each stage with a new paragraph.
- Decide where you will place the reader in relation to the action, and whether you will write in first, second, or third person.
- How will you include shifts in time or focus? Consider how you could use flashbacks or foreshadowing.
- How will you create tension or conflict? Without at least one of these, your story will not engage the reader. For example, an argument might trigger strong emotion or dramatic action.
- Think about how to *withhold* and *reveal* key information. Don't spill it all out at once.
- How will you end your writing? You might use a cliffhanger or reach a resolution.

Planning a description

Consider:

- How will you draw the reader in from the start? Perhaps with a surprising statement or a moment of intense emotion or drama.
- What will be the highlights of your description?
- How will you organise your description into sections that lead on from each other? For example, you could focus on a detail and then describe a wider perspective. Each section should begin with a new paragraph.
- Consider how you will set out different aspects of setting. Will you shift through place (location or view); or through time, describing the place at one point and then again later?
- Think carefully about how to use topic sentences and discourse markers to guide your reader through and across paragraphs.
- How will you bring your description to a satisfying conclusion?

TIP

As a writer, you can control the amount of information you give your reader. Sometimes, what you *don't* reveal or only reveal bit by bit, can help to create tension and suspense.

Key terms

Make sure you can write a definition for each of these key terms.

chronological cliffhanger climax crisis discourse marker flashback focus foreshadowing inciting incident opening suspense tension time frame

Use the following questions to check your understanding of the knowledge covered in this section. Then cover the answers column with a piece of paper and write down as many as you can. Check and repeat.

Questions

Answers

	Question	Answer
1	Narrative structure is the way that a writer organises and presents a story to a reader. True or false?	True.
2	Narrative structure can only be found in fiction texts. True or false?	False.
3	What is meant by 'focus' in narrative structure?	What the writer is concentrating on at any particular time.
4	What structural devices can be used to signal a change of focus?	A new paragraph; discourse markers.
5	What is foreshadowing and what effect does it create for the reader?	Foreshadowing is a narrative device that suggests what is going to happen later on in the story. It helps the reader anticipate how the story might unfold.
6	What is a circular narrative?	A story that ends in the same or similar place to where it began.
7	What narrative devices might a writer use to create tension and suspense?	Withholding information or giving small clues to keep the reader guessing and anticipating what might happen next.
8	What term describes the peak of excitement in a narrative?	The climax.
9	If a story starts *in media res*, what does this mean?	The story starts in the middle of the action. It then goes on to reveal what happened before and after this event.
10	What is a flashback and why might a writer use it?	A shift back in time in a story. A writer might use this to explain why a character acts as they do, or why a situation has arisen.

Put paper here

Previous questions

Now go back and use these questions to check your knowledge of previous topics.

Questions

Answers

	Question	Answer
1	What is a clause?	A sentence or part of a sentence that includes a subject (noun, noun phrase, or pronoun) and a verb.
2	What is a statement?	A sentence that states a fact, such as: *Birds have wings.*

Put paper here

Knowledge CONCEPT

8 Structuring an argument

What is an argument?

A written argument expresses an **opinion** and tries to persuade the reader to agree with it. It provides factual evidence and explains what, in the writer's view, this evidence proves.

An argument should:

- pick a point of view to argue, for example: the school day should be shorter
- argue consistently for it, giving numerous reasons, for example: students learn more effectively in the morning, students and teachers have homework as well.
- address the opposite point of view to build your argument
- give your personal opinion, ensuring it contributes to a coherent argument.

An argument should be logical, but to be effective it also needs to be expressed persuasively. This is why rhetorical language is often used in making an argument.

QUESTION CONNECTION

Look at page 168 for the steps to follow to answer Paper 2 Question 5, which asks you to write a text to argue or persuade.

LINK

You can read more about rhetorical language on pages 18-25.

Fact and opinion

In order to write about authors' arguments, or write one yourself, you need to be clear about the difference between facts and opinions.

Fact	Opinion
What is it?	
A **fact** is something that can be proved to be true.	An opinion is someone's viewpoint or judgement.
How is it used?	
Facts can be used to: – build strong evidence to support your point – build an authoritative tone in your argument	Opinions can be used to: – persuade the reader or listener, as they appeal to emotions.
What should I remember?	
Be accurate when using facts to make them believable.	As opinions are often someone's viewpoint or judgement, use them to argue your point by suggesting that many others already agree with you.

Both facts and opinions are hugely valuable when writing about a topic and are best used in combination. By using both, you can build a cohesive argument.

> The Earth is spherical. (Fact)
>
> Students should be given more homework. (Opinion)
>
> Asia is the largest continent in the world. (Fact)
>
> Lions deserve to be saved more than rhinos. (Opinion)

Topic sentences

A **topic sentence** is a sentence, usually at the start of a paragraph, that prepares the reader for what is coming next – usually for the rest of the paragraph.

An effective written argument leads the reader carefully through a series of connected ideas. A topic sentence in effect tells the reader, 'Now we're going on to this next big idea, which will be developed in this paragraph.'

> There are many reasons why it is good to recycle clothes. The first reason is …

Discourse markers

Discourse markers are words or phrases that link ideas in a text. They show the relationship between one idea and the next and are especially important when writing an argumentative or persuasive text. They can be used to:

- point out the direction in which the text is heading
- refer back to ideas that have come earlier.

Discourse markers are usually used at the start of the sentence, but can be used mid-sentence.

Some discourse markers are:

| however | despite | nonetheless | on the other hand | consequently |

| in addition | although | as a result | furthermore | similarly |

| by contrast | alternatively | ultimately | specifically | moreover |

> In addition, a later start to the school day will benefit teachers who need to plan the next school day.
>
> Similarly, students will be able to prepare for the next day as well.

8 Structuring an argument

What are the devices used in a written argument?

When you read a written argument, for example in a persuasive newspaper editorial or magazine article, you will recognise some typical structural features.

- An introduction stating what the issue is in a way that readers can relate to and which will capture their interest (approximately one paragraph).
- A development explaining more about the problem or issue, often providing evidence, perhaps in the form of examples, case studies, facts or opinions (approximately two or three paragraphs).
- A **counter-argument** anticipating what those opposing the writer's views might say, and why the writer thinks they are wrong (approximately one paragraph).
- A conclusion bringing the strands of the argument together, and perhaps suggesting what might be done – often using the word 'should' (approximately one paragraph).

Look at how these features appear in the following newspaper article.

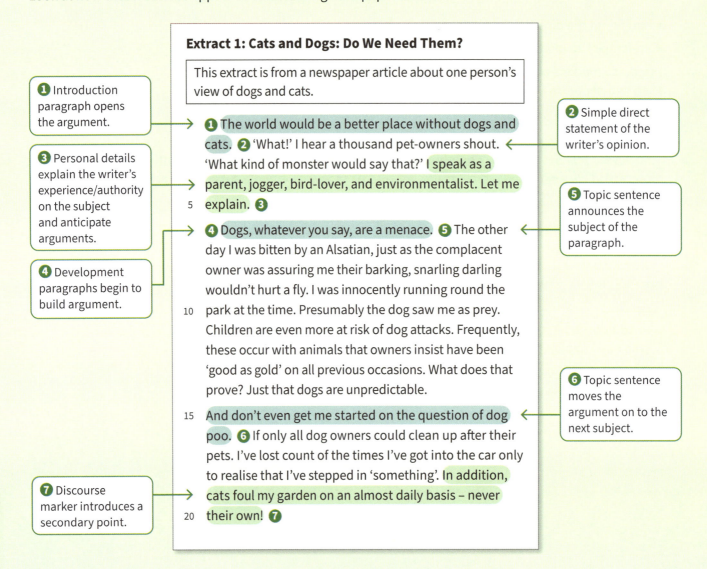

Extract 1: Cats and Dogs: Do We Need Them?

This extract is from a newspaper article about one person's view of dogs and cats.

❶ The world would be a better place without dogs and cats. ❷ 'What!' I hear a thousand pet-owners shout. 'What kind of monster would say that?' I speak as a parent, jogger, bird-lover, and environmentalist. Let me
5 explain. ❸

❹ Dogs, whatever you say, are a menace. ❺ The other day I was bitten by an Alsatian, just as the complacent owner was assuring me their barking, snarling darling wouldn't hurt a fly. I was innocently running round the
10 park at the time. Presumably the dog saw me as prey. Children are even more at risk of dog attacks. Frequently, these occur with animals that owners insist have been 'good as gold' on all previous occasions. What does that prove? Just that dogs are unpredictable.

15 And don't even get me started on the question of dog poo. ❻ If only all dog owners could clean up after their pets. I've lost count of the times I've got into the car only to realise that I've stepped in 'something'. In addition, cats foul my garden on an almost daily basis – never
20 their own! ❼

❶ Introduction paragraph opens the argument.

❸ Personal details explain the writer's experience/authority on the subject and anticipate arguments.

❹ Development paragraphs begin to build argument.

❼ Discourse marker introduces a secondary point.

❷ Simple direct statement of the writer's opinion.

❺ Topic sentence announces the subject of the paragraph.

❻ Topic sentence moves the argument on to the next subject.

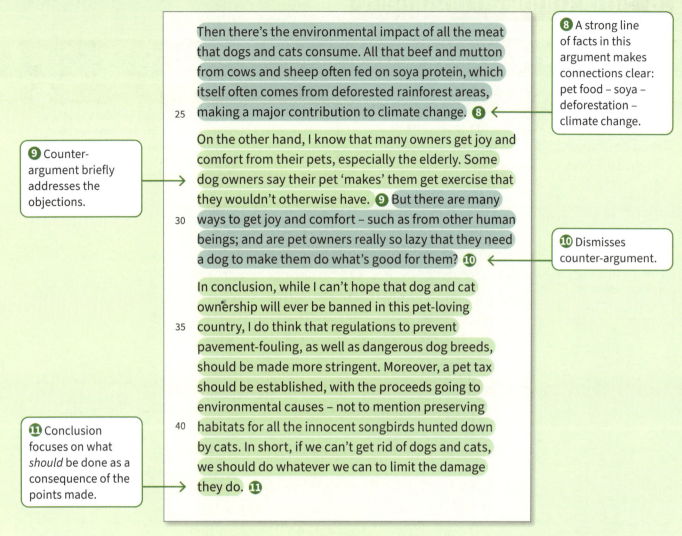

8 A strong line of facts in this argument makes connections clear: pet food – soya – deforestation – climate change.

Then there's the environmental impact of all the meat that dogs and cats consume. All that beef and mutton from cows and sheep often fed on soya protein, which itself often comes from deforested rainforest areas,
25 making a major contribution to climate change. **8**

9 Counter-argument briefly addresses the objections.

On the other hand, I know that many owners get joy and comfort from their pets, especially the elderly. Some dog owners say their pet 'makes' them get exercise that they wouldn't otherwise have. **9** But there are many
30 ways to get joy and comfort – such as from other human beings; and are pet owners really so lazy that they need a dog to make them do what's good for them? **10**

10 Dismisses counter-argument.

In conclusion, while I can't hope that dog and cat ownership will ever be banned in this pet-loving
35 country, I do think that regulations to prevent pavement-fouling, as well as dangerous dog breeds, should be made more stringent. Moreover, a pet tax should be established, with the proceeds going to environmental causes – not to mention preserving
40 habitats for all the innocent songbirds hunted down by cats. In short, if we can't get rid of dogs and cats, we should do whatever we can to limit the damage they do. **11**

11 Conclusion focuses on what *should* be done as a consequence of the points made.

This argument states its case at the outset. It then works its way paragraph by paragraph through the objections to dogs and cats: danger, faeces, and climate change. Then it considers a counter-argument and dismisses it, before concluding with recommendations for action.

TIP
If you're unsure of a **statistic** in your own writing, you could make a similar impact using a phrase such as 'The vast majority of …' or 'In most cases …'.

Knowledge CONCEPT

8 Structuring an argument

How can I write about the structure of an argument?

Here is one student's answer to how the point of view is conveyed in Extract 1 on pages 58-59. They draw attention to the structure of the argument, as well as how language and perspective are used to influence the reader.

QUESTION CONNECTION

In Paper 2 Question 4, you will be asked to write about how authors convey their point of view. In your response, you could comment on structure, but you could also write about other methods writers use, such as perspective and language.

❶ Identifies how the writer introduces her case.

The writer begins with a bold opening opinion: 'The world would be a better place without cats and dogs', which will succeed in capturing the attention of readers. ❶ The rest of this paragraph goes on to justify the opinion, acknowledging the opposite view in an exaggerated rhetorical question: 'What kind of monster would say that?' and listing four positive credentials of the writer: 'parent, jogger, bird-lover, environmentalist' with the aim of 'winning over' the reader. ❷ It invites them to see the argument in: 'Let me explain' to convey an established understanding between them both.

❷ Identifies rhetorical devices and effects.

❸ Identifies the argument structure.

The argument builds by including three paragraphs of both facts, as in 'The other day I was bitten', and opinions: 'don't even get me started on the question of dog poo'. ❸ A counter-argument is challenged briefly, beginning with a discourse marker: 'On the other hand, I know that many owners get joy' and dismissed. ❹ A summarising conclusion paragraph and statement ('In short, if we can't get rid of dogs and cats') emphasises the writer's personal opinion in a bold way to the reader, creating a cohesive argument, as this was the way the argument began. ❺

❹ Identifies the counter-argument and its dismissal.

❺ Identifies how the writer concludes, including her own feelings.

Notice how this student finds a variety of ways to sum up how the writer's argument progresses, identifying what each stage does. Look for the following sentence starters:

The writer begins …

The rest of this paragraph …

The argument builds …

A summarising conclusion …

TIP

When commenting on a writer's argument, remember to explain the effects of how it is presented, its structure, and how it leads the reader through a series of linked ideas in order to persuade them to adopt viewpoint.

How can I structure an argument in my own writing?

In Paper 2 Question 5, you will be asked to write your own text to express an opinion, present an argument or to persuade a reader to do or think something. It is essential to plan your response.

Explore the argument

First consider the question, and the text form, audience, and purpose of the response it asks you for.

For example, the question could be:

> 'Job satisfaction is much more important than how much you earn.'
>
> Write an article for a magazine in which you argue your point of view on this statement.

To plan an answer to this, first think about the question. It raises two main sub-questions:

- What *gives* job satisfaction?
- How much do you really need to earn?

You could see what ideas you can come up with for each of these using spider diagrams like the ones below.

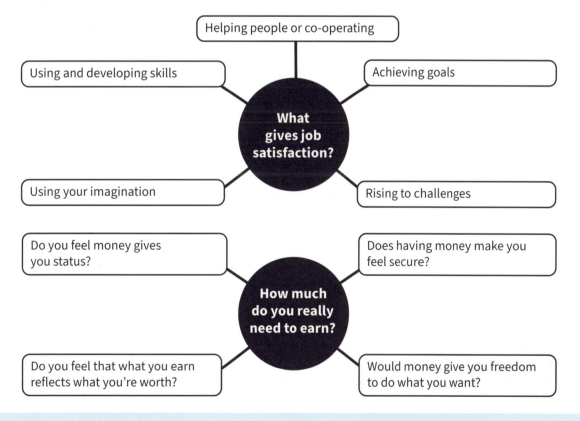

8 Structuring an argument

Build a cohesive argument

In your response, you need to focus on one main point of view to build a cohesive argument. You will address the opposite view in your one counter-argument paragraph, but the task requires you to have a particular opinion that you are arguing.

First, make sure you know the purpose of the text and its audience. Think about the ways that you can argue your point successfully and have the most impact, such as through rhetorical language and considering which tone and perspective to use. Refer to pages 18–41 for more details about these, and also page 168 (Paper 2 Question 5).

For the question on page 61, you could then structure your argument like this:

> 1. Introduction: how our society values wealth and celebrity and material possessions. Then asking if there is more to life.

> 2. Exploring some of the things you have listed that seem most important to you, with some examples from the world of work, e.g. a nurse helping others, or an artist using their imagination.

> 3. Counter-argument: exploring how people might argue in favour of money being important, e.g. gaining respect or admiration, freedom to travel, money to buy possessions. You could begin with a discourse marker, such as 'On the other hand …'.

> 4. Your reasons for preferring job satisfaction; for example, that it lasts long after material possessions have become boring, or that money is never satisfying on its own.

> 5. Conclusion: how you would advise others, for example a young person choosing a career, and why.

TIP

Check your plan to make sure that it is *cohesive* – that one idea leads on to the next and it makes sense as a whole.

Key terms

Make sure you can write a definition for each of these key terms.

counter-argument   discourse marker   fact
opinion   statistic   topic sentence

Use the following questions to check your understanding of the knowledge covered in this section. Then cover the answers column with a piece of paper and write down as many as you can. Check and repeat.

Questions

Answers

1 A topic sentence always comes at the end of a paragraph. True or false?

False. It normally comes at the start.

2 Is this a fact or an opinion?
It's always worthwhile to take a holiday abroad.

An opinion. This is because it cannot be proven or backed up with evidence.

3 Planning a response takes up valuable time that would be better spent on writing that response. True or false?

False. It is important to plan to organise your ideas and build a cohesive argument.

4 What is a *cohesive* argument? Choose from:
• One that you stick to.
• One that is passionately argued.
• One that makes sense as a whole.

One that makes sense as a whole.

5 What is a 'counter-argument'? Choose from:
• An opposing viewpoint to your own.
• An argument that disproves your own.
• An especially persuasive argument.

An opposing viewpoint to your own.

6 What is the effect of this discourse marker? 'On the other hand …'?

It warns the reader that you are about to explore a view that differs from the one you have just been writing about.

7 Discourse markers can only be used at the start of a sentence. True or false?

False. You could, for example, write: 'Cats, *on the other hand*, don't need to be taken for walks.'

8 What discourse marker could you use to indicate that you are going to introduce another similar point?

Possible answers include: 'In addition'; 'Additionally'; or 'Moreover'.

9 What would the discourse marker 'Consequently' indicate?

That you were about to write about something that was a result of the last thing you mentioned.

Put paper here

Previous questions

Now go back and use these questions to check your knowledge of previous topics.

Questions

Answers

1 What is a circular narrative?

A story that ends in the same or similar place to where it began.

2 If a story starts *in media res*, what does this mean?

The story starts in the middle of the action. It then goes on to reveal what happened before and after this event.

Put paper here

Knowledge

Paper 1: Overview

Structure

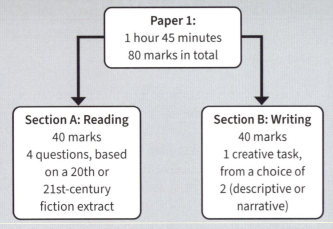

Paper 1:
1 hour 45 minutes
80 marks in total

Section A: Reading
40 marks
4 questions, based
on a 20th or
21st-century
fiction extract

Section B: Writing
40 marks
1 creative task,
from a choice of
2 (descriptive or
narrative)

Paper 1	Suggested timings	Marks	Skill tested
Reading the source	10 mins	-	-
Question 1	5 mins	4	AO1
Question 2	10 mins	8	AO2
Question 3	10 mins	8	AO2
Question 4	25 mins	20	AO4
Question 5	45 mins	40	AO5 AO6

Questions

In the exam, the questions will be printed in the exam booklet where you write your answers. The source text will be provided in a separate document.

The following are examples of the question types. They relate to the source text on page 176, *Dawn at Woolacombe Sands* by Jez Neumann. The exam papers will include the same question types in the same order each year. The source texts will be different.

LINK

The assessment objectives are explained in more detail on page 200.

Q1 | **Identify explicit information** | AO1

This question tests AO1 – identifying straightforward details from the opening lines of a source text.

Q1 Read again the first part of the source, from **lines 1 to 5.**

List **four** things Amir and Jane can see.

[4 marks]

This question tests your ability to:
- list four relevant pieces of **explicit information**
- choose the information from the right part of the source.

Q2 | **Comment on language** | AO2

This question tests one aspect of AO2 – commenting on the effects of a writer's language choices.

Q2 Look in detail at **lines 10 to 17** of the source.

How does the writer use language to describe Woolacombe Sands?

[8 marks]

This question tests your ability to:
- choose examples of language choices from the right part of the source
- clearly identify the language being used, using quotations and subject terms
- comment in detail on the effect created by these language choices.

Q3 | Comment on structure AO2

This question tests another aspect of AO2 – commenting on the effect of a writer's structural choices.

> **Q3** You now need to think about the **whole** of the source.
>
> How has the writer structured the text to interest you as a reader?
>
> **[8 marks]**

This question tests your ability to:
- choose examples of structural choices from the whole of the source
- clearly identify the structural choices using subject terms
- comment in detail on the effect created by these structural choices.

Q4 | Respond to a view AO4

This question tests AO4 – responding to (evaluating) an opinion about the source text using quotations and commenting on writer's methods.

> **Q4** Focus this part of your answer on **line 18 to the end**.
>
> A student said, 'In this part of the story, Amir and Jane have different reactions to Woolacombe Sands. The writer shows that Amir doesn't understand his wife and all of our sympathies are with Jane.'
>
> To what extent do you agree?
>
> **[20 marks]**

This question tests your ability to:
- give a detailed and clear response to the opinion given
- comment on how the writer uses language and/or structural methods
- use quotations to justify your opinion.

Q5 | Descriptive or Narrative writing AO5 AO6

This question tests AO5 – communicating imaginatively and structuring writing effectively. It also tests AO6 – using vocabulary, spelling, punctuation, and sentence types in an accurate and varied way.

> **Q5** Write a description of an interesting place to visit as suggested by this picture:
>
>
>
> **Or**
>
> Write a story about a memorable journey.
>
> **[40 marks]**

This question tests your ability to:
- write creatively in a way that sustains your reader's interest
- use words, punctuation, and sentence types in a varied and accurate way.

Paper 1: Reading the source / Question 1

Reading the source

In Paper 1, Section A: Reading, there will be four questions to answer about a source text. Before answering any questions, you must remember to read the source text in full.

Aim to spend the first 10 minutes of your exam carefully reading and annotating the text. It will be:

- about 700 words
- a fiction text from the 20th or 21st century.

There will be a short introduction to the source. This introduction will give you some important information, such as the setting, characters, or what is happening and where. Make sure you read it.

Some source texts include a glossary, which explains any unusual words. The glossed words will be starred, so use the glossary to double check their meaning when you come across them during your reading.

In the Paper 1 section of this book, Sources 1–4 will be used for learning and practice. These are on pages 176–183.

Question 1: Overview

? Focus	✓ Marks	🕐 Time	✳ AO
Ideas and information	4 marks	5 minutes	AO1

Question 1 tests your ability to find ideas and information in the source text. The ideas and information will be explicit (clearly stated), rather than implied (when you have to work them out).

Question 1 will always follow the same format:

> **Q1** Read again the first part of the source text, from **lines x to x**.
>
>   List **four** things …
>
>   **[4 marks]**

You are directed to the opening part of the source text and asked to select four pieces of specific information.

LINK

The knowledge section on pages 2–8 will remind you of the difference between explicit and implicit information.

TIP

Make sure you read the question carefully. At the start of an exam, it is easy to rush and miss the key focus of the question.

Question 1: Strategy

Follow the steps below to respond to a Question 1 task.

Step 1: Underline the key focus of the question. This is usually found at the end of the question, detailing exactly what you need to look for.

↓

Step 2: Look at the lines specified in the question. Bracket or draw a line beside the relevant lines in the source text, and slowly re-read the extract.

↓

Step 3: Select four things as specified in the question. You could underline or circle them in the source text.

↓

Step 4: Clearly list those four things in your answer booklet.

- List them in a short, precise way.
- You could use your own words or include short quotations from the text – whichever is quickest.

> **TIP**
>
> Do not copy out long sections of the text for Question 1. A short list of the four things will achieve the four marks.

Question 1: Example

Read the sample Question 1 and annotations below. In the exam, the relevant extract (e.g. lines 1–5) will not be printed out, so you will need to find it in the source text. You may find it helpful to mark the extract, so you keep looking at the right section of text.

> **LINK**
>
> This question refers to an extract from Source 1: *Dawn at Woolacombe Sands*. The full text is on pages 176–177.

Q1 Read again the first part of the source text, from **lines 1 to 5**.

List **four** things that Amir and Jane can see.

[4 marks]

This is the number of things you need to find. You will not receive any more marks for finding more.

This is the key focus of the question. Read it carefully to check you understand exactly what you are looking for. The word 'see' is important here.

This is where you should look in the source text. You will not get marks for anything outside these lines.

Source 1: *Dawn at Woolacombe Sands* by Jez Neumann

As Amir and Jane walked along the narrow sandy path, Amir began to feel vague anticipation somewhere inside him. The sea was obscured for now though, and all that they could see were tall dune grasses, a seabird pecking at something on the path, and the open grey sky. A faint sun drifted high
5 above them, lonely in the emptiness.

Paper 1: Question 1

Question 1: Sample answers

Sample answer 1

Now read the following sample answers to the Question 1 example question on page 67, alongside the examiner's comments.

This answer scores 2 marks out of 4.

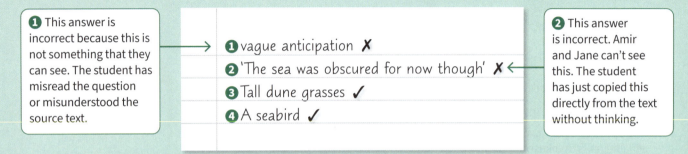

❶ This answer is incorrect because this is not something that they can see. The student has misread the question or misunderstood the source text.

❶ vague anticipation ✗

❷ 'The sea was obscured for now though' ✗

❸ Tall dune grasses ✓

❹ A seabird ✓

❷ This answer is incorrect. Amir and Jane can't see this. The student has just copied this directly from the text without thinking.

Sample answer 2

This answer scores full marks, as it correctly identifies four things that Amir and Jane can see.

❶ Tall dune grasses ✓

❷ A seabird ✓

❸ The grey sky ✓

❹ The faint sun ✓

Notice how the student has selected precise words from the source text which answer the question. Some descriptions can be long and detailed, but you only need to pick out the key words.

> **REMEMBER**
>
> - Keep your answers short. Answers do not need to be in full sentences.
> - You can use the exact words from the source text, but make sure you use only the part you need.
> - Do not copy out long chunks of text.
> - You can phrase answers in your own way as long as you are answering the question.

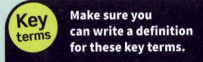
Key terms Make sure you can write a definition for these key terms.

explicit information

Paper 1: Question 1

Use the following questions to check your understanding of the knowledge covered in this section. Then cover the answers column with a piece of paper and write down as many as you can. Check and repeat.

Questions	Answers
1 How long should you spend on Question 1?	5 minutes.
2 How many marks are available for Question 1?	4 marks.
3 What is the focus of Question 1?	Finding ideas and information in the source text.
4 You should copy out long quotations. True or false?	False.
5 The information you need will be explicit. True or false?	True.
6 You need to select four precise bits of information. True or false?	True.
7 You must not make any marks on the source text. True or false?	False.
8 Summarise the four steps of the Question 1 strategy.	**Step 1:** underline the key focus of the question. **Step 2:** mark relevant lines in the source text. **Step 3:** choose four things in the source text. **Step 4:** list your answers.

Put paper here

Previous questions

Now go back and use these questions to check your knowledge of previous topics.

Questions	Answers
1 What type of source text will you be given to read and comment on in Paper 1?	Prose fiction – an extract from a novel or short story from the 20th or 21st century.
2 What is explicit information?	Information that is clearly stated. The reader does not have to work it out.

Put paper here

Practice EXAM

Exam-style questions

Answer the exam-style questions on pages 70–71. In the exam, the relevant extract (e.g. lines 1–4) for Question 1 will *not* be reprinted in the question paper, so you will need to find it in the source text. The extracts have been included here for easy reference.

> **REMEMBER** ❗
>
> In the exam, you will need to read the *whole* source text first, before you start looking at the questions and any specific extracts.

> **EXAM TIP**
>
> In your answer, you should:
>
> - check the question focus
> - select your answers from the correct part of the source text
> - clearly and precisely list your answers.

1.1

> **Q1** Read again the first part of the source text, from **lines 1 to 5**.
>
> List **four** things that Millie does.
>
> **[4 marks]**

> **LINK** 🔗
>
> This question refers to an extract from Source 2: *Millie*. The full text is on pages 178–179.

> **Source 2: *Millie* by Katherine Mansfield**
>
> Millie went back into the kitchen. She put some ashes on the stove and sprinkled them with water. Languidly, the sweat pouring down her face, and dropping off her nose and chin, she cleared away the dinner, and going into the bedroom, stared at herself in the fly-specked mirror […]. She didn't know
> 5 what was the matter with herself that afternoon.

1.2

> **Q1** Read again the first part of the source text, from **lines 1 to 9**.
>
> List **four** things that Rilla can see as she stands at the window.
>
> **[4 marks]**

> **LINK**
>
> This question refers to an extract from Source 3: *Facing the Light*. The full text is on pages 180–181.

> **Source 3: *Facing the Light* by Adele Geras**
>
> She is standing at the window. There's not even a breath of wind to move the white curtains and the grass outside lies dry and flat under the last of the sun. Summertime, and early evening, and she isn't in bed yet. She's nearly eight and it's too soon for sleeping. Everyone is doing something somewhere
> 5 else and no one is looking. The shadows of trees are black on the lawn and the late roses are edged with gold. There's a piece of silvery water glittering through the weeping willow leaves. That's the lake. Swans swim on the lake and she could go down to the water to see the white birds. No one would know and what you don't know can't hurt you.

1.3

> **Q1** Read again the first part of the source, from **lines 1 to 6**.
>
> List **four** things that Flora feels.
>
> **[4 marks]**

LINK

This question refers to an extract from Source 4: *The Bees*. The full text is on pages 182–183.

Source 4: *The Bees* by Laline Paull

The cell squeezed her and the air was hot [...]. All the joints of her body burned from her frantic twisting against the walls, her head was pressed into her chest and her legs shot with cramp, but her struggles had worked–one wall felt weaker. She kicked out with all her strength and felt something
5   crack and break. She forced and tore and bit until there was a jagged hole into fresher air beyond.

Paper 1: Question 2

? Focus	✓ Marks	🕐 Time	✳ AO
Language	8 marks	10 minutes	AO2

Question 2 tests your ability to comment in detail on the effects of the writer's choice of language in the source text. Question 2 will always follow the same format:

> **Q2** Look in detail at **lines x to x** of the source.
>
> How does the writer use language to …
>
> You could include the writer's choice of:
> - words and phrases
> - language features and techniques
> - sentence forms.   **[8 marks]**

> **LINK**
>
> The knowledge section on pages 10–16 will remind you of key **figurative language**, word choices and subject terms that will help you answer this type of question.

You will only have to refer to a set number of lines for Question 2, not the whole source. The specific part of the source you are focusing on is reprinted in your answer booklet.

Question 2: Strategy

Follow the steps below to respond to a Question 2 task.

> **Step 1**: Underline the key focus of the question.

> **Step 2**: Select three language features that:
> - are relevant to the focus of the question
> - you could say something thoughtful about, for example, the use of **figurative language** to create an image; or specific words, such as powerful **verbs**, **adverbs**, and **adjectives**.

> **Step 3**: Comment in detail on these features.
> - Clearly state the language features (e.g. **simile**) and use a quotation as an example.
> - Comment in detail on the effect of these language choices – this is what determines your mark. The more you explore the features you have identified, the higher your mark will be. Naming language features and choosing good quotations is useful but it is the comment on effect which earns marks.

> **TIP**
>
> Be careful which language features you choose. It can be hard to comment about features such as alliteration, punctuation, and sentence forms, unless they create very specific effects.

Question 2: Example

Read the sample Question 2 and annotations below. Before you complete Question 2, re-read the printed extract and underline any language features that are relevant to the key focus of the question.

Q2 Look in detail at **lines 10 to 17** of the source.

How does the writer use language to describe Woolacombe Sands?

You could include the writer's choice of:

- words and phrases
- language features and techniques
- sentence forms.

[8 marks]

LINK

This question refers to an extract from Source 1: *Dawn at Woolacombe Sands*. The full text is on pages 176–177.

Check these line references. You won't receive any marks for writing about language features that aren't in these lines.

These bullet points are suggestions – you do not have to cover all of them. It is quite hard to say anything detailed about sentence forms, so you are best sticking to word choices and language techniques, such as figurative language.

This is the focus of the question. You must select examples of language that are specifically describing Woolacombe Sands.

Source 1: *Dawn at Woolacombe Sands* by Jez Neumann

10 Woolacombe Sands is, as the cliché goes, a feast for the senses. When you see it in the early morning light, the wide beach gapes, smiling emptily; it opens out in front of you, introducing you to the quiet mystery of the sea that lies behind it. There's a loud silence that lures you in. A brisk air embraces you like a reluctant friend. The scene reveals itself to you on
15 its own terms and asks you to witness its empty magic. But Amir didn't feel this. Not a bit. To him, it was quite literally nothing. A huge, gigantic, overwhelming nothing. Nothing at all.

When selecting quotations to show the language feature, keep them short. It is best if you can incorporate a short quotation into a sentence, as you write. For example:

The adverb 'emptily' placed directly after 'smiling' undercuts the positivity and makes the beach a little ominous.

Paper 1: Question 2

Question 2: Sample answers

Sample answer 1

Now read the following sample answers to the Question 2 example question on page 73, alongside the examiner's comments.

This is one paragraph from a longer answer. It scores less than half the marks available.

❶ The student identifies an example of language but not precisely. They misunderstand what the writer means by this word in the context of the source.

❸ This is a potentially useful piece of language to comment on, but the student hasn't clearly labelled it and their comment is very general rather than specific to what's happening in the source.

The writer uses the word 'feast' as this shows that the people are hungry to see the sea. **❶** The writer also **personifies** the sea by saying it is 'smiling emptily' which makes it sound welcoming but also not welcoming. **❷** He also mentions 'empty magic' which sounds strange and makes the reader want to read on to find out what happens. **❸** The writer repeats the word 'nothing' to show how Amir feels. It shows us that he feels nothing and doesn't really want to be there at all. **❹**

❷ This is a potentially better point. The student has clearly identified and labelled a language feature. They begin to make a good comment, but it is not detailed, and they quickly move on instead of developing their point.

❹ This point is irrelevant. It is not about Woolacombe Sands but is instead about Amir. The student has lost sight of the focus of the question.

Examiner's comments

The quality of Sample answer 1 is quite mixed. Sometimes, the student makes a potentially good point, but they don't develop it. They don't clearly identify the language feature and occasionally write about irrelevant things.

It can sometimes help to start your answer with a comment on the overall effect of language choices – but be specific. See Sample answer 2 for how you might do this. Avoid writing very general comments such as 'The language choices help me to picture the scene'.

Sample answer 2

This is one paragraph from a longer answer to the same question. It scores high marks.

❶ The student begins by stating an overall impression of the beach – an opening statement that they develop in the next few sentences.

❸ This further extends the comment from the previous sentence with insightful comment on the effect of the word choices, which are labelled and referenced clearly.

> The writer presents Woolacombe Sands as an enigmatic place. ❶ The setting is personified as one that seems friendly, as it is shown as 'smiling' which suggests that it is amiable and the type of place that visitors may feel at home in. ❷ Yet the adverb 'emptily' placed directly after 'smiling' undercuts things and makes the beach a little ominous, as if there's something absent or slightly sinister about it — as if it's alive but also dead. ❸ The overall effect of this phrase is to present the beach as a mysterious place which appears superficially welcoming but also unknowable. ❹

❷ The language feature is clearly labelled with a precise quotation. The student spends some time explaining the effect of this language choice. The comment is specific to the events in the source – it's not generalised.

❹ This final comment clinches the point being made, explaining perceptively the way language choices have conveyed an impression of the beach.

Examiner's comments

Sample answer 2 clearly chooses and labels a rich piece of language. The student carefully unpicks the effects and ideas that the language creates. They extend their comments, and you can sense they are really thinking in depth.

The key to a better mark is developing your comments. Always extend your point; build up detail and show depth of thought. Coach yourself to do this by saying: 'What else can I add to this?' Sometimes adding an extra few sentences to a comment can push your mark higher.

TIP

In your answer, exploring an example in depth is better than trying to cover several examples in less detail.

REMEMBER

- The most important part of your answer is what you say about the *effect* of the language choices.
- Comment in detail on things such as what impression the language gives you of a character, place, or situation.
- Choose the three language techniques or words that you can say most about. Often, this means figurative language or individual words.

Key terms — Make sure you can write a definition for each of these key terms.

adjective   adverb   figurative language
personifies   simile   verb

Retrieval EXAM

Paper 1: Question 2

Use the following questions to check your understanding of the knowledge covered in this section. Then cover the answers column with a piece of paper and write down as many as you can. Check and repeat.

Questions	Answers
1 What is the focus of Question 2?	Commenting on the effect of the writer's language choices.
2 How long should you spend on Question 2?	10 minutes.
3 How many marks are available for Question 2?	8 marks.
4 Underline the question focus in this task: *How does the writer use language to describe Jamal's feelings about school?*	How does the writer use language to describe Jamal's feelings about school?
5 You need to identify as many language features as you can. True or false?	False. Aim to identify three language features.
6 You must write about sentence types in order to score highly. True or false?	False. It is better to focus on figurative language and individual words.
7 Figurative language and individual words are usually best to write about. True or false?	True. There is usually more you can say about figurative language and individual words.
8 Your mark heavily depends upon the quality of your comments. True or false?	True.
9 You don't need to label the language features or use a quotation. True or false?	False.
10 The best way to score highly is by extending your comments. True or false?	True.
11 Summarise the three steps of the Question 2 strategy.	**Step 1:** underline the key focus of the question. **Step 2:** select three language features. **Step 3:** comment in detail on these features.

Put paper here

Previous questions

Now go back and use these questions to check your knowledge of previous topics.

Questions	Answers
1 How is a metaphor different from a simile?	It speaks of a thing as if it *is* something else, without using 'like' or 'as'.
2 What does *infer* mean?	To work out meaning that is only hinted at, rather than explicitly stated.

Put paper here

Exam-style questions

Answer the exam-style questions on pages 77–79. In the exam, the relevant extract (e.g. lines 6-19) for Question 2 will be reprinted alongside the question in the answer booklet.

> **REMEMBER**
>
> In the exam, you will need to read the *whole* source text first, before you start looking at the questions and any specific extracts.

2.1

Q2 Look in detail at **lines 6 to 19** of the source.

How does the writer use language to describe the increasing tension?

You could include the writer's choice of:

- words and phrases
- language features and techniques
- sentence forms

[8 marks]

> **LINK**
>
> This question refers to an extract from Source 2: *Millie*. Remember to first read the full text on pages 178–179.

> **EXAM TIP**
>
> In your answer, you should:
>
> - select the most useful aspects of language
> - clearly label them and use a quotation
> - comment in detail on the effect created by these language choices.

Source 2: *Millie* by Katherine Mansfield

[…] *Tick-tick* went the kitchen clock, the ashes clinked in the grate, and the venetian blind knocked against the kitchen window. Quite suddenly Millie felt frightened. A queer trembling started inside her—in her stomach—and then spread all over to her knees and hands. "There's somebody about."

10 She tiptoed to the door and peered into the kitchen. Nobody there; the verandah doors were closed, the blinds were down, and in the dusky light the white face of the clock shone, and the furniture seemed to bulge and breathe … and listen, too. The clock—the ashes—and the venetian—and then again—something else, like steps in the back yard. […] She darted to

15 the back door, opened it, and at the same moment some one ducked behind the wood pile. "Who's that?" she cried, in a loud, bold voice. "Come out o' that! I seen yer. I know where y'are. [...] Come out from behind of that wood stack!" She was not frightened any more. She was furiously angry. Her heart banged like a drum.

Exam-style questions

2.2

> **Q2** Look in detail at this extract from **lines 10 to 20** of the source.
>
> How does the writer use language to describe the setting?
>
> You could include the writer's choice of:
>
> - words and phrases
> - language features and techniques
> - sentence forms.
>
> **[8 marks]**

LINK

This question refers to an extract from Source 3: *Facing the Light*. Remember to first read the full text on pages 180–181.

Source 3: *Facing the Light* by Adele Geras

10 She has to go, to flee, across the carpet woven with flowers and twisted trees, and then the door opens and she's in the corridor and it's dark there, always, even when the sun is shining outside, and a thick stillness takes up all the space and spreads down the staircase and she moves from step to step on tiptoe so as not to disturb it. Paintings on the walls stare at her as

15 she passes. Still life and landscapes spill strange colours and their own light into the silence and the portraits scream after her and she can't hear them. The marble floor in the hall is like a chess board of black and white and she makes sure to jump the black squares because if you don't, something bad is sure to happen, and maybe she just touched one black square on her way to

20 the garden but that wouldn't count, would it?

2.3

Q2 Look in detail at this extract from **lines 7 to 18** of the source.

How does the writer use language to describe Flora's experience of the hive?

You could include the writer's choice of:

- words and phrases
- language features and techniques
- sentence forms.

[8 marks]

LINK

This question refers to an extract from Source 4: *The Bees*. Remember to first read the full text on pages 182–183.

Source 4: *The Bees* by Laline Paull

She dragged her body through and fell out onto the floor of an alien world. Static roared through her brain, thunderous vibration shook the ground and a thousand scents dazed her. All she could do was breathe until gradually the
10 vibration and static subsided and the scent evaporated into the air. Her rigid body unlocked and she calmed as knowledge filled her mind.

This was the Arrivals Hall and she was a worker. Her kin was Flora and her number was 717. Certain of her first task, she set about cleaning out her cell. In her violent struggle to hatch she had broken the whole front wall, unlike
15 her neater neighbours. She looked, then followed their example, piling her debris neatly by the ruins. The activity cleared her senses and she felt the vastness of the Arrivals Hall, and how the vibrations in the air changed in different areas.

Paper 1: Question 3

Question 3: Overview

Focus	Marks	Time	AO
Structure	8 marks	10 minutes	AO2

Question 3 tests your ability to comment in detail on how the writer has structured the source text. Question 3 will always follow the same format:

> **Q3** You now need to think about the **whole** of the source.
>
> How has the writer structured the text to interest you as a reader?
>
> You could write about:
>
> - what the writer focuses your attention on at the beginning of the source
> - how and why the writer changes this focus as the source develops
> - any other structural features that interest you.
>
> **[8 marks]**

> **LINK**
>
> The knowledge section on pages 48–54 will remind you of some of the key structural features that will help you to answer this type of question.

For this question, you need to think about the *whole* of the source text provided, not just focus on some lines within it.

You need to think specifically about the **structure** of the source text, not the language features. The structure is the overall shape of the text – how the events of the story are sequenced.

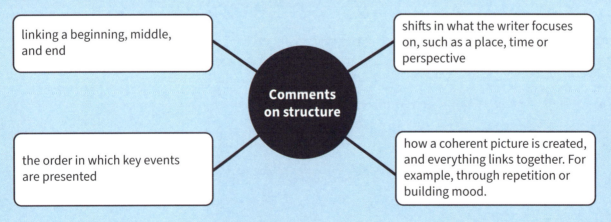

- linking a beginning, middle, and end
- shifts in what the writer focuses on, such as a place, time or perspective

Comments on structure

- the order in which key events are presented
- how a coherent picture is created, and everything links together. For example, through repetition or building mood.

Question 3: Strategy

Follow the steps below to respond to a Question 3 task.

Step 1: Briefly re-read the source text, looking out for key structural features.

Step 2: Select three key parts of the source's structure.

- The structural features you select should be taken from different sections of the extract, usually from the beginning, middle, and end.
- They should be features you feel you can say something thoughtful about – how they make the reader's experience interesting, for example, by switching perspective, increasing tension, changing the focus.

Step 3: Comment in detail on these structural features.

- Explain which part of the structure you are commenting on, using line numbers or a direct reference.
- Your comments should explore the effect of the structural choices – how that specific part of the structure helps you understand character and/or situation.
- Make sure your comments are detailed – this is what determines your mark. The more you explore the feature you have identified, the higher your mark will be.

You might find some of the sentence stems below helpful when thinking about how to present your ideas.

> In the opening paragraph, the writer introduces …
>
> Then the writer shifts the focus of the story and concentrates on …
>
> The problem that is established in the first part of the story is later developed further when …
>
> In the middle of the text, the writer focuses the reader's attention on …
>
> As the extract progresses, the writer builds up tension for the reader by …
>
> The ending of the story features a climax which …
>
> The earlier events in the story prepare the reader for the ending by …

Question 3: Example

Read the sample Question 3 and annotations below. Remember that Question 3 will always follow the same format; only the source text will change.

Q3 You now need to think about the **whole** of the source. ←

  How has the writer structured the text to interest you as a reader?

→ You could write about:

- what the writer focuses your attention on at the beginning of the source
- how and why the writer changes this focus as the source develops
- any other structural features that interest you.

[8 marks]

> You need to consider the *whole* extract, not just a few lines within it.

> Don't spend time talking about just what 'interests' you in the text. You need to comment on how the writer uses the structure of the text to help the reader understand the characters or situation at specific points in the text.

> These bullet points are useful suggestions. You can achieve high marks by writing in detail about how characters and situations are shown at the start of a source, how situations develop, and how things are by the end of the source.

> Keep your focus on the structure of the text. You will not gain marks focusing on anything else.

Source 1: *Dawn at Woolacombe Sands* by Jez Neumann

> This extract from a short story features Amir and Jane, a young married couple. They are visiting Woolacombe Sands, a beach in England.

As Amir and Jane walked along the narrow sandy path, Amir began to feel vague anticipation somewhere inside him. The sea was obscured for now though, and all that they could see were tall dune grasses, a seabird pecking at something on the path, and the open grey sky. A faint sun drifted high
5 above them, lonely in the emptiness.

Soon though, the path opened out and they emerged from the dunes. Amir realised he was finally there – standing on the beach at Woolacombe Sands at dawn alongside Jane, who had paused to take a single photo and then stood still, her eyes shut as if she was lost in some other unknown place.

10 Woolacombe Sands is, as the cliché goes, a feast for the senses. When you see it in the early morning light, the wide beach gapes, smiling emptily; it opens out in front of you, introducing you to the quiet mystery of the sea that lies behind it. There's a loud silence that lures you in. A brisk air embraces you like a reluctant friend. The scene reveals itself to you on
15 its own terms and asks you to witness its empty magic. But Amir didn't feel this. Not a bit. To him, it was quite literally nothing. A huge, gigantic, overwhelming nothing. Nothing at all.

"Don't talk. You'll only spoil the moment," Jane said, abruptly. She wasn't

looking at Amir, but was instead staring out to sea, as if it – *somehow* –
20 understood her spiritually. The morning light was on her face. She seemed
both present and elsewhere.

Amir began to open his mouth but closed it again. He wanted to speak but
felt that Jane had already decided that he was not allowed to be part of the
scene. His words and deeds were irrelevant. His thoughts were irrelevant too
25 apparently. Yet here they were, together and not together on a silent beach
with last night's row hovering between them.

The beach was not really that interesting to Amir. It seemed point-free. Car
parks had a purpose. Shops had a purpose. Sport did, too. But this was just
some sand and salty water. It was nothing really. Amir decided it would be
30 better if he kept this to himself though, because Jane was currently adopting
one of her many yoga poses and he knew from bitter experience that she
didn't like being interrupted in such spiritual moments. There was a ship on
the horizon and so Amir focused on this, wondering what was happening on
board and where they were heading.

35 Moments passed. He still hadn't spoken, but wanted to find the right words,
the right combination of words to make Jane happy again. Or at least one
that didn't spark her anger. They ought to be trying to make their marriage
work properly again. He wanted that, but now it seemed like they were in
different spheres.

40 "Well, what do you feel?" Jane asked eventually, much to Amir's surprise.
She wasn't looking at him and he couldn't tell if this was a trick question or
not. It felt like there was a dam somewhere, just about holding things back.

"It's quite big," Amir said, which seemed to him to be the form of words
which could do the least harm to the dam. A moment settled.

45 "Is that really the best thing you can find to say? It's quite big?" Amir still
couldn't see Jane's eyes but realised the magical repairing incantation had
eluded him.

He tried again. "I wonder where that ship is going," he said. A bit more of the
dam broke.

50 "We come to place of serenity and all you can tell me is it's big and there's a
ship?" Jane hissed.

"Well, what do you see?" Amir asked meekly.

"I don't see anything," Jane said eventually. "I feel it. I feel the inner
language of nature, the certainty of time and the feeling that humanity is
55 ultimately powerless." She seemed less angry now, but whether this was a
good thing, Amir didn't know.

"I understand that," Amir said, his hopes pinned to this bland statement.

When dams break, it's often a release.

"Amir. I want out. I can't live with you anymore."

Paper 1: Question 3

Question 3: Sample answers

Sample answer 1

Now read the following sample answers to the Question 3 example question on page 82, alongside the examiner's comments.

This is one paragraph from a longer answer. It receives less than half the marks available.

❶ The student identifies a very general area of structure – setting – but they say very little about the effect of this choice.

❸ This identifies a structural part – the middle – and makes a basic point about what is shown about the characters' relationship. The comment is very general.

> The writer interests me by writing a story set on a beach. I find this is intriguing as it seems mysterious. ❶ Before the writer describes the beach setting, he begins by introducing the two characters, which helps to build up a sense of anticipation and tension at the start. ❷ The middle part of the story shows how Amir and Jane are not in a good relationship. I think this is interesting because many people can relate to it and they will identify with this situation. ❸ The writer uses the words 'You'll only spoil it'. The word 'spoil' is a negative word and so it makes Jane seem unhappy at this point in the story. ❹

❷ The student makes a valid comment about structure and its effect here.

❹ This is about words rather than structure. It is a straightforward point about the character at this point in the source, but there isn't much detail.

Examiner's comments

This first sample answer does loosely identify a part of the source text structure, but the comments are often vague rather than precisely exploring the effect of the structure. The student also writes about words rather than structure at times.

In your answers, it is important that you make specific comments about the effects the writer is creating in the source text. Never write general comments that could apply to many texts, such as 'This part makes me want to read on' or 'The ending tells us what happens to the character'.

In Question 3, you need to keep your answers focused on specific structural features in the text, and the effects that they create for the reader. Sample answer 2 shows examples of this.

The very best answers comment on how parts of the structure fit together. This means commenting on things like how an event in the opening prepares you for what happens in the end, or how characters and/or situations change as the source develops.

TIP 💡

The best way to improve your mark is to develop the detail of your comments. Always look to extend the point you are making by saying a bit more about effect. You can see how to do this by comparing the two sample answers.

Sample answer 2

This is one paragraph from a longer answer. It receives high marks.

1 The student precisely pinpoints a key part of the story structure using narrative terms such as 'beginning' and 'introduces'. They give specific details, comment on the unsettling effect, and show how the opening has a structural link to the ending.

> At the beginning of the story the writer briefly introduces character and setting, providing the reader with indirect clues as to the couple's relationship which make more sense by the end of the story. For instance, in the opening paragraph we learn of Amir's 'vague anticipation' which alerts readers to potential conflict further into the narrative and, along with other details such as the lonely sky, seem a little unsettling. **1**
>
> It becomes clearer as the story develops that there is something wrong with their relationship. The first real sign of this occurs in the middle section where the writer uses dialogue to show Jane's displeasure at Amir, at which point the reader's impression of Jane becomes less sympathetic — the writer re-positions the characters at this point to paint Amir as a kind of victim figure. **2** This creates some tension as the reader begins to sense that trouble may lie ahead, something which is confirmed by the devastating line placed at the very end of the story which acts as a terrible climax. **3**

2 Another key moment in the structure is identified and is linked to the previous point. The student comments on the effect – how it tells us more about the relationship and how dialogue is a key part of the structure at this point.

3 This extends the comment on effect, noting a key structural device – tension. It also insightfully comments on how this is linked to the ending of the source, again using another structural term – climax.

Examiner's comments

This sample answer is much more successful as it clearly identifies parts of the story and makes perceptive comments about effect. The student can also see how the various parts of the source structure relate to each other.

 Key terms **Make sure you can write a definition for these key terms**

climax   problem
structure   tension

REMEMBER

- The most important part of your answer is about the *effect* of the structural choices.
- Comment in detail on things such as what impression the structural choices gives you of character and/or situation at three specific points in the source.
- The best answers comment on how the parts of the source text link together – how something at the start prepares you for what happens later in the source text.
- You don't need to use complex narrative terms – you can write about the beginning, middle, and end; links; and how things develop and changes in focus.

Retrieval

Paper 1: Question 3

Use the following questions to check your understanding of the knowledge covered in this section. Then cover the answers column with a piece of paper and write down as many as you can. Check and repeat.

Questions	Answers
1 What is the focus of Question 3?	Commenting on the effects of the writer's structural choices.
2 How long should you spend on Question 3?	10 minutes.
3 How many marks are available for Question 3?	8 marks.
4 Name four different aspects of a text that can relate to its structure.	Responses might include the development of tension, shifting perspective, change of location or viewpoint, beginning, middle or ending, climax.
5 You need to identify as many structural features as you can. True or false?	False. Aim to identify three structural features and discuss their effects.
6 Your mark heavily depends upon the quality of your comments. True or false?	True.
7 You must always use quotations, rather than line numbers or references. True or false?	False.
8 The best way to score highly is by extending your comments. True or false?	True.
9 Summarise the three steps of the Question 3 strategy.	**Step 1:** briefly re-read the source text. **Step 2:** select three structural features. **Step 3:** comment in detail on these features and their effects.

Put paper here

Previous questions

Now go back and use these questions to check your knowledge of previous topics.

Questions	Answers
1 Narrative structure is the way that a writer organises and sequences a story to a reader. True or false?	True.
2 What structural devices can be used to signal a change of focus?	A new paragraph; discourse markers.

Put paper here

Exam-style questions

Answer the exam-style questions on pages 87–91. To answer these questions you need to refer to the full source texts.

> **REMEMBER**
>
> In the exam, you will need to read the *whole* source text first, before you start looking at the questions.

3.1

> **Q3** You now need to think about the **whole** of the source.
>
> How has the writer structured the text to interest you as a reader?
>
> You could write about:
>
> - what the writer focuses your attention on at the beginning of the source
> - how and why the writer changes this focus as the source develops
> - any other structural features that interest you.
>
> **[8 marks]**

LINK

This question refers to the whole text of Source 2: *Millie*. This source can also be found on pages 178–179.

EXAM TIP

In your answer, you should:

- identify the three key parts of the structure you're going to comment on
- comment in detail on the effect of each part you've identified – how does it help you understand character and situation?
- comment on how the three parts you've identified link together and relate to each other.

Source 2: *Millie* by Katherine Mansfield

> This extract from a short story is set on a farm in New Zealand in 1913. There has been a murder on a neighbouring farm and the murderer is still at large. Millie's husband has gone out to help find the murderer, leaving Millie alone.

Millie went back into the kitchen. She put some ashes on the stove and sprinkled them with water. Languidly, the sweat pouring down her face, and dropping off her nose and chin, she cleared away the dinner, and going into the bedroom, stared at herself in the fly-specked mirror […]. She didn't
5 know what was the matter with herself that afternoon.

[…] *Tick-tick* went the kitchen clock, the ashes clinked in the grate, and the venetian blind knocked against the kitchen window. Quite suddenly Millie felt frightened. A queer trembling started inside her—in her stomach—and then spread all over to her knees and hands. "There's somebody about."
10 She tiptoed to the door and peered into the kitchen. Nobody there; the verandah* doors were closed, the blinds were down, and in the dusky light the white face of the clock shone, and the furniture seemed to bulge and breathe … and listen, too. The clock—the ashes—and the venetian—and then again—something else, like steps in the back yard. […] She darted to
15 the back door, opened it, and at the same moment some one ducked behind the wood pile. "Who's that?" she cried, in a loud, bold voice. "Come out o' that! I seen yer. I know where y'are. […] Come out from behind of that wood stack!" She was not frightened any more. She was furiously angry. Her heart banged like a drum.

Exam-style questions

20   "I'll teach you to play tricks with a woman," she yelled, [...] and dashed down the verandah steps, across the glaring yard to the other side of the wood stack. A young man lay there, on his stomach, one arm across his face. "Get up! You're shamming*!" [...] [S]he kicked him in the shoulders. He gave no sign. "Oh, my God, I believe he's dead." She knelt down, seized hold of him,

25   and turned him over on his back. He rolled like a sack. She crouched back on her haunches, staring; her lips and nostrils fluttered with horror.

He was not much more than a boy, with fair hair, and a growth of fair down on his lips and chin. His eyes were open, rolled up, showing the whites, and his face was patched with dust caked with sweat. He wore a cotton shirt and

30   trousers, with sandshoes on his feet. One of the trousers was stuck to his leg with a patch of dark blood.

[…] She bent over and felt his heart. "Wait a minute," she stammered, "wait a minute," and she ran into the house for a [...] pail of water. [...] She dipped a corner of her apron in the water and wiped his face and his hair

35   and his throat, with fingers that trembled. Under the dust and sweat his face gleamed, white as her apron, and thin, and puckered in little lines.

A strange dreadful feeling gripped Millie Evans' [chest]—some seed that had never flourished there, unfolded and struck deep roots and burst into painful leaf. The boy breathed sharply, half choked, his eyelids quivered, and he

40   moved his head from side to side.

[…] "You're better," said Millie, smoothing his hair. "Feeling fine now again, ain't you?" The pain in her [chest] half suffocated her. "It's no good you crying, Millie Evans. You got to keep your head." Quite suddenly he sat up and leaned against the wood pile, away from her, staring on the ground.

45   "There now!" cried Millie Evans, in a strange, shaking voice. The boy turned and looked at her, still not speaking, but his eyes were so full of pain and terror that she had to shut her teeth and clench her hands to stop from crying. After a long pause he said in the little voice of a child talking in his sleep, "I'm hungry." His lips quivered.

50   She scrambled to her feet and stood over him. "You come right into the house and have a sit down meal," she said. "Can you walk?"

"Yes," he whispered, and swaying he followed her across the glaring yard.

---

verandah: *an open-aired porch with a roof*

shamming: *pretending*

3.2

> **Q3** You now need to think about the **whole** of the source.
>
> How has the writer structured the text to interest you as a reader?
>
> You could write about:
>
> - what the writer focuses your attention on at the beginning of the source
> - how and why the writer changes this focus as the source develops
> - any other structural features that interest you. **[8 marks]**

LINK

This question refers to the whole text of Source 3: *Facing the Light*. This source can also be found on pages 180–181.

Source 3: *Facing the Light* by Adele Geras

> This is an extract from the beginning of a novel. Seven-year-old Rilla is visiting Willow Court, a grand old country house belonging to her family.

She is standing at the window. There's not even a breath of wind to move the white curtains and the grass outside lies dry and flat under the last of the sun. Summertime, and early evening, and she isn't in bed yet. She's nearly eight and it's too soon for sleeping. Everyone is doing something somewhere
5 else and no one is looking. The shadows of trees are black on the lawn and the late roses are edged with gold. There's a piece of silvery water glittering through the weeping willow leaves. That's the lake. Swans swim on the lake and she could go down to the water to see the white birds. No one would know and what you don't know can't hurt you.

10 She has to go, to flee, across the carpet woven with flowers and twisted trees, and then the door opens and she's in the corridor and it's dark there, always, even when the sun is shining outside, and a thick stillness takes up all the space and spreads down the staircase and she moves from step to step on tiptoe so as not to disturb it. Paintings on the walls stare at her as
15 she passes. Still life and landscapes spill strange colours and their own light into the silence and the portraits scream after her and she can't hear them. The marble floor in the hall is like a chess board of black and white and she makes sure to jump the black squares because if you don't, something bad is sure to happen, and maybe she just touched one black square on her way to
20 the garden but that wouldn't count, would it?

Then she's on the grass and the air is soft, and she runs as fast as she can down the steps of the terrace and over the lawn and past all the flowers and between high hedges clipped into cones and balls and spirals until she reaches the wild garden where the plants brush her skirt, and she's running and running to
25 where the swans always are and they've gone. They have floated over to the far bank. She can see them. It's not too far away so she starts walking.

Something catches her eye. It's in the reeds and it's like a dark stain in the water and when she gets a little nearer it looks like a sheet or a cloth and there are waterplants and grey-green willow branches with skinny-finger
30 leaves hiding some of it. If only she can get nearer to where the water meets the bank she can reach in and pull it and see what it is. The water is cool on her hand and there's something that looks like a foot poking out from under the material. Could it be someone swimming? No one swims without moving.

Exam-style questions

> Suddenly there's cold all around her and what she doesn't know won't
> 35 hurt her but she knows this is wrong. This is bad. She should run and fetch
> someone but she can't stop her hand from reaching out to the dark cloth that
> lies on the surface of the lake. She pulls at it and something heavy comes
> towards her and the time is stretched so long that the moment goes on for
> ever and ever and there's a face with glassy open eyes and pale greenish skin,
> 40 and she feels herself starting to scream but no sound comes out and she
> turns and runs back to the house. Someone must come. Someone must help,
> and she runs to call them to bring them and she's screaming and no one can
> hear her. Wet drowned fingers rise up from the lake and stretch out over the
> grass and up into the house to touch her and she will always feel them, even
> 45 when she's very old. Now she knows and she can't ever stop knowing.

3.3

Q3 You now need to think about the **whole** of the source.

How has the writer structured the text to interest you as a reader?

You could write about:

- what the writer focuses your attention on at the beginning of the source
- how and why the writer changes this focus as the source develops
- any other structural features that interest you.   **[8 marks]**

LINK

This question refers to the whole text of Source 4: *The Bees*. This source can also be found on pages 182–183.

Source 4: *The Bees* by Laline Paull

> This story set in a beehive and all the characters are bees. In this extract, the writer describes Flora 717, a worker bee, being born. After a struggle, Flora emerges from her cell and starts to learn about life inside a beehive.

> The cell squeezed her and the air was hot [...]. All the joints of her body
> burned from her frantic twisting against the walls, her head was pressed into
> her chest and her legs shot with cramp, but her struggles had worked–one
> wall felt weaker. She kicked out with all her strength and felt something
> 5 crack and break. She forced and tore and bit until there was a jagged hole
> into fresher air beyond.

> She dragged her body through and fell out onto the floor of an alien world.
> Static roared through her brain, thunderous vibration shook the ground and
> a thousand scents dazed her. All she could do was breathe until gradually the
> 10 vibration and static subsided and the scent evaporated into the air. Her rigid
> body unlocked and she calmed as knowledge filled her mind.

> This was the Arrivals Hall and she was a worker. Her kin was Flora and her
> number was 717. Certain of her first task, she set about cleaning out her cell.
> In her violent struggle to hatch she had broken the whole front wall, unlike her

15   neater neighbours. She looked, then followed their example, piling her debris neatly by the ruins. The activity cleared her senses and she felt the vastness of the Arrivals Hall, and how the vibrations in the air changed in different areas.

Row upon row of cells like hers stretched into the distance, and there the cells were quiet but resonant as if the occupants still slept. Immediately
20   around her was great activity with many recently broken and cleared-out chambers, and many more cracking and falling as new bees arrived. The differing scents of her neighbours also came into focus, some sweeter, some sharper, all of them pleasant to absorb.

With a hard erratic pulse in the ground, a young female came running down
25   the corridor between the cells, her face frantic.

'Halt!' Harsh voices reverberated from both ends of the corridor and a strong astringent* scent rose in the air. Every bee stopped moving but the young bee stumbled and fell across Flora's pile of debris. Then she clawed her way into the remains of the broken cell and huddled in the corner, her little hands up.

30   Cloaked in a bitter scent which hid their faces and made them identical, the dark figures strode down the corridor towards Flora. Pushing her aside, they dragged out the weeping young bee. At the sight of their spiked gauntlets, a spasm of fear in Flora's brain released more knowledge.

They were police.

35   'You fled inspection.' One of them pulled at the girl's wings, while another examined the four still-wet membranes. The edge of one was shrivelled.

'Spare me,' she cried. 'I will not fly, I will serve in any other way—' [...]

Before the bee could speak the two officers pressed her head down until there was a sharp crack. She hung limp between them and they dropped her
40   body in the corridor.

'You.' A peculiar rasping voice addressed Flora and she did not know which one spoke, but stared at the black hooks on the backs of their legs. 'Hold still.' Long black callipers* […] measured her height. 'Excessive variation. Abnormal.'

45   'That will be all, officers.' At the kind voice and fragrant smell, the police released Flora. They bowed to a tall and well-groomed bee with a beautiful face.

'Sister Sage, this one is obscenely ugly.'

'And excessively large.'

'It would appear so. Thank you, officers, you may go.'

50   Sister Sage waited for them to leave. She smiled at Flora.

'To fear them is good. Be still while I read your kin—'

'I am Flora 717.'

Sister Sage raised her antennae. 'A sanitation worker who speaks. Most notable …'

55   Flora stared at her tawny and gold face with its huge dark eyes. 'Am I to be killed?'

---

astringent: *dry and bitter*   **callipers:** *measuring instrument*

Paper 1: Question 4

Question 4: Overview

Focus	Marks	Time	AO
Responding to an opinion	20 marks	25 minutes	AO4

Question 4 tests your ability to respond to (**evaluate**) an **opinion** about a source text. This will include commenting on the writer's choice of language and/or structure. This question is sometimes called 'the evaluation question'.

Question 4 will always follow the same format:

- It will ask you to focus on a section of the extract, giving you line numbers, which you may wish to mark on your source text.
- It will then include an opinion in speech marks.
- It will ask 'to what extent' (how much) you agree with the opinion.
- You will be given a bulleted list of what you could do in your answer.

LINK

The knowledge section on pages 56–62 will remind you of key concepts and terms that will help you answer this type of question.

Q4   Focus this part of your answer on **line x to the end**.

A student said, 'xx.'

To what extent do you agree?

In your response, you could:

- consider …
- evaluate …
- support your response with references to the text.

[20 marks]

This question needs you to:

- give a detailed and clear response to the opinion given.
- comment on how the writer uses language and/or structural methods.
- use quotations to justify your opinions.

Question 4: Strategy

Follow the steps below to respond to a Question 4 task.

Step 1: Underline the opinion, which is presented inside quotation marks in the question. You need to think very carefully about the opinion given, checking you understand its meaning.

↓

Step 2: Bracket the specific part of the source you are writing about and re-read it.

↓

Step 3: Plan your **argument**, to ensure it is coherent. Consider the following:

- Do you agree, partly agree, or disagree with the point of view presented?
- Make a list of reasons to include to support your argument.

↓

Step 4: You will need to find 'evidence' to back up your own opinion in the form of quotations from the source text. You will need to think how the writer's use of language and/or structure influences your opinion.

↓

Step 5: Write in detail, developing your argument over a number of paragraphs. The most important thing is the quality of your 'argument' – how well you give evidence to support and explain your opinion.

TIP

Whether you agree or disagree with the opinion given in the question doesn't matter. What does matter is how well you give your response. The quality of the points you make and the detail of your response determine your mark.

LINK

The knowledge section on pages 56–62 will remind you of how to structure an argument.

Paper 1: Question 4

Question 4: Example

Read the sample Question 4 and annotations below. Remember that Question 4 will ask you to focus on one section of the extract. In the exam question, you will have to look back at the relevant part of the source text. Here we have included the extract to help you.

LINK

This question refers to an extract from Source 1: *Dawn at Woolacombe Sands*. The full text is on pages 176–177.

Q4 Focus this part of your answer on **line 18 to the end**.

A student said, 'In this part of the story, Amir and Jane have different reactions to Woolacombe Sands. The writer shows that Amir doesn't understand his wife and all of our sympathies are with Jane.'

To what extent do you agree?

In your response, you could:

- consider Amir and and Jane's reactions to Woolacombe Sands
- evaluate how the writer presents Amir's and Jane's relationship
- support your response with references to the text.

[20 marks]

You are given a specific part of the source text to work with. Make sure you focus only on these lines.

These are the focuses of this question. These are the opinions that you need to respond to in your answer.

The word 'evaluate' can be confusing. Use it as a reminder to write about how the author has used language and/or structure to present the relationship.

These bullet points are useful suggestions.

Source 1: *Dawn at Woolacombe Sands* by Jez Neumann

"Don't talk. You'll only spoil the moment," Jane said, abruptly. She wasn't looking at Amir, but was instead staring out to sea, as if it – *somehow* –
20 understood her spiritually. The morning light was on her face. She seemed both present and elsewhere.

Amir began to open his mouth but closed it again. He wanted to speak but felt that Jane had already decided that he was not allowed to be part of the scene. His words and deeds were irrelevant. His thoughts were irrelevant too
25 apparently. Yet here they were, together and not together on a silent beach with last night's row hovering between them.

The beach was not really that interesting to Amir. It seemed point-free. Car parks had a purpose. Shops had a purpose. Sport did, too. But this was just some sand and salty water. It was nothing really. Amir decided it would be
30 better if he kept this to himself though, because Jane was currently adopting one of her many yoga poses and he knew from bitter experience that she didn't like being interrupted in such spiritual moments. There was a ship on the horizon and so Amir focused on this, wondering what was happening on board and where they were heading.

35   Moments passed. He still hadn't spoken, but wanted to find the right words, the right combination of words to make Jane happy again. Or at least one that didn't spark her anger. They ought to be trying to make their marriage work properly again. He wanted that, but now it seemed like they were in different spheres.

40   "Well, what do you feel?" Jane asked eventually, much to Amir's surprise. She wasn't looking at him and he couldn't tell if this was a trick question or not. It felt like there was a dam somewhere, just about holding things back.

"It's quite big," Amir said, which seemed to him to be the form of words which could do the least harm to the dam. A moment settled.

45   "Is that really the best thing you can find to say? It's quite big?" Amir still couldn't see Jane's eyes but realised the magical repairing incantation had eluded him.

He tried again. "I wonder where that ship is going," he said. A bit more of the dam broke.

50   "We come to place of serenity and all you can tell me is it's big and there's a ship?" Jane hissed.

"Well, what do you see?" Amir asked meekly.

"I don't see anything," Jane said eventually. "I feel it. I feel the inner language of nature, the certainty of time and the feeling that humanity is
55   ultimately powerless." She seemed less angry now, but whether this was a good thing, Amir didn't know.

"I understand that," Amir said, his hopes pinned to this bland statement.

When dams break, it's often a release.

"Amir. I want out. I can't live with you anymore."

Paper 1: Question 4

Question 4: Sample answers

Sample answer 1

Now read the following sample answers to the Question 4 example question on page 94, alongside the examiner's comments.

This is one paragraph from a longer Question 4 answer. It receives less than half the marks available.

1 This attempts to answer the question, but the comment is very simple.

3 The student is focusing on the writer's language choices. They have picked out the image of a dam. They've commented that the writer's word choices are good, rather than explaining how the language shapes the reader's understanding.

> The beach seems very atmospheric but it is not interesting to Amir, which shows his reaction. **1** Jane loves the beach and does some 'yoga poses' which shows she is at home there. This shows how her reaction is different to Amir's. **2** The writer uses some really good words to describe their relationship such as 'a dam'. This is a really thoughtful way to describe it and I think it helps the reader understand things really well. **3** I do have sympathy for both of the characters. They seem to want different things. **4**

2 This is more focused on the question, but the point made is not developed. The student's response is brief and basic.

4 This is focused, but the view has no detail. The student needed to argue this view more thoroughly using references to the text.

Examiner's comments

Sample answer 1 begins to answer the question in part, but there is no depth to the points made. There is a vague attempt to write about word choices.
For Question 4, it is important to try and write a lengthy, detailed answer. Try to develop the quality and depth of the points you make. This will help you to gain more marks.

TIP

You must make points about the language or structure used by the writer in this question. Some students forget to do this, and it lowers their mark.

Sample answer 2

This is one paragraph from a longer answer. It scores high marks.

❶ This point is directly relevant to the question about sympathy. It is developed with some well-chosen quotations which help to build the argument.

❷ A strong view is offered here with a well-chosen quotation that show how the writer's language choices affect how the reader sees Jane.

❸ A structural point is made about the climax of the source and how it affects the way Jane is portrayed. The student is firmly focused on the question and makes a strong point.

> Although the story is written in third person, the writer allows us to see Amir's point of view more clearly than Jane's. As we are allowed access to his thoughts rather than Jane's, we are likely to sympathise more with Amir because we can see that he doesn't feel 'part of the scene' and learn that he wants to 'make their marriage work properly'. ❶ Jane does have a different reaction to the beach, but I don't feel much sympathy for her. The writer presents her as dismissive and self-interested, using verb choices such as 'hissed' to describe the way she talks to Amir, suggesting animalistic, aggressive qualities that make her appear unlikeable. ❷ The climactic part where she bluntly says to Amir that she 'wants out' makes any sympathy for her vanish. Although they do have different reactions, it seems to me that our sympathy lies more with Amir than Jane, and yet the writer does, in some ways, problematise our reaction to both characters: we are allowed to glimpse how Amir's unemotional reaction to the location seems a little odd. In doing so, the writer invites the reader to see how faltering relationships are rarely one partner's fault and that miscommunication is not just Jane's problem. ❸

Examiner's comments

Sample answer 2 is a detailed response. It uses the text well and builds points by explaining them clearly. The student is very sharply focused on the opinion and makes some perceptive points about sympathy. It also has a good understanding of language and structural choices.

REMEMBER

- This task is worth 20 marks, 25% of the whole of Paper 1. Allow 25 minutes to complete it.
- The clarity and quality (depth and thoughtfulness) of your response is important.
- Detail is important – use plenty of well-chosen quotations to support your argument.
- It doesn't matter if you agree or disagree with the opinion. What matters is how well and thoroughly you give your view.
- Write about the way the writer has used language and/or structure – but it must be relevant to the question.

 Key terms Make sure you can write a definition for these key terms

argument   evaluate   opinion

Retrieval EXAM

Paper 1: Question 4

Use the following questions to check your understanding of the knowledge covered in this section. Then cover the answers column with a piece of paper and write down as many as you can. Check and repeat.

	Questions	Answers
1	How long should you spend on Question 4?	25 minutes.
2	How any marks are available for Question 4?	20 marks.
3	What is the focus of Question 4?	Responding to an opinion about the source text.
4	You don't always need to write about language and structure. True or false?	False.
5	The question will ask you to write about a certain part of the source. True or false?	True.
6	Your mark heavily depends upon the quality of your comments. True or false?	True.
7	Summarise the five steps of the Question 4 strategy.	**Step 1:** underline the key focus of the question. **Step 2:** mark and re-read relevant lines in the source text. **Step 3:** decide on your opinion and plan your argument. **Step 4:** select quotations and references. **Step 5:** write your answer in full.

Put paper here

Previous questions

Now go back and use these questions to check your knowledge of previous topics.

	Questions	Answers
1	What is a flashback and why might a writer use it?	A shift back in time in a story. A writer might use this to explain why a character acts as they do, or why a situation has arisen.
2	What structural devices can be used to signal a change of focus?	A new paragraph; discourse markers.

Put paper here

Exam-style questions

Answer the exam-style questions on pages 99–103. In the exam, the relevant extract (e.g. lines 20 to the end) for Question 4 will not be reprinted in the question paper, so you will need to find it in the source text. The extracts have been included here for easy reference.

4.1

> **Q4** Focus this part of your answer on the second part of the source text, from **line 20 to the end**.
>
> A student said, 'This part of the story, where Millie confronts the boy, shows that Millie is more caring than aggressive. She is foolish to take the boy into her house.'
>
> To what extent do you agree?
>
> In your response, you could:
>
> - consider Millie's reactions to the boy
> - evaluate how the writer presents Millie's actions
> - support your response with references to the text.
>
> **[20 marks]**

LINK

This question refers to an extract from Source 2: *Millie*. The full text is on pages 178–179.

REMEMBER !

In the exam, you will need to read the *whole* source text first before you start looking at the questions and any specific extracts.

EXAM TIP

In your answer, you should:

- give your view on the precise parts in the question. Make sure you stick to the question focus.
- give a detailed response. This is a 20-mark question.
- use quotations from the source text to build your case.
- comment on how the writer has used language and/or structure.

Source 2: *Millie* by Katherine Mansfield

20 "I'll teach you to play tricks with a woman," she yelled, [...] and dashed down the verandah* steps, across the glaring yard to the other side of the wood stack. A young man lay there, on his stomach, one arm across his face. "Get up! You're shamming*!" [...] [S]he kicked him in the shoulders. He gave no sign. "Oh, my God, I believe he's dead." She knelt down, seized hold of

25 him, and turned him over on his back. He rolled like a sack. She crouched back on her haunches, staring; her lips and nostrils fluttered with horror.

He was not much more than a boy, with fair hair, and a growth of fair down on his lips and chin. His eyes were open, rolled up, showing the whites, and his face was patched with dust caked with sweat. He wore a cotton shirt and

30 trousers, with sandshoes on his feet. One of the trousers was stuck to his leg with a patch of dark blood.

[…] She bent over and felt his heart. "Wait a minute," she stammered, "wait a minute," and she ran into the house for [...] a pail of water. [...] She dipped a corner of her apron in the water and wiped his face and his hair

35 and his throat, with fingers that trembled. Under the dust and sweat his face gleamed, white as her apron, and thin, and puckered in little lines.

A strange dreadful feeling gripped Millie Evans' [chest]—some seed that had never flourished there, unfolded and struck deep roots and burst into painful leaf. The boy breathed sharply, half choked, his eyelids quivered, and he

40 moved his head from side to side.

[…] "You're better," said Millie, smoothing his hair. "Feeling fine now again,

Exam-style questions

ain't you?" The pain in her [chest] half suffocated her. "It's no good you crying, Millie Evans. You got to keep your head." Quite suddenly he sat up and leaned against the wood pile, away from her, staring on the ground.

45 "There now!" cried Millie Evans, in a strange, shaking voice. The boy turned and looked at her, still not speaking, but his eyes were so full of pain and terror that she had to shut her teeth and clench her hands to stop from crying. After a long pause he said in the little voice of a child talking in his sleep, "I'm hungry." His lips quivered.

50 She scrambled to her feet and stood over him. "You come right into the house and have a sit down meal," she said. "Can you walk?"

"Yes," he whispered, and swaying he followed her across the glaring yard.

---

verandah: *an open-aired porch with a roof*

shamming: *pretending*

Q4 Focus this part of your answer on the second part of the source text, from **line 28 to the end**.

A student said, 'This part of the story, where Rilla finds the body in the lake, is really eerie. The most horrific moment is where she sees the face.'

To what extent do you agree?

In your response, you could:

- consider your own impressions of Rilla's reaction to finding the body
- evaluate how the writer creates a scary atmosphere
- support your response with references to the text.

[20 marks]

LINK

This question refers to an extract from Source 3: *Facing the Light*. The full text is on pages 180–181.

Source 3: *Facing the Light* by Adele Geras

Something catches her eye. It's in the reeds and it's like a dark stain in the water and when she gets a little nearer it looks like a sheet or a cloth and
30   there are waterplants and grey-green willow branches with skinny-finger leaves hiding some of it. If only she can get nearer to where the water meets the bank she can reach in and pull it and see what it is. The water is cool on her hand and there's something that looks like a foot poking out from under the material. Could it be someone swimming? No one swims
35   without moving.

Suddenly there's cold all around her and what she doesn't know won't hurt her but she knows this is wrong. This is bad. She should run and fetch someone but she can't stop her hand from reaching out to the dark cloth that lies on the surface of the lake. She pulls at it and something heavy
40   comes towards her and the time is stretched so long that the moment goes on for ever and ever and there's a face with glassy open eyes and pale greenish skin, and she feels herself starting to scream but no sound comes out and she turns and runs back to the house. Someone must come. Someone must help, and she runs to call them to bring them and she's
45   screaming and no one can hear her. Wet drowned fingers rise up from the lake and stretch out over the grass and up into the house to touch her and she will always feel them, even when she's very old. Now she knows and she can't ever stop knowing.

Exam-style questions

4.3

Q4 Focus this part of your answer on the second part of the source text, from **line 25 to the end.**

A student said: 'This part of the text, from when the police arrive, shows how violent and controlled bee society is, but it is Sister Sage who is the most powerful.'

To what extent do you agree?

In your response, you could:

- consider your own impressions of bee society
- evaluate how the writer has created these impressions
- support your opinions with references to the text.

[20 marks]

LINK

This question refers to an extract from Source 4: *The Bees.* The full text is on pages 182–183.

Source 4: *The Bees* by Laline Paull

25 With a hard erratic pulse in the ground, a young female came running down the corridor between the cells, her face frantic.

'Halt!' Harsh voices reverberated from both ends of the corridor and a strong astringent* scent rose in the air. Every bee stopped moving but the young bee stumbled and fell across Flora's pile of debris. Then she clawed her way into the
30 remains of the broken cell and huddled in the corner, her little hands up.

Cloaked in a bitter scent which hid their faces and made them identical, the dark figures strode down the corridor towards Flora. Pushing her aside, they dragged out the weeping young bee. At the sight of their spiked gauntlets, a spasm of fear in Flora's brain released more knowledge.

35 They were police.

'You fled inspection.' One of them pulled at the girl's wings, while another examined the four still-wet membranes. The edge of one was shrivelled.

'Spare me,' she cried. 'I will not fly, I will serve in any other way—' [...]

Before the bee could speak the two officers pressed her head down until
40 there was a sharp crack. She hung limp between them and they dropped her body in the corridor.

'You.' A peculiar rasping voice addressed Flora and she did not know which one spoke, but stared at the black hooks on the backs of their legs. 'Hold still.' Long black callipers* [...] measured her height. 'Excessive variation.
45 Abnormal.'

'That will be all, officers.' At the kind voice and fragrant smell, the police released Flora. They bowed to a tall and well-groomed bee with a beautiful face.

'Sister Sage, this one is obscenely ugly.'

50 'And excessively large.'

'It would appear so. Thank you, officers, you may go.'

Sister Sage waited for them to leave. She smiled at Flora.

'To fear them is good. Be still while I read your kin—'

'I am Flora 717.'

55 Sister Sage raised her antennae. 'A sanitation worker who speaks. Most notable …'

Flora stared at her tawny and gold face with its huge dark eyes. 'Am I to be killed?'

---

astringent: *dry and bitter*
callipers: *measuring instrument*

Question 5: Overview

Focus: Descriptive or narrative writing

Marks: 40 marks

Time: 45 minutes

AO: AO5, AO6

Question 5 tests both your creative writing skills (AO5) and technical skills (AO6). Question 5 will always follow the same format:

Q5   Either

Write a description of ... as suggested by this picture:

Or

Write (part of) a story about....   **[40 marks]**

> **TIP**
>
> In some exam papers, the choice is between two narrative options, or two descriptive options. Make sure you are prepared for both types of writing.

The same skills are being tested whichever option you choose, but think carefully about your choice. Pick the option that allows you to best show off your abilities.

There are 40 marks available. Of this total, 24 marks are for the quality of your ideas and 16 marks are for the accuracy and variety of your technical skills, which include word choice, spelling, punctuation, and sentence types.

Question 5: Strategy

Follow the steps below to respond to a Question 5 task.

Step 1: Make a choice. Consider which question option will best show off your imagination and creative abilities.

Step 2: Plan the structure of your response.

- Work out what you will write about in each paragraph.
- Decide how you will end your writing.

Step 3: Write your response. Make sure everything you write engages your reader and uses language accurately.

- Include effective detail, such as imagery and figurative language.
- Vary word, punctuation, and sentence structure to show off your range of vocabulary and technical skills.

Step 4: Proof-read your work to ensure your spelling and punctuation are accurate and everything makes sense.

LINK

The knowledge section on the following pages of this book will help you with your writing task.

For figurative language, please see pages 10–16.

For character, please see pages 26–32.

For sentence structure, please see pages 42–46.

For narrative structure, please see pages 48–54.

TIP

Aim to write a detailed answer. Most successful responses are around two to three sides in length.

Question 5: Key skills

Whether you choose to write a descriptive or narrative response, the same key skills are being assessed. They are detailed below.

Skill	What this means you need to do	Assessment objective
Clear communication	Make sure everything you write is clear and makes sense.	AO5
Quality of ideas	Engage your reader with interesting ideas. Spend time planning how you will use setting, character, or events to make your response engaging.	AO5
Quality of expression	Show that you can phrase your response in interesting ways. Take time to craft what you are writing. Use interesting words.	AO5
Structure and sequence	Plan the sequence of your response – what will happen in what order. Show that you can 'shape' a response by giving it an interesting structure.	AO5
Technical accuracy	Make sure that spelling, punctuation, and expression are as accurate as possible.	AO6
Technical variety	Show that you can use a range of punctuation and sentence types.	AO6

Think about these skills while you are planning and writing your response. It is important to 'consciously craft' your writing, even though it takes time.

Paper 1: Question 5

Question 5: Planning a response

Planning a response is an essential part of this Question 5 task. Before you begin writing your response, spend at least 5 minutes planning. This will ensure you keep focused on the task while you are writing and don't run out of time.

Planning a description

- If you choose to write a description, read the focus of the task carefully, as well as looking at the picture. Write down a few possible ideas that you have. Decide which one interests you most and you feel is most imaginative or unusual.

- Work out the order of your writing. Plan the sequence of what you'll write about, so it is carefully shaped and ordered.

- Think about three main events or stages to your writing, and how you will link them. Even if you are writing a description, there still needs to be a flow to your text. Think of taking your reader on a journey, and deciding what you will show them, where, and how.

- You might find it helpful to plan how to craft a successful opening and closing to your description, the shifts in focus, and how to appeal to senses. Refer back to pages 48–54 on narrative structure to remind yourself of these devices.

Here is a sample task and three possible ideas:

Q5 Write a description of a busy city at night as suggested by this picture:

[40 marks]

> **TIP**
> The picture is just a starting point for your response. It is just there to inspire your own writing. You do not have to write about all the detail in it and you can add your own ideas.

1. The excitement of bright lights and people rushing everywhere. The smell of food.

2. Getting lost in a crowd. The feeling of panic. The sound of sirens.

3. The moments where shops begin to close, people go home, and the city becomes quieter.

> **TIP**
> Remember that descriptive writing relies on atmosphere, phrasing, emotion, figurative language, and interesting expression.

All three ideas could lead to interesting descriptions. They are relevant to the question. The third idea approaches the task in an interesting way. It allows for a sense of 'journey' in the response and may lead to a clearer structure.

Planning a narrative

- If you choose to write a narrative, you need to think about a character and a problem or challenge they face. Write down a few possible ideas and choose the one you think is most interesting or unusual.

- Work out the order of your writing. Plan the sequence of what you'll write about, so it is carefully shaped and ordered.

- Think about an opening, middle, and ending. Remember that you are only writing two or three sides, so go for a compact structure but one that has interesting elements.

- You might find it helpful to plan how to open and close your narrative, the shifts in focus, and how to build suspense and tension in the story. This can be done through some of the following structural devices:

LINK

You can see some of these structural methods used in sample answers on pages 110–113.

- Echoes – using a similar phrase or idea at both the start and end of your response
- Repetition – of an image or phrase
- Withholding information – gradually revealing it, giving hints or clues
- Focus shift – introducing a new idea, character, or problem
- Flashback in time to something that happened earlier
- **Flashforward** in time to something that happens later
- Tension – building the suspense by suggesting growing danger
- Climax – a 'high point' of drama.

Here is a sample task and three possible ideas.

> **Q5** Write a story with the title 'Lost'. **[40 marks]**

1. A lost dog who finds his way home to his worried owner.

2. A woman loses her winning lottery ticket but then finds it.

3. A boy feels emotionally lost after a terrible event but rediscovers happiness.

All three ideas could lead to interesting stories and are relevant to the question but the third idea interprets the word 'lost' in a metaphorical way. This is an interesting way to tackle the question. Examiners mark lots of similar responses and so choosing an idea that is imaginative and unusual (when done well) can impress them.

Paper 1: Question 5

Question 5: Writing a response

Once you have planned your response, you will be able to write it.

Openings

Craft an interesting opening. Try to engage your reader from the start with something imaginative, intriguing, or unusual.

Here are two sample questions with some approaches to writing an opening. These approaches can be applied to both descriptive and narrative writing.

> **TIP** 💡
>
> Avoid using obvious sentence openers such as 'There was a …' or 'I was walking along …'.

Q5 Either

Write a description of a journey as suggested by this picture:

Or

Write a story set in a dangerous place. **[40 marks]**

Approach	Example
Focusing on a place / situation	Death Valley was the last place you wanted to break down.
Focusing on the weather	The sun, already fiendishly unbearable, seemed to be enjoying its cruel reign.
Focusing on scenery	The mountains loomed, an ominous presence on the horizon.
Focusing on feelings	I really didn't want to be here, but had little choice.
Focusing on an event in the middle of the story, (known as *in media res*)	It was then that the car spluttered to a halt and I knew I was in trouble.

Endings

You can bring your writing to a close in several different ways. It's important that you produce something that feels like you have brought your response 'to a rest'. You don't need to write a story ending where all problems are resolved.

Here are some approaches for endings based on the exam task opposite.

Approach	Example
Upbeat ending	Finally, the end of the road was in sight and the clouds lifted.
Downbeat ending	The light faded and the mountains became mere silhouettes.
Cliffhanger	But just as I felt freedom course through my veins, a figure appeared in the distance.
Open ending	And so I was free. But where I went from here, heaven only knew.
Flashforward	All that happened many years ago, and if things had been different, I'd be telling you a very different story.
Echoed ending	Death Valley was the last place you wanted to break down.

Style

Whether you are writing a description or a narrative, it is important to demonstrate variety in your writing. You need to craft your writing with care.

Here are some aspects of style and how you can demonstrate them.

TIP

Be careful not to over-use interesting vocabulary. Make sure you choose ambitious words well and use them correctly where they are appropriate.

Word choice: Use a selection of 'ambitious' vocabulary. Choose unusual words that show the breadth of your vocabulary.

Punctuation: Use brackets, speech marks, colons, and semi-colons.

Aspects of style

Images: Use metaphor/simile/ personification as appropriate. Show that you can enrich your descriptions with figurative language and imagery.

Sentences: Vary the length and variety of sentences. Make sure you can use complex sentences accurately.

Make sure you revisit the basics of punctuation as you revise. You need to know how to use full stops, capitals, commas, colons, semi-colons, and paragraphs. Ensure you know how to punctuate dialogue correctly.

Remember that some of your mark is dependent on technical accuracy. Always leave time to double-check spelling and punctuation.

LINK

You can see some of these style aspects used in sample answers on pages 110–113.

Question 5: Sample answers

Read the sample Question 5 (descriptive task) and annotations below.

Q5 Write a description of an unusual place to visit as suggested by this picture:

[40 marks]

This word is important. You do not have to write about this exact picture. You can use another idea that has been triggered by this picture.

This is the key focus of your writing. The picture may help with your ideas, but this is the main task.

The picture may contain a setting and/or a character. It may contain lots of detail and busy situations, or it may show a peaceful scene.

Sample answer 1 (descriptive)

Now read the following sample answers to the Question 5 (descriptive) example question above, alongside the examiner's comments. This is one paragraph from a longer answer. It receives less than half the marks available.

❶ This is accurately written but not as interesting as it could be. The student is describing things in a straightforward way.

❸ This time shift seems abrupt and although the student is trying to create tension, they have used very obvious images.

❺ This repetition of an earlier idea could work if it was done more interestingly. Here, it seems random.

I stood outside the building and looked at the stones on the front of it. They were quite rough and grey. ❶ It was beginning to rain and I felt a bit wet. ❷ Suddenly, it was dark and I could hear an owl hooting. I felt the hairs on the back of my neck stand up. ❸ I could also smell someone cooking food inside the building, it smelt like heaven, my mouth began to sallivait. ❹ I looked again at the grey stones but they looked even darker at night. ❺

❷ The student uses another sense to describe here but the word choices are basic.

❹ Another sense type is used to describe and a simple simile is used. There are punctuation errors and a spelling mistake here.

Examiner's comments

Sample answer 1 reads like a list of sense impressions rather than a shaped description. The ideas and expression are largely straightforward rather than shaped. The student uses figurative language, but not in a very imaginative way. There are some technical errors, but there is an attempt to use some interesting vocabulary. A better answer would develop the parts of the description featured. It would choose some less obvious descriptions, use more interesting words and a better range of punctuation and sentences types.

Sample answer 2 (descriptive)

This is a section from a longer answer. It receives high marks.

1 The student has set up an interesting scenario inspired by the picture. Figurative language is used well to convey precise details of the scene.

> In flickering light, my eyes traced the cracks on the ceiling. I was helplessly falling into sleep after a long day's travel. Somewhere downstairs, a monotonous clock, like a mother's gentle lullaby, was beckoning me to sleep. I'd soon surrender. **1**
> The wind outside played a melancholy air, the tune whistling through the ivy that adorned the front of the hotel. There was music in the night: the mewl of a fox somewhere in the hills; the rhythmic crunch of gravel (probably the night porter); the hushed tenor of a late-night arrival. **2**
> But hush.
> Those hypnotic ceiling cracks drew me in.
> Hush. **3**
> Earlier today, the sunlight had peered over the hills and touched the face of the hotel. It looked imperious, but the lush greenery softened its forbidding glare and once inside, I felt home. Day turned into evening and sleep awaited. **4**

2 The description is developed here using an extended metaphor. The student demonstrates a variety of accurate punctuation.

3 The use of short sentences and the single word paragraph creates a distinctive structure here. The echoing of the first sentence also aids structure.

4 The time shift here also contributes to the overall structural effect. A range of interesting words are used here.

Examiner's comments

Sample answer 2 is well-shaped. The student has taken the general idea of the picture and offered something imaginative. It feels like there is a 'journey' in the description. The figurative language, the word choices, and the structural effects are very effective.

TIP

Using single word sentences and paragraphs can be a quick way to show variety. However, be careful not to overuse them!

Read the sample Question 5 (narrative task) and annotations below.

This doesn't necessarily mean a full story. Focusing on just one part of a wider story is usually best as you only have 45 minutes. For example, you might choose to focus on an exciting event that happened in the journey.

Q5 Write a story about a memorable journey.

[40 marks]

The prompt might be a title, a setting, or a situation. Remember, the prompt is just a starting point. Your job is to bring the idea to life.

Paper 1: Question 5

Sample answer 3 (narrative)

Now read the following sample answers to the Question 5 (narrative) example question on page 111, alongside the examiner's comments. This is a section from a longer answer. It receives less than half marks.

❶ This is a simple opening to a story. The idea is relevant but not very imaginative. There is an attempt to create a sense of excitement.

> One day my dad asked if we wanted to go to London. I said yes! I'd never been to London and was excited to see all the sights I'd seen in films. I hardly slept that night. ❶
>
> We set off early the next day in my dad's car. There were four of us, my parents, me and my brother, and we were a bit tired but still excited. After an our, we stopped at the service station to strech our legs and have a coffee. ❷
>
> All of a sudden I couldn't believe my eyes. There was my favourite footballer having a burger. I was speechless. I went up to him and asked for his autograph. He gave it to me and we talked for ten minutes about football. Then my dad said we had to travel on. ❸

❷ Characters are introduced, but they're not described at all and are just names. There is some attempt to create a sense of situation. There are misplaced commas and some spelling errors.

❸ The student tries to create excitement, but it's not built up and the idea is a basic one. Again, there is no real sense of character.

TIP

Try to engage your reader with emotional content. Stories are much more effective when there is some powerful emotional energy attached to them, such as love, fear, or envy.

Examiner's comments

Sample answer 3 contains lots of events but no real detail. The idea is a simple one and it's difficult to picture the characters as there is so little detail. The language is straightforward with no figurative language or variation in sentence structure. There are some punctuation and spelling errors.

Sample answer 4 (narrative)

This is a section from a longer answer. It receives high marks.

❶ This opening quickly introduces the situation and begins to build tension. Brief description helps to convey situation and character.

> Autumn
>
> Amina and me on a crisp autumn day. Me driving and her in the back seat, smiling nervously. The low sunlight. I'll never forget that journey. In one sense, we knew where we were going. Hospital. In another sense, we had no idea how the journey would end. ❶

By the time December arrived, I'd made the same journey every day for three long weeks. The features of the road had become totems; familiar things I'd acknowledge each time in a kind of superstitious hope that my daughter would live. Those totems will live long in my mind: the dilapidated garage on the bend; the mansion shrouded by increasingly bare trees.

And the journeys down that long hospital corridor were tedious in their familiarity. Walking down them, I felt like I was in an airlock, suspended somewhere in space in an alternate reality where none of this was happening to the real me. The institutional smells of hospital food and medical concoctions would bring me back to reality. At the end of the corridor was the ward where Amina lay. Sometimes, I didn't want to enter it. ❸

The worst thing was, as always, the waiting. And then one day, it was here. That day. The one where we'd find out what Amina's future held.

In the next hour, we'd know the shape of things to come. I could see Amina's consultant at the other end of the ward. She looked across but neither smiled nor acknowledged us. It seemed to me that time was slowing down, and the nurses all knew something.

❷ Effective description and word choice help to engage the reader. A range of punctuation is used.

❸ The shift in setting here adds more interest, as do effective description of place and emotion.

TIP

Flashbacks and echoing are effective ways to add structural interest to narratives. See how the writer of Sample answer 4 has achieved this.

❹ The student builds tension well here.

Examiner's comments

Sample answer 4 is very effective at building tension and using language to describe situations and feelings. A range of interesting descriptions and words are used. The range and accuracy of technical English is very good.

 Key terms Make sure you can write a definition for these key terms.

cliffhanger   flashforward   *in media res*

REMEMBER

- Allow 45 minutes to complete Question 5. It is worth 50% of the Paper 1 marks.
- Planning is essential. Work out the structure of your response before you begin writing.
- Aim to engage your reader with your content – imaginative ideas always impress.
- Use a range of interesting words and language techniques.
- Use a range of punctuation and sentence types.
- Always proof-read your work – accuracy is important.

Retrieval EXAM

Paper 1: Question 5

Use the following questions to check your understanding of the knowledge covered in this section. Then cover the answers column with a piece of paper and write down as many as you can. Check and repeat.

Questions	Answers
1. What is the focus of Question 5?	Writing a description or narrative.
2. How long should you spend on Question 5?	45 minutes.
3. How many marks are available for Question 5?	40 marks.
4. How many marks are available for technical ability?	16 marks.
5. How many marks are available for the quality of your ideas?	24 marks.
6. Structuring your work in an interesting way is less important in descriptive writing. True or false?	False.
7. Clear communication is important for good marks. True or false?	True.
8. You can only write about what is in the picture. True or false?	False.
9. Always plan your ideas before you write. True or false?	True.
10. Stories that end happily always get better marks. True or false?	False.
11. Summarise the four steps of the Question 5 strategy.	**Step 1:** make a choice. **Step 2:** plan the structure of your response. **Step 3:** write your response. **Step 4:** proof-read your work.

Put paper here

Previous questions

Now go back and use these questions to check your knowledge of previous topics.

Questions	Answers
1. Name at least four different genres of fiction.	Possible answers include: science fiction, fantasy, romance, historical fiction, thriller, mystery, horror.
2. Is the following an example of pathetic fallacy or personification, and why? *Time waits for no one.*	This is personification because it makes time sound like a person but does not describe it as having any human emotion.

Put paper here

Exam-style questions

Answer the exam-style questions on pages 115–117.

5.1

Q5 **Either**

Write a description of being lost in an unfamiliar place as suggested by this picture:

Or

Write part of a story about a special occasion.

[40 marks]

Exam-style questions

5.2

Q5 Either

Write a description of a busy parent as suggested by this picture:

Or

Write a story where something unexpected happens.

[40 marks]

5.3

Q5 Either

Write a description of a dangerous event as suggested by this picture:

Or

Write a story with the title 'The present'.

[40 marks]

Paper 2: Overview

Structure

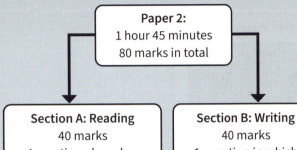

Paper 2	Suggested timings	Marks	Skill tested
Reading the source	10 mins	-	-
Question 1	5 mins	4	AO1
Question 2	10 mins	8	AO1
Question 3	15 mins	12	AO2
Question 4	20 mins	16	AO3
Question 5	45 mins	40	AO5 AO6

Paper 2:
1 hour 45 minutes
80 marks in total

Section A: Reading
40 marks
4 questions, based on
two non-fiction extracts
(one 20th or 21st-century
and one 19th century)

Section B: Writing
40 marks
1 question in which
you present a
viewpoint in response
to a prompt

Questions

In the exam, the questions will be printed in the exam booklet where you write your answers. The source texts will be provided to you in a separate document.

The following are examples of the question types. They relate to the sources on pages 184–187.

LINK
The assessment objectives are explained in more detail on page 200.

Q1 | **Interpret information** AO1

This question tests the first part of AO1 – interpreting **implicit** and **explicit** information from a source.

Q1 Read again the first part of **Source A**, from **lines 1 to 11**.

Choose **four** statements below which are **true**.

Shade the **circles** in the boxes of the ones that you think are **true**.

A There was water on the road they drove along. ○

B The writer and her son are travelling in a car. ○

C This is the first time the writer has been to London. ○

D The writer and her son set off in the morning. ○

E Their journey had been held up by traffic problems. ○

F The writer wouldn't mind if the journey took a bit longer. ○

G Robbie is staying in London for more than a year. ○

H The writer is excited about returning home. ○

[4 marks]

This question tests your ability to:
- select four correct options from a choice of eight
- use both explicit and implicit reading skills.

Q2 | Synthesise information

AO1

This question tests AO1 – identifying and interpreting ideas and information from two sources and synthesising them (bringing them together).

Q2 You need to refer to **Source A** and **Source B** for this question.

The colleges in **Source A** and **Source B** are very different.

Use details from **both** sources to write a summary of what you understand about the differences between the two colleges' buildings and locations. **[8 marks]**

This question tests your ability to:
- make inferences about the individual texts in relation to the task
- clearly identify links between the texts
- comment in detail on differences between the texts.

Q3 | Comment on language

AO2

This question tests AO2 – commenting on the effect of a writer's language choices using subject terms.

Q3 You now need to refer only to **Source B** from **lines 35 to 52**.

How does the writer use language to describe Mr Brownlow?

[12 marks]

This question tests your ability to:
- select examples of language choices from the right part of the source
- clearly identify the language being used, using quotations and subject terms
- comment in detail on the effect created by these language choices.

Q4 | Compare perspectives

AO3

This question tests AO3 – comparing writers' perspectives and how they are conveyed.

Q4 For this question, you need to refer to the **whole of Source A**, together with the **whole of Source B**.

Compare how the two writers convey their different thoughts and feelings about their sons.

[16 marks]

This question tests your ability to:
- clearly identify each writer's perspective on the topic they write about
- use details from both texts to exemplify and draw comparisons between these perspectives
- comment in detail on what these perspectives show and reveal
- comment on how each writer uses language and structure to convey their perspectives.

Q5 | Present a viewpoint

AO5 AO6

This question tests AO5 – communicating clearly and structuring writing effectively. It also tests AO6 – using vocabulary, spelling, punctuation, and sentence types in an accurate and varied way.

Q5 'Schools are great places to be. They are places where close friendships are made, memorable events happen, and young people learn how to become successful adults.'

Write an article for a magazine in which you argue your point of view on this statement.

[40 marks]

This question tests your ability to:
- write an argument in response to the given statement
- write in a way that sustains your reader's interest
- structure and sequence your response in an effective way
- use words, punctuation, and sentence types in a varied and accurate way.

Paper 2: Reading the source / Question 1

Reading the source

In Paper 2, Section A: Reading, there will be four questions to answer about two linked source texts. Before answering any questions, you must remember to read both source texts in full.

Aim to spend the first 10 minutes of your exam carefully reading the texts. Each source text will be:

- about 700 words
- a non-fiction text (one from the 19th century and one from either the 20th or 21st century).

TIP

There will be a short introduction to the source. This introduction will give you some critical information, which is useful when answering the questions about the whole source.

Question 1: Overview

? Focus	✓ Marks	🕒 Time	✳ AO
Interpret ideas	4 marks	5 minutes	AO1

Question 1 tests your ability to interpret explicit and some implicit information. You are directed to the opening part of the source and asked to select the four correct statements from a choice of eight. The eight possible answers are listed in the same order as the information appears in the text. Read each of them carefully, as some require you to 'process' or **infer** information, rather than simply find it.

Question 1 will always follow the same format:

Q1 Read again the first part of **Source x**, from **lines x to x**.

Choose **four** statements below which are **true**.

Shade the **circles** in the boxes of the ones that you think are **true**.

A .... ⬭

B .... ⬭

C .... ⬭

D .... ⬭

E .... ⬭

F .... ⬭

G .... ⬭

H .... ⬭

[4 marks]

LINK

The knowledge section on pages 2–8 will remind you of the difference between explicit and implicit information that will help you to answer this type of question.

TIP

If you make an error in the exam, you should cross out the whole box. If you change your mind and require a statement that has been crossed out, then draw a circle around the box.

Question 1: Strategy

Follow the steps below to respond to a Question 1 task.

> **Step 1**: Look at the lines specified in the question. Draw brackets or draw a line beside the key lines of the source and re-read them.

⬇

> **Step 2**: Carefully read each option before selecting any answers. The eight options will be arranged in the order in which the information appears in the text. Track each option in order against the source. Doing this can make this question easier to manage.

⬇

> **Step 3**: Select four statements that are true.

Question 1: Example

Read the sample Question 1 and annotations below. In the exam, the relevant lines will not be printed out in the question, so you will need to find them in the source text. You may find it helpful to mark the relevant lines to make sure you keep looking at the right section of text.

LINK

This question refers to an extract from Source 5A: *Endings*. The full text is on pages 184–185.

Q1 Read again the first part of **Source 5A**, from **lines 1 to 11**.

Choose **four** statements below which are **true**.

Shade the **circles** in the boxes of the ones that you think are **true**.

A There was water on the road they drove along. ◯

B The writer and her son are travelling in a car. ◯

C This is the first time the writer has been to London. ◯

D The writer and her son set off in the morning. ◯

E Their journey had been held up by traffic problems. ◯

F The writer wouldn't mind if the journey took a bit longer. ◯

G Robbie is staying in London for more than a year. ◯

H The writer is excited about returning home. ◯

[4 marks]

These are the key lines of the source you must select from. Always double check you are selecting from the right source and the right lines.

Options like this require you to read carefully as both 'car' and 'van' are mentioned in the first two lines of the source.

Options like this require you to process information. Line 5 in the source expresses this idea but in different words, so you will need to carefully read and interpret what is said.

Source 5A: *Endings* by Petra Swift

Yet another car steamed past us in the outside lane, throwing rainwater up the sides of our van. It was going to be a long journey from Berwick to London and although it was one we'd done a few times before, we'd usually go by train. But this time was different.

5 We left home at 6.30am with the intention of being in London by midday and so far, all was going well. We'd stopped once for coffee and so far, had encountered no traffic jams. I wished we had, just to put off the moment that lay ahead. In essence, this was a mum-and-son trip with a difference: at the end of the road, I'd drop Robbie, my teenage son, off at the music college

10 that would be his place of study – and home – for the next three years. I'd be returning home without him. I can't say I was thrilled.

Paper 2: Question 1

Question 1: Sample answers

Sample answer 1

Now read the following sample answers to the Question 1 example question on page 121, alongside the examiner's comments.

This answer scores 2 marks out of 4.

A	There was water on the road they drove along.	◐
B	The writer and her son are travelling in a car.	◐
C	This is the first time the writer has been to London.	○
D	The writer and her son set off in the morning.	○
E	Their journey had been held up by traffic problems.	◐
F	The writer wouldn't mind if the journey took a bit longer.	◐
G	Robbie is staying in London for more than a year.	○
H	The writer is excited about returning home.	○

❶ The student has not read the source closely enough – although 'another car' is mentioned in the opening line, the source makes it clear they are travelling in a van.

❷ The student has not processed the source information properly – they needed to work out that 'had encountered no traffic jams' means they had not been held up by traffic problems.

TIP 💡

After selecting four answer options, re-read your choices and check them against the source extract. Make sure you only select four statements.

Sample answer 2

This answer scores full marks as all of the correct options have been selected.

A	There was water on the road they drove along.	◐
B	The writer and her son are travelling in a car.	○
C	This is the first time the writer has been to London.	○
D	The writer and her son set off in the morning.	◐
E	Their journey had been held up by traffic problems.	○
F	The writer wouldn't mind if the journey took a bit longer.	◐
G	Robbie is staying in London for more than a year.	◐
H	The writer is excited about returning home.	○

REMEMBER ❗

- Make sure you select from the right source and lines.
- Carefully read the options and source text.
- Shade only four options.

Key terms Make sure you can write a definition for these key terms

explicit   implicit   infer

Paper 2: Question 1

Use the following questions to check your understanding of the knowledge covered in this section. Then cover the answers column with a piece of paper and write down as many as you can. Check and repeat.

	Questions	Answers
1	How long should you spend on Question 1?	5 minutes.
2	How many marks are available for Question 1?	4 marks.
3	You will need to process some of the information in the options.	True.
4	The information needs to be selected from anywhere in the source.	False. The question will tell you which lines to focus on.
5	You need to select four correct options from a choice of eight.	True.
6	You should put a bracket around the key lines in the source.	True.
7	Summarise the three steps of the Question 1 strategy.	**Step 1:** identify the key lines of the source. **Step 2:** read each option and double check it against the source. **Step 3:** select four true statements.

Put paper here (×3)

Previous questions

Now go back and use these questions to check your knowledge of previous topics.

	Questions	Answers
1	What is explicit information?	Information that is clearly stated. The reader does not have to work it out.
2	What does *infer* mean?	To work out meaning that is only hinted at, rather than explicitly stated.

Put paper here

Practice

Exam-style questions

Answer the exam-style questions on pages 124–125. In the exam, the relevant extract (e.g. lines 1–13) for Question 1 will *not* be reprinted in the question paper, so you will need to find them in the source text. They have been included here for easy reference.

REMEMBER

In the exam, you will need to read the *whole* source text first, before you start looking at the questions and any specific extracts.

1.1

> **Q1**   Read again the first part of **Source 6A**, from **lines 1 to 13**.
>
> Choose **four** statements below which are **true**.
>
> Shade the **circles** in the boxes of the ones that you think are **true**.
>
> **A** Tudor is more than seven years old.   ⬭
>
> **B** Tudor has been picked for fewer than three Premier League junior teams.   ⬭
>
> **C** Tolu is bursting with pride at Tudor's achievements.   ⬭
>
> **D** *Child Genius* is a Channel 5 TV show.   ⬭
>
> **E** The TV show features children being subjected to lots of unpleasant tests.   ⬭
>
> **F** Tolu shows some sympathy with Tudor's experience in the test. ⬭
>
> **G** Tolu does not do very well in the test.   ⬭
>
> **H** Tolu judges Tudor to be less able than he thought.   ⬭
>
> **[4 marks]**

LINK

This question refers to an extract from Source 6A: *Cruellest reality TV show ever*. The full text is on pages 188-189.

Source 6A: *Cruellest reality TV show ever* by Tanith Carey

At the tender age of eight, Tudor has been picked to play soccer for no fewer than three Premier League junior teams: QPR, Tottenham and Chelsea. This achievement alone would be enough to make most fathers' hearts burst with pride. But, unfortunately for Tudor, he appears to have a very long way to go
5 before he meets the sky-high expectations of his demanding dad, Tolu.

So far, the most heart-rending scenes on Channel 4's reality series Child Genius – in which 20 children are subjected to a terrifying barrage of tests – have been the sight of this small boy hiding his face in his hands as he weeps. The reason? He has not scored as well as his father tells him he
10 should have done. […] Yet rather than commiserate with his son after a disappointing performance, it is Tolu, who declares that he finds the contest 'emotionally draining'. He then tells Tudor: 'Maybe you're not as good as we thought.' […]

1.2

> **Q1** Read again the first part of **Source 7A**, from **lines 1 to 7**.
>
> Choose **four** statements below which are **true**.
>
> Shade the **circles** in the boxes of the ones that you think are **true**.
>
> **A** The writer thought London was an up-to-date place. ◯
>
> **B** The writer grew up in Bradford. ◯
>
> **C** As a child, the writer owned a bike, a football, and a computer. ◯
>
> **D** The writer doesn't enjoy using technology these days. ◯
>
> **E** The writer wishes she had a phone when she was younger. ◯
>
> **F** The writer never uses social media as an adult. ◯
>
> **G** The writer thinks social media poses challenges for teenagers. ◯
>
> **H** The writer didn't want her daughter to have a phone. ◯
>
> **[4 marks]**

LINK

This question refers to an extract from Source 7A: *The future is here*. The full text is on pages 192–193.

Source 7A: *The future is here* by Hannah Hussein

In 1972 we didn't have computers. Well, they had them in London probably, but we certainly never had them when I was a kid in Bradford. A bike? Yes. A football? Yes. A computer? Definitely not. I love all things technological now, but I'm not sure I would have liked to grow up surrounded by phones, tablets
5   and laptops. And definitely not social media. I'm never off it these days, but I think it's a difficult world for teenagers to negotiate. That's why I was initially reluctant for my daughter to get a phone.

1.3

> **Q1** Read again the first part of **Source 8A**, from **lines 1 to 5**.
>
> Choose **four** statements below which are **true**.
>
> Shade the **circles** in the boxes of the ones that you think are **true**.
>
> **A** The rain is not too heavy. ◯
>
> **B** The waves rise above the kayak. ◯
>
> **C** The writer begins to sink along with her boat. ◯
>
> **D** The wind pushes the water forwards. ◯
>
> **E** The writer has water thrown in her face. ◯
>
> **F** The writer has to work hard to move the boat forward. ◯
>
> **G** The boat makes substantial movements forward. ◯
>
> **H** The writer feels the physical demands of the journey. ◯
>
> **[4 marks]**

LINK

This question refers to an extract from Source 8A: *The Cruelest Journey*. The full text is on pages 196–197.

Source 8A: *The Cruelest Journey* by Kira Salak

Torrential rains. Waves higher than my kayak, trying to capsize me. But my boat is self-bailing and I stay afloat. The wind drives the current in reverse, tearing and ripping at the shores, sending spray into my face. I paddle madly, crashing and driving forward. I travel inch by inch, or so it seems, arm
5   muscles smarting and rebelling against this journey.

Paper 2: Question 2

Question 2: Overview

Focus	Marks	Time	AO
Interpret and synthesise information	8 marks	10 minutes	AO1

Question 2 tests your ability to **interpret** and **synthesise** information from two sources. It does not require you to comment on techniques or effects used by the writer. Synthesising means bringing together elements from two sources, finding links between them, and commenting on the information in the sources in a summary. Question 2 will follow a format like below:

> **Q2** You need to refer to **Source A** and **Source B** for this question.
>
> Use details from **both** sources to write a summary...
>
> **[8 marks]**

You will have to select relevant material from anywhere in the two source texts.

Question 2: Strategy

Follow the steps below to respond to a Question 2 task.

> **Step 1**: Underline the key focus of the question.

⬇

> **Step 2**: Select key information and ideas that are relevant to the focus of the question in both sources. It might be easiest to do this for each source separately first.
>
> - Skim read each source text, with this focus in mind.
> - Underline key information and ideas.
> - Make a note of relevant links.

⬇

> **Step 3**: Decide on two or three links between both sources that are relevant to the focus of the question. Make sure you are combining 'like with like'. This means links that correspond with each other.

⬇

> **Step 4**: Summarise these links in your response.
>
> - You should clearly show each point of connection using quotations to do so.
> - Comment in detail on the information you have selected from each source. You are trying to show what you have inferred and understood about the information or examples you have selected.

Question 2: Example

Read the sample Question 2 and annotations below. Before you complete Question 2, re-read both sources and look for any links that are relevant to the focus of the question.

> **Q2** You need to refer to **Source 5A** and **Source 5B** for this question.
>
> The ==colleges== in **Source 5A** and **Source 5B** are ==very different==. ←
>
> → Use details from both sources to write a summary of ==what you understand about the differences between the two colleges' buildings and locations==. ←
>
> **[8 marks]**

LINK

This question refers to the whole text of Source 5A: *Endings*, and the whole text of Source 5B: *A Gentleman's Journal*. These sources can also be found on pages 184–187.

This is the focus of the question. You must select links and source details which relate to this focus. You won't receive any marks for writing about things that don't relate to the focus of the question.

'What you understand' is a prompt to say 'show what you can interpret and infer'. This is the most important aspect of Question 2, so detail is expected.

Some exam papers might ask for 'similarities' rather than 'differences', but examiners will reward comments on both similarities and differences regardless of what the question asks for.

Source 5A: *Endings* by Petra Swift

> Source 5A is an extract from *Endings* in which Petra Swift describes taking her son to music college in London where he will begin a new stage in his life.

Yet another car steamed past us in the outside lane, throwing rainwater up the sides of our van. It was going to be a long journey from Berwick to London and although it was one we'd done a few times before, we'd usually go by train. But this time was different.

5 We left home at 6.30am with the intention of being in London by midday and so far, all was going well. We'd stopped once for coffee and so far, had encountered no traffic jams. I wished we had, just to put off the moment that lay ahead. In essence, this was a mum-and-son trip with a difference: at the end of the road, I'd drop Robbie, my teenage son, off at the music college

10 that would be his place of study – and home – for the next three years. I'd be returning home without him. I can't say I was thrilled.

We'd visited the college the previous spring before he'd applied. The place itself was little more than ten years old and still looked state-of-the-art. I remember thinking how my amazingly talented no-longer-little boy would

15 thrive there. I pictured him in one of the practice rooms, its lush carpet dampening the sound of the voices and instruments as fresh-faced students found their way through songs, initiating friendships that would hopefully last a lifetime – or at least three years. For that was the whole point of this place; its aim was to bring like-minded kids together and help them find a

20 career in music. Along the way, fun was guaranteed.

The college itself nestles in a busy part of the capital city, a lively, bustling building where a variety of students push confidently through the glass doors and spill out in the nearby high street in search of food, drink and fun.

Question 2: Example

25 The sober redbrick buildings of my college experience are nowhere to be seen. Instead, a comfortable newness is exuded.

When we visited last year, we met one of the tutors, a laid-back guy who told us his job was to inspire and facilitate the success of the students in his care. The tutors looked less like teachers and more like the kindly, slightly scruffy musicians Robbie spends most of his time with. I knew he'd love this college. It seemed to
30 exude freedom and commitment at the same time. The bright neon college sign promised a world of joy and an excitement that couldn't be had at home.

And yet now, more than a year later as we finally pulled up outside the college and looked around for the accommodation block, it felt less welcoming, as if it was waiting to take away my boy. It was, I knew, a ridiculous and selfish
35 feeling on my part but it was true that this was a bittersweet day. If Robbie was to have a future in music, he needed to be here in the capital at the heart of the country's music scene. It was a big achievement for him to get here and one that made me glow. It was a new beginning. But it was also an ending. The end of childhood and a loosening of the child-parent ties.

40 It didn't take too long to unload the van, much less to place his few belongings into his new room. Underneath Robbie's teenage bravado there was uncertainty though. We both knew the significance of the day but didn't need to voice it. We'd always had a tacit understanding of such things. A final cup of coffee in a nearby café put off the departure by half an hour. I resisted
45 any foolish shows of emotion. He needed to focus on how exciting things were going to be, not feel guilt or worry for a tearful parent.

Anyway, the much-dreaded moment was over quickly. A quick hug and a few words and then he was off into a new world. As I drove away, a host of memories from years past played through the screen in my head: his first
50 steps, a holiday in Dorset, the time we nearly lost him to pneumonia.

A different road now lay ahead.

Source 5B: *A Gentleman's Journal* by Finlay Graham

Source B is an extract from *A Gentleman's Journal*, written in 1872 by the Scottish writer Finlay Warner. In it, he describes his old college and the departure of his son, also called Finlay, to study there.

Another unremarkable day, notable only for the departure of Finlay, my youngest and my namesake, to his new place of study in the highlands. Like his four brothers before him, he was always destined to study at my old college, a forbidding stone stepmother that would make him a man. I recall
5 the day I left home as if it were yesterday, like him, a wet-behind-the-ears boy of eight, lugging my leathery old suitcase and heading off to live in that same strange world with strange rules.

The college itself is a sight to behold. It sits in gallant loneliness amongst the cold highlands, as if waiting patiently for those few weeks of the year when

10 the sun shines. Its isolation is part of its charm. Until the real snows come, you can rely on a train once a day to take you to the little station at the end of the line, from which the college is a short journey on foot. As you arrive, the first thing you see is a long, gravelled driveway, invariably wet with rain, that leads you to an imposing but slightly dilapidated entrance way. There was

15 always something frightfully gothic about that view, and the mild terror I felt as entered the building for the first time remains with me even now.

Finlay's new life will challenge him; he is a dear boy, but he has never been what you might call engaging. Of the five brothers, he is the most introverted, keeping his own company and often spending hours in his room,

20 avoiding sport and much preferring reading, which in itself is a fine pursuit, but not one which easily endears you to others. His brothers are more outgoing and – I hesitate to say – more academic. I do fear he will struggle a little against the notable reputations of his brothers, but as a father, you have to accept these things and find joy where you can.

25 I imagine Finlay will experience the same things as I did at the college: the draughty windows, the meagre* food and the occasional bouts of homesickness. Yet he will also experience the joy of boyish company, the rigour of lessons and the feeling of belonging to a tradition. The college did become a thing of beauty to me over time; it seemed enormous in my first year, but six years later it had

30 become my dominion*, one I was desperately sad to leave behind. Finlay will, like me, learn to resent the summers spent at home, those long days away from his college friends and the busy rooms where true friendships are made.

Finlay will be lucky if he experiences the schoolmasters of my youth. [M]y teachers were heroic, if that doesn't sound too sentimental. Mr Brownlow

35 was the finest of them. A whirlwind of a man, one for whom life held no fear. But *he* did inspire fear, at least at first. It's true to say that I dreaded his lessons in my first year, his deep, gruff voice echoing across the room as he insisted on publicly humiliating those whose work was less than acceptable.

To look at, old Brownlow seemed insubstantial. Slight, balding and with a face as

40 red as a post box, he would stand at the door as you entered his room. There was no familiar greeting, little warmth and certainly a feeling that you had entered his territory. The start of each lesson was always a quiet affair, until he warmed to his theme. Typically, we would sit silent in our rows, and he'd parade up and down, winding himself up like a Catherine wheel*, sparks beginning to fly as his passion

45 for his subject took hold. He was very much the boss, the expert, the sergeant major and interruptions were not welcome. As I grew older, my fear for him gave way to respect. The fearsome energy was merely an act; he was playing a part and once you'd earned his respect, he allowed you to see his gentle side, which manifested itself in a fascination for insects and a deep love of the highlands.

50 Heaven knows what old Brownlow would make of Finlay if he taught him. Perhaps he would do the boy good. Although I missed Finlay's departure earlier, I do know that he'll be in safe hands and hope to see a more assured young man when he returns at Christmas.

---

meagre: *not very much*

dominion: *a place where someone has control*

Catherine wheel: *a fast spinning firework*

Paper 2: Question 2

Question 2: Sample answers

Sample answer 1

Now read the following sample answers to the Question 2 example question on page 127, alongside the examiner's comments.

This is one paragraph from a longer answer. It scores less than half the marks available.

❶ The student identifies a 'like with like' link and makes a general point about locations.

❸ This is also a relevant point, but again there is very limited interpretation of detail here.

> The first college is in the city but the second one is in the country. Cities are busy places, but the countryside is much quieter. ❶ You can see this when the writer in Source 5A says 'a busy part of the capital' which shows that there'll be lots going on and it could be exciting. ❷ In Source 5B it says the college is in 'isolation' which shows that there's nothing there. ❸ Also, the college in Source 5A has 'practice rooms' but the college in Source 5B has a 'gravelled driveway' which shows that they have different things at each college. ❹

❷ Here the student gives a specific example from the source and begins to show some interpretive skills – they are inferring that 'busy' suggests 'lots going on' and 'exciting'. This is potentially good but needs much more development.

❹ This is a very loose difference. Although there is some merit in it, the student could have made a better choice.

Examiner's comments

Sample answer 1 is partly successful. The first comparison is relevant and shows some interpretive comment. The second comparison is less successful. The main shortcoming is the lack of inferential detail in the comments. To improve the answer, the student would need to include more detailed comments on the information in the source texts.

It helps to start your answer by clearly stating the point of comparison. This directly shows the examiner your overarching point and frees you up to concentrate on your comments. Instead of moving on to a second link in one paragraph, always try to add relevant detail to show the depth of your thinking. Building up your interpretations and inferences results in a higher mark.

As mentioned above, the quality of your comments is the most important part of your answer. This means you need to show insight about the details and information you select. You are demonstrating your interpretive skills – showing what you understand about those details. The more thoughtful details you include for each point, the better your mark is likely to be.

Sample answer 2

This is one paragraph from a longer answer. It receives high marks.

1 The student begins by making a clear 'like with like' comparison.

2 Precise references from the source are used. A series of inferences and interpretations are offered. The student is showing the quality of their thinking here.

3 Direct comparison is made with the second college. Some perceptive comments are made based on precisely chosen references.

4 A perceptive comment on the differences between the buildings' appearances.

> The two colleges seem very different in appearance. **1** The London college seems to be much more modern, with its 'state-of-the-art' appearance and 'glass doors' suggesting a cutting-edge, innovative place to learn. It implies that the college is forward-looking and exclusive, perhaps having had lots of money spent on it. **2** By contrast, the highland college seems more austere and sounds authoritarian. Its 'dilapidated' entrance and 'gothic' view imply it is unkempt and forbidding, and make it sound almost prison-like. **3** The differences in the buildings' appearance suggest how the nature of educational institutions can have a significant impact on students' feelings towards education. **4**

Examiner's comments

Sample answer 2 makes a clear and focused link at the start of the paragraph. It then gives detail which is interpreted in a comprehensive and perceptive way. The detail of the comments, supported by carefully-chosen evidence, is what makes this successful.

REMEMBER

- You need to make a sensible 'like with like' link.
- Refer to both texts in detail.
- Clearly state the comparison you're making.
- The most important part of your answer is your interpretation of the details you select.

Key terms Make sure you can write a definition for each of these key terms.

interpret   synthesise

Paper 2: Question 2

Use the following questions to check your understanding of the knowledge covered in this section. Then cover the answers column with a piece of paper and write down as many as you can. Check and repeat.

Questions	Answers
1 How long should you spend on Question 2?	10 minutes.
2 How many marks are available for Question 2?	8 marks.
3 You need to include quotations in your answer. True or false?	True.
4 You need to make clear, sensible links between both sources. True or false?	True.
5 You must write about language choices. True or false?	False.
6 Your mark heavily depends upon the quality of your comments. True or false?	True.
7 The best way to score highly is by extending your comments. True or false?	True.
8 Summarise the four steps of the Question 2 strategy.	**Step 1:** underline the key focus of the question. **Step 2:** select key details and information from both sources. **Step 3:** select two or three relevant links between both sources. **Step 4:** summarise these links in your response.

Put paper here

Previous questions

Now go back and use these questions to check your knowledge of previous topics.

Questions	Answers
1 You should skim-read both sources before reading the question. True or false?	False. You should read the sources in full, read the question, then skim-read the sources.
2 What are the three key features to identify in a text and why are they important?	Text form, audience, purpose. They strongly influence the structure, language, and style of a text.

Put paper here

Exam-style questions

Answer the exam-style questions on pages 133–141. Before you answer each of these questions, you should have already read both source texts. For this question, you need to think about the *whole* of both source texts provided, not just focus on some lines within each text.

2.1

> **Q2** You need to refer to **Source 6A** and **Source 6B** for this question.
>
> The attitudes of parents in **Source 6A** and **Source 6B** are similar.
>
> Use details from **both** sources to write a summary of what you understand about the similarities in the attitudes of parents.
>
> **[8 marks]**

LINK

This question refers to the whole text of Source 6A: *Cruellest reality TV show ever*, and the whole text of Source 6B: *Children*. These sources can also be found on pages 188–190.

EXAM TIP

In your answer, you should:

- make clear, sensible links between both sources
- use relevant quotations
- comment in detail – show your interpretive skills.

Source 6A: *Cruellest reality TV show ever* by Tanith Carey

> The following newspaper article was written by Tanith Carey, a parenting expert, in response to the Channel 4 programme, *Child Genius*.

At the tender age of eight, Tudor has been picked to play soccer for no fewer than three Premier League junior teams: QPR, Tottenham and Chelsea. This achievement alone would be enough to make most fathers' hearts burst with pride. But, unfortunately for Tudor, he appears to have a very long way to
5 go before he meets the sky-high expectations of his demanding dad, Tolu.

So far, the most heart-rending scenes on Channel 4's reality series *Child Genius* – in which 20 children are subjected to a terrifying barrage of tests – have been the sight of this small boy hiding his face in his hands as he weeps. The reason? He has not scored as well as his father tells him he
10 should have done. […] Yet rather than commiserate with his son after a disappointing performance, it is Tolu, who declares that he finds the contest 'emotionally draining'. He then tells Tudor: 'Maybe you're not as good as we thought.' […]

Even for a nation well used to the mercenary* exploitation of spy-on-the-wall
15 television, this has raised concern. As one worried viewer pointed out, the series would more aptly be named 'Pushy Parents'. For it is really all about the Eagle Dads and Tiger Mums, who want to show off how much work they have invested in their youngsters.

The show first aired in its current format last year, and – as the author of
20 a book looking at the damage caused by competitive parenting – I had thought we would not see a return of this toxic* mix of reality TV and hot-housing*. I had expected the sight of children as young as eight crying to prick the conscience of the commissioning editors.

A vain hope, of course. […]

25 *Child Genius* has tapped into an increasingly dangerous trend in parenting; the misguided belief that your offspring is a blank slate and if you hot-house

Exam-style questions

them enough, you can be solely responsible for their success. Parenting is turning into a form of product development. Increasingly, we are falling for the notion that if we cram enough facts into their little brains we can make
30 sure they come out on top. The end result is a rise in depression and anxiety among a generation who believe they are losers if they fail, or could always do better if they win.

Like all offspring of pushy parents, who feel their family's affection is conditional on their success, children like Tudor are not just weeping
35 because they didn't score well. When he tries to cover his tears with his hands, saying 'What I achieved was absolutely terrible', he is facing a much darker fear: That he will lose his father's love if he does not come up to scratch. […]

Of course, the goal of reality TV is to entertain — but should dramatic story-
40 lines really come ahead of a child's emotional well-being?

Perhaps it's a measure of their state of mind that some parents, such as psychologists Shoshana and Sacha, who featured in the first two episodes, saw nothing harmful in describing their approach to bringing up their daughter Aliyah, nine, as though she is 'a well-bred race-horse'. Shoshana
45 openly pities parents left to bring up children without her skill set. She was blissfully oblivious to the fact that the rest of us were watching, slack-jawed in disbelief at how hard she pushes her child. Far from rushing to adopt such techniques, parents have reacted in horror. The internet has been buzzing with viewers saying they found the series 'upsetting to watch',
50 'heartbreaking' and expressing concern […]

No doubt the reality is that Tolu is also a loving father, who sincerely believes he is doing the best for his son, and the producers have edited the programme to make him look like the ultimate caricature of an overbearing father.

55 But for me, one question remains: How much longer are we going to allow Channel 4 to encourage extreme parents to push their helpless children to breaking point in the name of entertainment?

---

mercenary: *money-grabbing*
toxic: *poisonous*
hot-housing: *intensely educating a child*

Source 6B: *Children*

The following newspaper article was written in the 19th century. It offers views on how to raise children.

It is a mistake to think that children love the parents less who maintain a proper authority over them. On the contrary, they respect them more. It is a cruel and unnatural selfishness that indulges children in a foolish and hurtful way. Parents are guides and counsellors to their children. As a guide
5 in a foreign land, they undertake to pilot them safely through the shoals and quicksands of inexperience. If the guide allows his followers all the freedom they please; if, because they dislike the constraint of the narrow path of safety, he allows them to stray into holes and precipices* that destroy them, to quench their thirst in brooks that poison them, to loiter in woods full of
10 wild beasts or deadly herbs, can he be called a sure guide?

And is it not the same with our children? They are as yet only in the preface, or as it were, in the first chapter of the book of life. We have nearly finished it, or are far advanced. We must open the pages for these younger minds.

If children see that their parents act from principle – that they do not find
15 fault without reason – that they do not punish because personal offence is taken, but because the thing in itself is wrong – if they see that while they are resolutely but affectionately refused what is not good for them, there is a willingness to oblige them in all innocent matters – they will soon appreciate such conduct. If no attention is paid to the rational wishes – if no
20 allowance is made for youthful spirits – if they are dealt with in a hard and unsympathising manner – the proud spirit will rebel, and the meek spirit be broken. […]

A pert or improper way of speaking ought never to be allowed. Clever children are very apt to be pert, and if too much admired for it, and laughed
25 at, become eccentric and disagreeable. It is often very difficult to check our own amusement, but their future welfare should be regarded more than our present entertainment. It should never be forgotten that they are tender plants committed to our fostering care, that every thoughtless word or careless neglect may destroy a germ of immortality*.

precipices: *steep, dangerous places*
immortality: *living forever*

Exam-style questions

2.2

Q2 You need to refer to **Source 7A** and **Source 7B** for this question.

The children in **Source 7A** and **Source 7B** live in very different places.

Use details from **both** sources to write a summary of what you understand about the differences in the places where the children live.

[8 marks]

LINK

This question refers to the whole text of Source 7A: *The future is here*, and the whole text of Source 7B: *Acrobats*. These sources can also be found on pages 192–195.

Source 7A: *The future is here* by Hannah Hussein

This extract is about how children use technology for entertainment.

In 1972 we didn't have computers. Well, they had them in London probably, but we certainly never had them when I was a kid in Bradford. A bike? Yes. A football? Yes. A computer? Definitely not. I love all things technological now, but I'm not sure I would have liked to grow up surrounded by phones, tablets
5 and laptops. And definitely not social media. I'm never off it these days, but I think it's a difficult world for teenagers to negotiate. That's why I was initially reluctant for my daughter to get a phone.

Gradually, of course, Basma wore me down. Kids are good at that. If you could see our house right now, you'd see a plethora* of technology. Phones
10 plugged in to chargers, an expensive computer sitting on my antique desk, a tablet lying on the floor just waiting to be stood on. Very much like the houses of our friends, no doubt – technologically and materially rich but time-poor. We've got a doorbell that means I can see who's outside, even when I'm miles from home. I've got the ability to make a Hollywood
15 quality movie on my phone. I've got a state-of-the-art recording studio on my computer. I can switch the heating on from work. And as is typical, my daughter can work all of these tools much faster and better than me.

Basma is currently in that funny teen phase now, but when I look back at her childhood, I view it with a mixture of fondness *and* horror. Nappies
20 and CBeebies I could do without, but the anarchy, creativity and general stupidity of having a toddler in the house is brilliant. Well, to a point.

The magic of snow delighted Basma. Making snowdogs, sledging, snow angels … I'm not sure how I kept up to be honest. It was always her play that fascinated me. She was always creative, making robots out of toilet rolls,
25 building a plasticine house for the hamster, and trying to dig a well in the back garden. She did it with a knowing smirk, reserving her most energy-sapping efforts until I'd just sat down after a hard day at work.

Somewhere along the line though, plasticine gave way to gaming and drawing became Tiktok. Basma still plays, but the games she plays are not
30 in the family home, they're somewhere in the digital ether. It's a world I'm no longer required to be part of, the messaging and memes out of reach. The

screen of her phone is also out of my reach, often tilted away from my view, and hidden behind a passcode. I'm still not sure what I think about children, parents and privacy.

35 Everyone thinks their childhood was better than their own kids. Less technologically advanced, but more creative. Outdoors rather than indoors. Yet when I really think about it, I reckon the children of this generation have got much to celebrate. Technology has made them communicate, albeit in a different way. Social media is primarily about feelings. And
40 Basma is fantastic at reading people. She knows how to challenge, comfort and entertain.

My daughter's digital teen years are mainly good ones. At the swipe of a screen, she finds a recipe for the occasional family meals she makes, she learns how to do CPR* (let's hope I'm not the first recipient of her new-found
45 skills) and also engages with the issues I want her to know about: global poverty, justice and equality. Most profoundly, the thing her childhood has taught her most is to love. Basma is a carer. She cares for people, animals and anything that exists.

A friend of mine has recently become an older mother. She loves it, but I can
50 see the tell-tale weariness in her eyes. The lack of sleep, the nappies, the sheer graft of parenthood. Part of me would like to be building snowdogs again in a carefree past, but would I really swap the precocious, maddening, self-absorbed, yet deeply caring fourteen-year-old daughter of now for the four-year-old of the past? No chance.

---

plethora: *a very large amount of something*
CPR: *cardiopulmonary resuscitation (a lifesaving technique)*

Source 7B: *Acrobats* by Albert Smith

> This extract was written in the 19th century and is about children playing in the streets of Victorian London.

As you pass through one of those [...] narrow dirty streets [...] you will be struck, above all things, by the swarms of children everywhere collected. They scuffle about, and run across your path, and disappear, like rabbits in a warren, in obscure holes. They wait on the kerb until a cab approaches,
5 and run under the very knees of the horse. They collect round the open water plug, and spend the entire day there, all returning wet through to the skin. [...]

[...] You occasionally see a girl of seven or eight years staggering under the weight of a baby whose sole nurse she is; but seldom find them with
10 brothers and sisters. They are only acquaintances. Their parents live huddled up in dirty single rooms, [...] they turn their children out to find means of amusement and subsistence, at the same time, in the streets.

Of all their favourite haunts, there is not one more popular than the bit of open ground where a mass of houses have been pulled down to make room

15   for a new street or building. If they find an old beam of timber, so much the better. They [...] turn it into a see-saw, and, this accomplished, a policeman is the only power that can drive them from the spot. They build forts [...]. They scuffle the mounds of rubbish perfectly smooth by running, or being dragged up and down them; they [...] make huts; and know of nothing in

20   the world capable of affording such delight, except it be the laying down, or taking up, of some wooden pavement.

Picture such a bit of ground, on a fine afternoon, alive with children. Amongst the revellers there is a boy, who for the last five minutes has been hanging by his legs to a bit of temporary railing, with his hair sweeping the ground.

25   Others would have had a fit long before, but this appears to be his natural position. On quitting it, without caring for the empty applause of the crowd, he goes to a retired corner of the plot, and, gravely putting his head and hands upon the ground, at a short distance from the wall, turns his heels up in the air, until he touches the house with his feet. This accomplished, he [...] claps

30   his shoeless soles together [...] and then calmly resumes his normal position, and walks away, not caring whether anybody regards him or not.

This boy is destined to become an Acrobat – at a more advanced period of his life to perform feats of suppleness and agility in the mud of the streets, the sawdust of the circus, or the turf of a race-course. His life will pass in a

35   marvellous series of positions, and its ordinary level course will be unknown to him. He will look upon chairs as articles of furniture only used to support people with the crown of their heads on the top back rail, or their legs on the seats of two stretched out to the utmost extent allowed by their length. Ladders, with him, will in future only be ascended by twisting in and out the

40   rounds like a serpent [...]

The Acrobats are generally seen in London after the racing season, or when the metropolis lies in their way from one course to another. Some go to the sea-side [...] Others join travelling companies [...] who go from town to town [...] When the pantomimes begin, the Acrobats find a new field for

45   employment. [...] They do not, however, always have the good fortune to appear as principals. [...] It is not until the stage-manager at rehearsal wants some daring spirit to tumble from the sky-borders on to the stage; to go round on the sails of a windmill amidst fireworks; or to be knocked through a door, or out of a window, or down a trap, that a pale man, in an old coat that

50   you have seen before, steps forward from the crowd at the wings, and says that he will undertake it, and that he can do any tumbling business required, for he is an Acrobat.

2.3

Q2 You need to refer to **Source 8A** and **Source 8B** for this question.

Nature and the natural world in **Source 8A** and **Source 8B** are shown to be different.

Use details from **both** sources to write a summary of what you understand about the differences in nature and the natural world.

[8 marks]

LINK

This question refers to the whole text of Source 8A: *The Cruelest Journey*, and the whole text of Source 8B: *On Sledge and Horseback to Outcast Siberian Lepers*. These sources can also be found on pages 196–199.

Source 8A: *The Cruelest Journey* by Kira Salak

This extract is about writer and adventurer Kira Salak, at the beginning of her 600-mile journey travelling solo in a kayak from Old Segou in Mali to Timbuktu. She follows the same route taken along the River Niger by the 19th century explorer, Mungo Park.

Torrential rains. Waves higher than my kayak, trying to capsize me. But my boat is self-bailing and I stay afloat. The wind drives the current in reverse, tearing and ripping at the shores, sending spray into my face. I paddle madly, crashing and driving forward. I travel inch by inch, or so it seems, arm
5 muscles smarting and rebelling against this journey.

A popping feeling now and a screech of pain. My right arm lurches from a ripped muscle. But this is no time and place for such an injury, and I won't tolerate it, stuck as I am in a storm. I try to get used to the metronome*-like pulses of pain as I fight the river. There is only one direction to go: forward.

10 I wonder what we look for when we embark on these kinds of trips. There is the pat answer that you tell the people you don't know: that you're interested in seeing a place, learning about its people. But then the trip begins and the hardship comes, and hardship is more honest: it tells us that we don't have enough patience yet, nor humility, nor gratitude. And
15 we thought that we had. Hardship brings us closer to truth, and thus is more difficult to bear, but from it alone comes compassion. And so I already discover one important reason why I'm here on this river, and I've told the world that it can do what it wants with me if only, by the end, I have learned something further. A bargain, then. The journey, my teacher.

20 And where is the river of just this morning, with its whitecaps that would have liked to drown me, with its current flowing backwards against the wind? Gone to this: a river of smoothest glass, a placidity unbroken by wave or eddy, with islands of lush greenery awaiting me like distant Xanadus*.

I know there is no turning back now. The journey to Timbuktu binds me. It
25 deceives me with images of the end, reached at long last. The late afternoon sun settles complacently over the hills to the west. Paddling becomes a sort of meditation now, a gentle trespassing over a river that slumbers. The Niger gives me its beauty almost in apology for the violence of the earlier storms,

and I'm treated to the peace and silence of this wide river, the sun on me, a
30 breeze licking my toes when I lay back to rest, the current as negligible as a
faint breath. Somono fishermen, casting out their nets, puzzle over me as I
float by.

"*Ça va, madame*?" they yell.

Each fisherman carries a young son perched in the back of his pointed canoe
35 to do the paddling. The boys stare at me, transfixed; they have never seen
such a thing. A white woman. Alone. In a red, inflatable boat. Using a two-
sided paddle.

I'm an even greater novelty because Malian women don't paddle here, not
ever. It is a man's job. So there is no good explanation for me, and the people
40 want to understand. They gather on the shore in front of their villages to
watch me pass, the kids screaming and jumping in excitement, the adults
yelling out questions in Bambarra which by now I know to mean: "Where
did you come from? Where's your husband?" And of course they will always
ask: "Where are you going?" "Timbuktu!" I yell out to the last question and
45 paddle on.

---

metronome: *a device that measures time with regular ticks*
Xanadus: *a beautiful and magnificent place*

**Source 8B: *On Sledge and Horseback to Outcast Siberian Lepers* by
Kate Marsden**

> Kate Marsden was a British missionary and explorer in the
> 19th century, who set out on an expedition to Siberia to try to find a cure
> for leprosy. This extract is about her journey through mosquito-infested
> marshes and forests.

On again for a few more miles; but I began to feel the effects of this sort of
travelling – in a word, I felt utterly worn out. It was as much as I could do to
hold on to the horse, and I nearly tumbled off several times in the effort. The
cramp in my body and lower limbs was indescribable, and I had to discard
5 the cushion under me, because it became soaked through and through
with the rain, and rode on the broad, bare, wooden saddle. What feelings of
relief arose when the time of rest came, and the pitching of tents, and the
brewing of tea! Often I slept quite soundly till morning, awaking to find that
the mosquitoes had been hard at work in my slumbers, in spite of veil and
10 gloves, leaving great itching lumps, that turned me sick. Once we saw two
calves that had died from exhaustion from the bites of these pests, and the
white hair of our poor horses was generally covered with clots of blood, due
partly to mosquitoes and partly to prodigious horse-flies. But those lepers –
they suffered far more than I suffered, and that was the one thought, added
15 to the strength that God supplied, that kept me from collapsing entirely ...

My second thunderstorm was far worse than the first. The forest seemed on fire, and the rain dashed in our faces with almost blinding force. My horse plunged and reared, flew first to one side, and then to the other, dragging me amongst bushes and trees, so that I was in danger of being caught by

20 the branches and hurled to the ground. After this storm one of the horses, carrying stores and other things, sank into a bog nearly to its neck; and the help of all the men was required to get it out ...

Soon after the storm we were camping and drinking tea, when I noticed that all the men were eagerly talking together and gesticulating*. I asked

25 what it all meant, and was told that a large bear was supposed to be in the neighbourhood, according to a report from a post-station close at hand. There was a general priming of firearms, except in my case, for I did not know how to use my revolver, so thought I had better pass it on to someone else, lest I might shoot a man in mistake for a bear. We mounted again and went

30 on. The usual chattering was exchanged for a dead silence, this being our first bear experience; but we grew wiser as we proceeded, and substituted noise for silence. We hurried on, as fast as possible, to get through the miles of forests and bogs. I found it best not to look about me, because, when I did so, every large stump of a fallen tree took the shape of a bear. When my

35 horse stumbled over the roots of a tree, or shied at some object unseen by me, my heart began to gallop.

---

gesticulating: *using gestures to communicate*

Paper 2: Question 3

Question 3: Overview

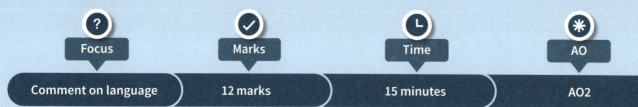

Focus	Marks	Time	AO
Comment on language	12 marks	15 minutes	AO2

Question 3 tests your ability to comment in detail on the writer's choice of language, using subject terms as you do so. Question 3 will always follow the same format:

> **Q3** You now need to refer only to **Source x** from **lines xx to xx**.
>
> How does the writer use language to …?
>
> **[12 marks]**

This is a similar type of question to that found in Paper 1 Question 2. Both questions ask you to explore the writer's use of language to create an impression or achieve effects. You will use the same skills. The key difference is that in Paper 2, there are no bullet points to guide you and there are more marks available. This means you are expected to write a more extended answer. You will only have to refer to a set number of lines for Question 3 from one source.

LINK

The knowledge section on pages 10–16 will remind you of figurative language that will help you answer this type of question.

TIP

Remember that 'commenting on the effect of language' means commenting on *why* a writer has chosen that feature of language. Consider how the language feature works by analysing the connotations, contrasts, or imagery it creates.

Question 3: Strategy

Follow the steps below to respond to a Question 3 task.

> **Step 1**: Underline the key focus of the question.

> **Step 2**: Select three language features that:
> - are relevant to the focus of the question
> - allow you to say something thoughtful. Be selective about which language features you use. **Figurative language**, mood, and imagery are good techniques to comment on. It can be harder to explain in detail the effects of features such as alliteration or punctuation.

> **Step 3**: Comment in detail on these features as you write your answer. Make sure you:
> - clearly state the language features (e.g. **simile**) and use a quotation to exemplify
> - comment in detail on the effect of these language choices – the more you explore the feature you have identified, the higher your mark.

Question 3: Example

Read the sample Question 3 and annotations below.

Q3 You now need to refer only to **Source 5B** from **lines 35 to 52**.

How does the writer use language to describe Mr Brownlow?

[12 marks]

> Make sure that you only refer to this source and these lines. You won't receive any marks for writing about language features that aren't in these lines.

> This is the focus of the question. You must select examples of language that specifically describe Mr Brownlow. No marks are given for writing about language features that are not relevant to the focus of the question.

A Gentleman's Journal by Finlay Graham

35 Finlay will be lucky if he experiences the schoolmasters of my youth. [My] teachers were heroic, if that doesn't sound too sentimental. Mr Brownlow was the finest of them. A whirlwind of a man, one for whom life held no fear. But *he* did inspire fear, at least at first. It's true to say that I dreaded his lessons in my first year, his deep, gruff voice echoing across the room as he

40 insisted on publicly humiliating those whose work was less than acceptable.

To look at, old Brownlow seemed insubstantial. Slight, balding and with a face as red as a post box, he would stand at the door as you entered his room. There was no familiar greeting, little warmth and certainly a feeling that you had entered his territory. The start of each lesson was always a

45 quiet affair, until he warmed to his theme. Typically, we would sit silent in our rows, and he'd parade up and down, winding himself up like a Catherine wheel*, sparks beginning to fly as his passion for his subject took hold. He was very much the boss, the expert, the sergeant major and interruptions were not welcome. As I grew older, my fear for him gave way to respect. The

50 fearsome energy was merely an act; he was playing a part and once you'd earned his respect, he allowed you to see his gentle side, which manifested itself in a fascination for insects and a deep love of the highlands.

Catherine wheel: *a fast spinning firework*

LINK

This question refers to an extract from Source 5B: *A Gentleman's Journal*. The full text is on pages 186–187.

As with the Paper 1 Question 2, be very careful which language features you choose. Figurative language and individual word choices are usually best to write about. Features such as alliteration, punctuation, and sentence types often lead to thin comments which are difficult to analyse in detail.

Use quotations to show the language feature, keeping them short. Precisely identifying the specific feature within the body of your own writing is best. For example:

> The writer makes Mr Brownlow seem like he is a force of nature, using metaphorical language such as 'whirlwind' and also 'Catherine wheel'.

TIP

Remember – it helps to label the language feature using terms such as **metaphor**, **personification**, or **verb**.

Paper 2: Question 3

Question 3: Sample answers

Sample answer 1

Now read the following sample answers to the Question 3 example question on page 143, alongside the examiner's comments.

This is one paragraph from a longer answer. It scores less than half the marks available.

❶ This is a potentially useful piece of language to comment on, but the student needed to label it more precisely. Their comment is simplistic.

❸ This is a sensible piece of language to comment on, but the comment is very general rather than specific to what's happening in the source. It would also benefit from further analysis.

> The writer calls Mr Brownlow 'a whirlwind of a man' which means he's always in a hurry. **❶** He is also described as having a face as 'red as a post box' which is a simile. This suggests he is angry or has high blood pressure. **❷** Another way he is described is as being 'like a Catherine wheel' which is a very interesting description and helps the reader to picture the teacher. **❸** I think he fits into the college well because both the college and Mr Brownlow seem old.

❷ This example is precisely labelled but their comment is not detailed or thoughtful. They attempt some analysis of the simile, but this is relatively basic.

Examiner's comments

Sample answer 1 has some potentially good points, but the student doesn't always clearly identify the language feature and, more importantly, makes thin comments which do not fully explore the writer's language choices. Some of the answer is too general rather than specifically about the language in the extract, and some is irrelevant. To improve this answer, they should make more detailed comment on the effect of the language examples identified.

Sample answer 2

This is one paragraph from a longer answer to the same question. It scores high marks.

1 The student begins by stating an overall impression of Mr Brownlow based on specific examples from the source that are correctly labelled.

3 The student further explores the effect of the language choice with an extended and detailed comment on the effect of the metaphor.

> The writer makes Mr Brownlow seem like he is a force of nature, using metaphorical language such as 'whirlwind' and also 'Catherine wheel'. **1** The comparison to an unstoppable wind makes him seem very powerful but also unpredictable, as if he is uncontrollable and furious. They also imply that the students are very wary of his manner and view him as aggressive. **2** The comparison to a spinning, fiery Catherine wheel makes him seem bright and energetic, but there is a feeling that his fiery nature suggests dangerous qualities. **3** The overall effect of these metaphors makes him seem both intriguing and powerful but also fearsome. **4**

2 Several effects are identified here. The student builds up a selection of impressions of the teacher all of which derive from the language feature identified.

4 This final comment clinches the overall point the student has made. It is specific to the source and focus of the question.

Examiner's comments

Sample answer 2 clearly identifies and labels a useful language feature which is explored with sophistication. The student has written developed comments, making perceptive and detailed observations. By stating the overall effect of language choices at the beginning of the answer, it clearly sets up the comments and analysis that follows.

TIP 💡

Always try to extend your comments; build up detail and show the quality of your thinking. Adding an extra few sentences to explain the effect and how it works can increase your mark.

REMEMBER ❗

- Choose the three most useful language techniques or words – the ones that you can say most about. Often, this means things such as figurative language or individual words.
- The most important part of your answer is what you say about the effect of the language choices.
- Comment in detail on things such as what impression the language gives you of character or situation.

Key terms

Make sure you can write a definition for each of these key terms.

figurative language   metaphor
personification   simile   verb

Paper 2: Question 3

Use the following questions to check your understanding of the knowledge covered in this section. Then cover the answers column with a piece of paper and write down as many as you can. Check and repeat.

	Questions	Answers
1	How long should you spend on Question 3?	15 minutes.
2	How many marks are available for Question 3?	12 marks.
3	What should you underline in the exam question?	The question focus.
4	You need to identify as many language features as you can. True or false?	False. Aim to identify three language features.
5	You must write about sentence types in order to score highly. True or false?	False. It is better to focus on figurative language and individual words.
6	Figurative language and individual words are usually best to write about. True or false?	True. There is usually more you can say about figurative language and individual words.
7	Your mark heavily depends upon the quality of your comments. True or false?	True.
8	You don't need to label the language features or use a quotation. True or false?	False.
9	The best way to score highly is by extending your comments. True or false?	True.
10	Summarise the three steps of the Question 3 strategy.	**Step 1:** underline the key focus of the question. **Step 2:** select three language features. **Step 3:** comment in detail on these features.

Put paper here

Previous questions

Now go back and use these questions to check your knowledge of previous topics.

	Questions	Answers
1	What technique is used here, and what is its effect? *The students swarmed into the dining hall.*	Metaphor. It suggests that a crowd of students moves quickly and all at once, like swarming insects.
2	You should aim to include as many rhetorical features in your writing as possible. True or false?	False.

Put paper here

Exam-style questions

Answer the exam-style questions on pages 147–149. In the exam, the relevant lines in the extract for Question 3 will *not* be reprinted in the question paper so you will need to find them in the source text. They have been included here for easy reference.

> **REMEMBER**
>
> In the exam, you will need to read the *whole* source text first, before you start looking at the questions and any specific extracts. You should only select content from the relevant lines of the source.

3.1

> **Q3** You now need to refer only to **Source 6B** from **lines 1 to 10**.
>
> How does the writer use language to describe the relationship between parents and children?
>
> **[12 marks]**

LINK

This question refers to an extract from Source 6B: *Children*. The full text is on page 190.

EXAM TIP

In your answer, you should:

- select the most useful aspects of language
- clearly label them and use a quotation
- comment in detail on the effect created by these language choices.

Source 6B: *Children*

It is a mistake to think that children love the parents less who maintain a proper authority over them. On the contrary, they respect them more. It is a cruel and unnatural selfishness that indulges children in a foolish and hurtful way. Parents are guides and counsellors to their children. As a guide
5 in a foreign land, they undertake to pilot them safely through the shoals and quicksands of inexperience. If the guide allows his followers all the freedom they please; if, because they dislike the constraint of the narrow path of safety, he allows them to stray into holes and precipices that destroy them, to quench their thirst in brooks that poison them, to loiter in woods full of
10 wild beasts or deadly herbs, can he be called a sure guide?

---

precipices: *steep, dangerous places*

Exam-style questions

3.2

Q3 You now need to refer only to **Source 7B** from **lines 8 to 21**.

How does the writer use language to describe children's lives?

[12 marks]

LINK

This question refers to an extract from Source 7B: *Acrobats*. The full text is on pages 194–195.

Source 7B: *Acrobats* by Albert Smith

[…] You occasionally see a girl of seven or eight years staggering under the weight of a baby whose sole nurse she is; but seldom find them with
10 brothers and sisters. They are only acquaintances. Their parents live huddled up in dirty single rooms, […] they turn their children out to find means of amusement and subsistence, at the same time, in the streets.

Of all their favourite haunts, there is not one more popular than the bit of open ground where a mass of houses have been pulled down to make room
15 for a new street or building. If they find an old beam of timber, so much the better. They […] turn it into a see-saw, and, this accomplished, a policeman is the only power that can drive them from the spot. They build forts […]. They scuffle the mounds of rubbish perfectly smooth by running, or being dragged up and down them; they […] make huts; and know of nothing in the world
20 capable of affording such delight, except it be the laying down, or taking up, of some wooden pavement.

Q3 You now need to refer only to **Source 8B** from **lines 1 to 15**.

How does the writer use language to describe difficult experiences?

[12 marks]

LINK

This question refers to an extract from Source 8B: *On Sledge and Horseback to Outcast Siberian Lepers*. The full text is on pages 198–199.

Source 8B: *On Sledge and Horseback to Outcast Siberian Lepers* by Kate Marsden

On again for a few more miles; but I began to feel the effects of this sort of travelling – in a word, I felt utterly worn out. It was as much as I could do to hold on to the horse, and I nearly tumbled off several times in the effort. The cramp in my body and lower limbs was indescribable, and I had to discard
5 the cushion under me, because it became soaked through and through with the rain, and rode on the broad, bare, wooden saddle. What feelings of relief arose when the time of rest came, and the pitching of tents, and the brewing of tea! Often I slept quite soundly till morning, awaking to find that the mosquitoes had been hard at work in my slumbers, in spite of veil and
10 gloves, leaving great itching lumps, that turned me sick. Once we saw two calves that had died from exhaustion from the bites of these pests, and the white hair of our poor horses was generally covered with clots of blood, due partly to mosquitoes and partly to prodigious horse-flies. But those lepers – they suffered far more than I suffered, and that was the one thought, added
15 to the strength that God supplied, that kept me from collapsing entirely...

Paper 2: Question 4

Question 4: Overview

? Focus	✓ Marks	🕐 Time	✳ AO
Compare perspectives	16 marks	20 minutes	AO3

Question 4 tests your ability to **compare** the **perspectives** of two writers, analysing the **methods** used by the writers to **convey** these perspectives. To do this, you will need to comment on the choice of language and/or structure.

You will have to refer to the whole of both source texts.

Question 4 will always follow the same format:

- the question will ask you to refer to the whole of both sources
- it will give you a focus for what ideas and perspectives should be compared.
- you will be given a bulleted list which can be used to guide what you include in your answer.

> **Q4** For this question, you need to refer to the **whole of Source A**, together with the **whole of Source B**.
>
> Compare how the writers....
>
> **[16 marks]**

It is important to clear identify each writer's perspective, so make sure you explicitly state this in your answer. There may be more than one perspective taken throughout the text and, as the perspective changes, there will be shifts in focus that are interesting to the reader. It is essential that you identify perspectives which relate to the focus in the question and compare corresponding perspectives from both sources.

It is also important that you explore each perspective and how it is conveyed in detail. It might help to consider how you as a reader responded to the perspectives and how they are conveyed. The more you analyse the writers' methods, the higher your mark should be. Most successful answers are around two to three pages long, which should give you an idea of the level of detail needed.

LINK

The knowledge section on pages 34–40 will remind you about the writer's perspectives and the methods used to convey this. This will help you to answer this type of question.

TIP

Unlike Question 2, this question requires you to comment on the way the authors present their topic. This means you need to be alert to how the authors use language and/or structure.

Question 4: Strategy

Follow the steps below to respond to a Question 4 task.

Step 1: Underline the key focus of the question.

Step 2: Select key details and information in each source relevant to the focus of the question.

Step 3: Identify 'like for like' perspectives in both sources that are relevant to the focus of the question.

Step 4: Identify language and/or structural choices made by both writers that are relevant to the focus of the question.

Step 5: Summarise these comparisons in your response. You should:

- explicitly state each writer's perspective
- clearly show the point of comparison using relevant quotations to do so
- comment in detail on the information you have selected from each source
- comment on relevant aspects of language and/or structure.

> **TIP**
>
> Remember that 'perspectives' means how the writer sees things/ their attitudes/their feelings/their thoughts. These terms are often used in the question.

You might find some of the words and sentence stems below helpful when thinking about how to compare perspectives.

both writers ...	on the other hand ...	similarly ...
whereas ...	the writer of Source A ...	in Source B ...
however ...	just as x does, ...	

Paper 2: Question 4

Read the sample Question 4 and annotations below. Remember that Question 4 will ask you to refer to the whole of both sources. In the exam question, you will have to look back at the source texts in the insert. Here we have provided both source texts to help you.

LINK

This question refers to the whole text of Source 5A: *Endings*, and the whole text of Source 5B: *A Gentleman's Journal*. These sources can also be found on pages 184–187.

Q4 For this question, you need to refer to the **whole of Source 5A**, together with the **whole of Source 5B**.

Compare how the writers convey their different thoughts and feelings about their sons.

In your answer, you could:

- compare their different thoughts and feelings about their sons
- compare the methods they use to convey their thoughts and feelings
- support your response with references to both texts.

[16 marks]

Although you are dealing with the whole of both sources, you will need to carefully select the most useful bits of each one.

These are the words that prompt you to write about the writers' 'perspectives'. In some questions, the word 'attitudes' or 'ideas' might be used.

Remember that you need to draw comparisons, so clearly state the thoughts and feelings you identify, showing the difference between each writer's perspective.

This is the question focus. It is very specific, so always select parts of the sources that are relevant to this question focus.

This is a reminder to comment on the way the authors present their topic. 'Methods' means things like language and structural choices.

You do not need to *compare* methods as a priority. It is more important to compare perspectives and comment about the methods in each text.

Source 5A: *Endings* by Petra Swift

Source 5A is an extract from *Endings* in which Petra Swift describes taking her son to music college in London where he will begin a new stage in his life.

Yet another car steamed past us in the outside lane, throwing rainwater up the sides of our van. It was going to be a long journey from Berwick to London and although it was one we'd done a few times before, we'd usually go by train. But this time was different.

5 We left home at 6.30am with the intention of being in London by midday and so far, all was going well. We'd stopped once for coffee and so far, had encountered no traffic jams. I wished we had, just to put off the moment that lay ahead. In essence, this was a mum-and-son trip with a difference: at the end of the road, I'd drop Robbie, my teenage son, off at the music college
10 that would be his place of study – and home – for the next three years. I'd be returning home without him. I can't say I was thrilled.

We'd visited the college the previous spring before he'd applied. The place itself was little more than ten years old and still looked state-of-the-art. I remember thinking how my amazingly talented no-longer-little boy would
15 thrive there. I pictured him in one of the practice rooms, its lush carpet dampening the sound of the voices and instruments as fresh-faced students found their way through songs, initiating friendships that would hopefully last a lifetime – or at least three years. For that was the whole point of this place; its aim was to bring like-minded kids together and help them find a
20 career in music. Along the way, fun was guaranteed.

The college itself nestles in a busy part of the capital city, a lively, bustling building where a variety of students push confidently through the glass doors and spill out in the nearby high street in search of food, drink and fun. The sober redbrick buildings of my college experience are nowhere to be
25 seen. Instead, a comfortable newness is exuded.

When we visited last year, we met one of the tutors, a laid-back guy who told us his job was to inspire and facilitate the success of the students in his care. The tutors looked less like teachers and more like the kindly, slightly scruffy musicians Robbie spends most of his time with. I knew he'd love this college.
30 It seemed to exude freedom and commitment at the same time. The bright neon college sign promised a world of joy and an excitement that couldn't be had at home.

And yet now, more than a year later as we finally pulled up outside the college and looked around for the accommodation block, it felt less
35 welcoming, as if it was waiting to take away my boy. It was, I knew, a ridiculous and selfish feeling on my part but it was true that this was a bittersweet day. If Robbie was to have a future in music, he needed to be here in the capital at the heart of the country's music scene. It was a big achievement for him to get here and one that made me glow. It was a new
40 beginning. But it was also an ending. The end of childhood and a loosening of the child-parent ties.

It didn't take too long to unload the van, much less to place his few belongings into his new room. Underneath Robbie's teenage bravado there was uncertainty though. We both knew the significance of the day but didn't
45 need to voice it. We'd always had a tacit understanding of such things. A final cup of coffee in a nearby café put off the departure by half an hour. I resisted any foolish shows of emotion. He needed to focus on how exciting things were going to be, not feel guilt or worry for a tearful parent.

Anyway, the much-dreaded moment was over quickly. A quick hug and a
50 few words and then he was off into a new world. As I drove away, a host of memories from years past played through the screen in my head: his first steps, a holiday in Dorset, the time we nearly lost him to pneumonia.

A different road now lay ahead.

Question 4: Example

Source 5B: *A Gentleman's Journal* by Finlay Graham

Source 5B is an extract from *A Gentleman's Journal*, written in 1872 by the Scottish writer Finlay Graham. In it, he describes his old college and the departure of his son, also called Finlay, to study there.

Another unremarkable day, notable only for the departure of Finlay, my youngest and my namesake, to his new place of study in the highlands. Like his four brothers before him, he was always destined to study at my old college, a forbidding stone stepmother that would make him a man. I recall
5 the day I left home as if it were yesterday, like him, a wet-behind-the-ears boy of eight, lugging my leathery old suitcase and heading off to live in that same strange world with strange rules.

The college itself is a sight to behold. It sits in gallant loneliness amongst the cold highlands, as if waiting patiently for those few weeks of the year
10 when the sun shines. Its isolation is part of its charm. Until the real snows come, you can rely on a train once a day to take you to the little station at the end of the line, from which the college is a short journey on foot. As you arrive, the first thing you see is a long, gravelled driveway, invariably wet with rain, that leads you to an imposing but slightly dilapidated
15 entrance way. There was always something frightfully gothic about that view, and the mild terror I felt as entered the building for the first time remains with me even now.

Finlay's new life will challenge him; he is a dear boy, but he has never been what you might call engaging. Of the five brothers, he is the most
20 introverted, keeping his own company and often spending hours in his room, avoiding sport and much preferring reading, which in itself is a fine pursuit, but not one which easily endears you to others. His brothers are more outgoing and – I hesitate to say – more academic. I do fear he will struggle a little against the notable reputations of his brothers, but as a father, you have
25 to accept these things and find joy where you can.

I imagine Finlay will experience the same things as I did at the college: the draughty windows, the meagre* food and the occasional bouts of homesickness. Yet he will also experience the joy of boyish company, the rigour of lessons and the feeling of belonging to a tradition. The college did
30 become a thing of beauty to me over time; it seemed enormous in my first year, but six years later it had become my dominion*, one I was desperately sad to leave behind. Finlay will, like me, learn to resent the summers spent at home, those long days away from his college friends and the busy rooms where true friendships are made.

35 Finlay will be lucky if he experiences the schoolmasters of my youth. [M]y teachers were heroic, if that doesn't sound too sentimental. Mr Brownlow

was the finest of them. A whirlwind of a man, one for whom life held no fear. But *he* did inspire fear, at least at first. It's true to say that I dreaded his lessons in my first year, his deep, gruff voice echoing across the room as he
40 insisted on publicly humiliating those whose work was less than acceptable.

To look at, old Brownlow seemed insubstantial. Slight, balding and with a face as red as a post box, he would stand at the door as you entered his room. There was no familiar greeting, little warmth and certainly a feeling that you had entered his territory. The start of each lesson was always a
45 quiet affair, until he warmed to his theme. Typically, we would sit silent in our rows, and he'd parade up and down, winding himself up like a Catherine wheel*, sparks beginning to fly as his passion for his subject took hold. He was very much the boss, the expert, the sergeant major and interruptions were not welcome. As I grew older, my fear for him gave way to respect. The
50 fearsome energy was merely an act; he was playing a part and once you'd earned his respect, he allowed you to see his gentle side, which manifested itself in a fascination for insects and a deep love of the highlands.

Heaven knows what old Brownlow would make of Finlay if he taught him. Perhaps he would do the boy good. Although I missed Finlay's departure
55 earlier, I do know that he'll be in safe hands and hope to see a more assured young man when he returns at Christmas.

---

meagre: *not very much*
dominion: *a place where someone has control*
Catherine wheel: *a fast spinning firework*

Paper 2: Question 4

Question 4: Sample answers

Sample answer 1

Now read the following sample answers to the Question 4 example question on page 152, alongside the examiner's comments.

This is one paragraph from a longer answer. It receives less than half the marks available.

① The student has identified thoughts and feelings and uses a relevant quotation but makes no further comment. There is some awareness of how the author is using language to convey their perspective.

③ This is another relevant but underdeveloped point. The student has missed an opportunity to comment on what the metaphor shows about the author's feelings.

> In source 5A, the writer feels sad that her son is leaving home, but she also seems proud. She uses the words 'amazingly talented' which shows she is really proud. **①** However, the writer of source 5B is not impressed with his son and says he will 'struggle'. This shows the writer doesn't think much of his son. **②** In source 5A, the writer also says that 'a different road now lay ahead' which shows that her son is leaving and she is sad. **③** In source 5B, the writer also seems sad at the end as he says he 'missed Finlay'. **④**

② The student identifies a feeling and has pinned it down with a quotation. The comment attached to it is simple and would benefit from being extended.

④ The student has misread the source here and so this point is not convincing.

Examiner's comments

Sample answer 1 identifies thoughts and feelings in both sources and uses relevant quotations to exemplify these, drawing a superficial comparison. There is an awareness of the writer's methods, specifically how the author uses language, but there is no exploration of what they reveal about thoughts and feelings. There is some misreading. The least successful aspect of this is the comments – there is little detail or exploration here.

A better answer would make more detailed comments about thoughts and feelings, contain more comments on language and/or structure, and make more comments on the differences between the texts.

Points about authors' methods must be relevant to the thoughts and feelings you identify. One way to do this is to 'lead with methods'. This means that once you've identified a perspective with a quotation, you can then pinpoint a word choice or language technique and develop your comment from there. You can see examples of this in Sample answer 2.

TIP

A good structure for this response is to write three substantial paragraphs – one for each point of comparison. Make sure that in each one you write about both sources and make explicit comparisons.

Sample answer 2

This is one paragraph from a longer answer. It scores high marks.

① The student begins by focusing on a specific part of both sources. They clearly identify thoughts and feelings and tie them down to well-chosen quotations. There is a good grasp of how language is used to convey these thoughts and feelings.

③ A clear point of comparison is made here followed by a perceptive reading of how social attitudes inform the perspectives shown in both texts.

The endings of both texts reveal the differences in the writers' attitudes. Text 5A is quite sentimental and uses metaphors like 'new world' and 'different road' to suggest the emotional nature her son's departure has, perhaps suggesting that their own world is changing and that their life paths are diverging, which suggests a poignant, emotional attitude on the part of the writer. **①** Combined with 'my boy' and the image of 'loosening' ties, it seems the writer has a very deep bond with her son and is struggling to come to terms with the magnitude of his departure. **②** However, the writer of text 5B is far less emotionally involved in his child. Although he uses the image of 'safe hands' which suggests that he does have some care for him and the phrase 'dear boy' earlier in the source, there seems a distance between them. This is perhaps indicating how the social attitudes towards parenthood involved much less emotional engagement than is seen in text 5A, where the mother seems to be heavily involved in the life of her son. **③**

② This extends the comments made in the previous sentence, making a perceptive point about the writer's feelings. There is a sharp sense of how the language conveys these feelings. Apt quotations are used.

TIP

Very occasionally, a writer will explicitly state their feelings, but most of the time you will need to infer them. Practise your skills of inference by guessing what a writer is implying about thoughts and feelings in different texts.

Examiner's comments

Sample answer 2 clearly identifies thoughts and feelings, making detailed, perceptive comments on them. There is a very good explanation of how the language choices of the writers convey these perspectives. The quality of your thinking largely determines your mark. When you write about perspectives, try to show the depth of your understanding. Make points that really get to the heart of the writers' thoughts and feelings.

REMEMBER

- This task is worth 16 marks, the most marks of any question in Section 1. Allow 20 minutes to complete it.
- Identify the perspectives of both writers and give evidence, clearly describing them. Write detailed and thoughtful comments on these perspectives and the writer's methods, such as language or structure, used to convey them. Make a comparison between the sources in each paragraph.

 Key terms Make sure you can write a definition for each of these key terms.

compare   convey   method   perspective

Paper 2: Question 4

Use the following questions to check your understanding of the knowledge covered in this section. Then cover the answers column with a piece of paper and write down as many as you can. Check and repeat.

	Questions	Answers
1	How long should you spend on Question 4?	20 minutes.
2	How many marks are available for Question 4?	16 marks.
3	Sometimes the words 'ideas' and 'feelings' are used in the question. True or false?	True.
4	The question will ask you to write about a certain part of the source.	False.
5	You must clearly state both writers' perspectives. True or false?	True.
6	Most good answers are around two sides in length. True or false?	True.
7	Your mark heavily depends upon the quality of your comments. True or false?	True.
8	Summarise the five steps of the Question 4 strategy.	**Step 1:** underline the key focus of the question. **Step 2:** select key details and information from both sources that are relevant to the question. **Step 3:** identify perspectives in each source that are relevant to the focus on the question. **Step 4:** identify language choices made by both writers that are relevant to the focus of the question. **Step 5:** summarise these comparisons in your response.

Put paper here

Previous questions

Now go back and use these questions to check your knowledge of previous topics.

	Questions	Answers
1	What is meant by the writer's attitude?	Their thoughts and feelings about the topic they are writing about.
2	A text that is written from a first-person viewpoint will use the pronouns 'I' and 'we'. True or false?	True.

Put paper here

Exam-style questions

Answer the exam-style questions on pages 159–167. In the exam, Question 4 will be about both source texts. They have been included here for easy reference but will be included in your booklet in the exam.

> **REMEMBER**
>
> In the exam, you will need to read the *whole* of each source text first before you start looking at the questions and specific extracts.

4.1

> **Q4** For this question, you need to refer to the **whole of Source 6A**, together with the **whole of Source 6B**.
>
> Compare how the writers convey their different thoughts and attitudes about talented children.
>
> In your answer, you could:
>
> - compare their different thoughts and attitudes about talented children
> - compare the methods they use to convey their thoughts and attitudes
> - support your response with references to both texts.
>
> **[16 marks]**

> **LINK**
>
> This question refers to the whole text of Source 6A: *Cruellest reality TV show ever*, and the whole text of Source 6B: *Children*. These sources can also be found on pages 188–190.

> **EXAM TIP**
>
> In your answer, you should:
>
> - clearly identify the perspectives of both authors
> - exemplify these perspectives with quotations
> - write detailed and thoughtful comments, comparing these perspectives
> - comment on the way the writer's methods, such as language or structure, have been used to convey these perspectives.

Source 6A: *Cruellest reality TV show ever* by Tanith Carey

> The following newspaper article was written by Tanith Carey, a parenting expert, in response to the Channel 4 programme, *Child Genius*.

At the tender age of eight, Tudor has been picked to play soccer for no fewer than three Premier League junior teams: QPR, Tottenham and Chelsea. This achievement alone would be enough to make most fathers' hearts burst with pride. But, unfortunately for Tudor, he appears to have a very long way to go

5 before he meets the sky-high expectations of his demanding dad, Tolu.

So far, the most heart-rending scenes on Channel 4's reality series *Child Genius* – in which 20 children are subjected to a terrifying barrage of tests – have been the sight of this small boy hiding his face in his hands as he weeps. The reason? He has not scored as well as his father tells him he

10 should have done. […] Yet rather than commiserate with his son after a disappointing performance, it is Tolu, who declares that he finds the contest 'emotionally draining'. He then tells Tudor: 'Maybe you're not as good as we thought.' […]

Even for a nation well used to the mercenary* exploitation of spy-on-the-wall

15 television, this has raised concern. As one worried viewer pointed out, the series would more aptly be named 'Pushy Parents'. For it is really all about the Eagle Dads and Tiger Mums, who want to show off how much work they have invested in their youngsters.

Exam-style questions

The show first aired in its current format last year, and – as the author of
20 a book looking at the damage caused by competitive parenting – I had
thought we would not see a return of this toxic* mix of reality TV and hot-
housing*. I had expected the sight of children as young as eight crying to
prick the conscience of the commissioning editors.

A vain hope, of course. [...]

25 *Child Genius* has tapped into an increasingly dangerous trend in parenting;
the misguided belief that your offspring is a blank slate and if you hot-house
them enough, you can be solely responsible for their success. Parenting is
turning into a form of product development. Increasingly, we are falling for
the notion that if we cram enough facts into their little brains we can make
30 sure they come out on top. The end result is a rise in depression and anxiety
among a generation who believe they are losers if they fail, or could always
do better if they win.

Like all offspring of pushy parents, who feel their family's affection is
conditional on their success, children like Tudor are not just weeping
35 because they didn't score well. When he tries to cover his tears with his
hands, saying 'What I achieved was absolutely terrible', he is facing a much
darker fear: That he will lose his father's love if he does not come up to
scratch. [...]

Of course, the goal of reality TV is to entertain — but should dramatic story-
40 lines really come ahead of a child's emotional well-being?

Perhaps it's a measure of their state of mind that some parents, such as
psychologists Shoshana and Sacha, who featured in the first two episodes,
saw nothing harmful in describing their approach to bringing up their
daughter Aliyah, nine, as though she is 'a well-bred race-horse'. Shoshana
45 openly pities parents left to bring up children without her skill set. She
was blissfully oblivious to the fact that the rest of us were watching, slack-
jawed in disbelief at how hard she pushes her child. Far from rushing to
adopt such techniques, parents have reacted in horror. The internet has
been buzzing with viewers saying they found the series 'upsetting to watch',
50 'heartbreaking' and expressing concern [...]

No doubt the reality is that Tolu is also a loving father, who sincerely
believes he is doing the best for his son, and the producers have edited
the programme to make him look like the ultimate caricature of an
overbearing father.

55 But for me, one question remains: How much longer are we going to allow
Channel 4 to encourage extreme parents to push their helpless children to
breaking point in the name of entertainment?

---

mercenary: *money-grabbing*
toxic: *poisonous*
hot-housing: *intensely educating a child*

Source 6B: *Children*

> The following newspaper article was written in the 19th century. It offers views on how to raise children.

It is a mistake to think that children love the parents less who maintain a proper authority over them. On the contrary, they respect them more. It is a cruel and unnatural selfishness that indulges children in a foolish and hurtful way. Parents are guides and counsellors to their children. As a guide

5 in a foreign land, they undertake to pilot them safely through the shoals and quicksands of inexperience. If the guide allows his followers all the freedom they please; if, because they dislike the constraint of the narrow path of safety, he allows them to stray into holes and precipices* that destroy them, to quench their thirst in brooks that poison them, to loiter in woods full of

10 wild beasts or deadly herbs, can he be called a sure guide?

And is it not the same with our children? They are as yet only in the preface, or as it were, in the first chapter of the book of life. We have nearly finished it, or are far advanced. We must open the pages for these younger minds.

If children see that their parents act from principle – that they do not find

15 fault without reason – that they do not punish because personal offence is taken, but because the thing in itself is wrong – if they see that while they are resolutely but affectionately refused what is not good for them, there is a willingness to oblige them in all innocent matters – they will soon appreciate such conduct. If no attention is paid to the rational wishes – if no

20 allowance is made for youthful spirits – if they are dealt with in a hard and unsympathising manner – the proud spirit will rebel, and the meek spirit be broken. [...]

A pert or improper way of speaking ought never to be allowed. Clever children are very apt to be pert, and if too much admired for it, and laughed

25 at, become eccentric and disagreeable. It is often very difficult to check our own amusement, but their future welfare should be regarded more than our present entertainment. It should never be forgotten that they are tender plants committed to our fostering care, that every thoughtless word or careless neglect may destroy a germ of immortality*.

---

precipices: *steep, dangerous places*
immortality: *living forever*

Exam-style questions

4.2

> **Q4** For this question, you need to refer to the **whole of Source 7A**, together with the **whole of Source 7B**.
>
> Compare how the writers convey different attitudes towards children's pastimes.
>
> In your answer, you could:
>
> - compare their different thoughts and feelings about children's pastimes
> - compare the methods they use to convey their thoughts and feelings
> - support your response with references to both texts.
>
> **[16 marks]**

LINK

This question refers to the whole text of Source 7A: *The future is here*, and the whole text of Source 7B: *Acrobats*. These sources can also be found on pages 192–195.

Source 7A: *The future is here* by Hannah Hussein

> This extract is about how children use technology for entertainment.

In 1972 we didn't have computers. Well, they had them in London probably, but we certainly never had them when I was a kid in Bradford. A bike? Yes. A football? Yes. A computer? Definitely not. I love all things technological now, but I'm not sure I would have liked to grow up surrounded by phones, tablets
5 and laptops. And definitely not social media. I'm never off it these days, but I think it's a difficult world for teenagers to negotiate. That's why I was initially reluctant for my daughter to get a phone.

Gradually, of course, Basma wore me down. Kids are good at that. If you could see our house right now, you'd see a plethora* of technology. Phones
10 plugged in to chargers, an expensive computer sitting on my antique desk, a tablet lying on the floor just waiting to be stood on. Very much like the houses of our friends, no doubt – technologically and materially rich but time-poor. We've got a doorbell that means I can see who's outside, even when I'm miles from home. I've got the ability to make a Hollywood
15 quality movie on my phone. I've got a state-of-the-art recording studio on my computer. I can switch the heating on from work. And as is typical, my daughter can work all of these tools much faster and better than me.

Basma is currently in that funny teen phase now, but when I look back at her childhood, I view it with a mixture of fondness *and* horror. Nappies
20 and CBeebies I could do without, but the anarchy, creativity and general stupidity of having a toddler in the house is brilliant. Well, to a point.

The magic of snow delighted Basma. Making snowdogs, sledging, snow angels … I'm not sure how I kept up to be honest. It was always her play that fascinated me. She was always creative, making robots out of toilet rolls,
25 building a plasticine house for the hamster, and trying to dig a well in the

back garden. She did it with a knowing smirk, reserving her most energy-sapping efforts until I'd just sat down after a hard day at work.

Somewhere along the line though, plasticine gave way to gaming and drawing became Tiktok. Basma still plays, but the games she plays are not
30 in the family home, they're somewhere in the digital ether. It's a world I'm no longer required to be part of, the messaging and memes out of reach. The screen of her phone is also out of my reach, often tilted away from my view, and hidden behind a passcode. I'm still not sure what I think about children, parents and privacy.

35 Everyone thinks their childhood was better than their own kids. Less technologically advanced, but more creative. Outdoors rather than indoors. Yet when I really think about it, I reckon the children of this generation have got much to celebrate. Technology has made them communicate, albeit in a different way. Social media is primarily about feelings. And Basma
40 is fantastic at reading people. She knows how to challenge, comfort and entertain.

My daughter's digital teen years are mainly good ones. At the swipe of a screen, she finds a recipe for the occasional family meals she makes, she learns how to do CPR* (let's hope I'm not the first recipient of her new-found
45 skills) and also engages with the issues I want her to know about: global poverty, justice and equality. Most profoundly, the thing her childhood has taught her most is to love. Basma is a carer. She cares for people, animals and anything that exists.

A friend of mine has recently become an older mother. She loves it, but I can
50 see the tell-tale weariness in her eyes. The lack of sleep, the nappies, the sheer graft of parenthood. Part of me would like to be building snowdogs again in a carefree past, but would I really swap the precocious, maddening, self-absorbed, yet deeply caring fourteen-year-old daughter of now for the four-year-old of the past? No chance.

---

plethora: *a very large amount of something*
CPR: *cardiopulmonary resuscitation (a lifesaving technique)*

Source 7B: *Acrobats* **by Albert Smith**

> This extract was written in the 19th century and is about children playing in the streets of Victorian London.

As you pass through one of those […] narrow dirty streets […] you will be struck, above all things, by the swarms of children everywhere collected. They scuffle about, and run across your path, and disappear, like rabbits in a warren, in obscure holes. They wait on the kerb until a cab approaches,
5   and run under the very knees of the horse. They collect round the open water plug, and spend the entire day there, all returning wet through to the skin. […]

[…] You occasionally see a girl of seven or eight years staggering under the weight of a baby whose sole nurse she is; but seldom find them with
10   brothers and sisters. They are only acquaintances. Their parents live huddled up in dirty single rooms, […] they turn their children out to find means of amusement and subsistence, at the same time, in the streets.

Of all their favourite haunts, there is not one more popular than the bit of open ground where a mass of houses have been pulled down to make room
15   for a new street or building. If they find an old beam of timber, so much the better. They […] turn it into a see-saw, and, this accomplished, a policeman is the only power that can drive them from the spot. They build forts […]. They scuffle the mounds of rubbish perfectly smooth by running, or being dragged up and down them; they […] make huts; and know of nothing in
20   the world capable of affording such delight, except it be the laying down, or taking up, of some wooden pavement.

Picture such a bit of ground, on a fine afternoon, alive with children. Amongst the revellers there is a boy, who for the last five minutes has been hanging by his legs to a bit of temporary railing, with his hair sweeping the
25   ground. Others would have had a fit long before, but this appears to be his natural position. On quitting it, without caring for the empty applause of the crowd, he goes to a retired corner of the plot, and, gravely putting his head and hands upon the ground, at a short distance from the wall, turns his heels up in the air, until he touches the house with his feet. This accomplished,
30   he […] claps his shoeless soles together […] and then calmly resumes his normal position, and walks away, not caring whether anybody regards him or not.

This boy is destined to become an Acrobat – at a more advanced period of his life to perform feats of suppleness and agility in the mud of the streets,
35   the sawdust of the circus, or the turf of a race-course. His life will pass in a marvellous series of positions, and its ordinary level course will be unknown to him. He will look upon chairs as articles of furniture only used to support people with the crown of their heads on the top back rail, or their legs on the seats of two stretched out to the utmost extent allowed by their length.

40 Ladders, with him, will in future only be ascended by twisting in and out the rounds like a serpent […]

The Acrobats are generally seen in London after the racing season, or when the metropolis lies in their way from one course to another. Some go to the sea-side […] Others join travelling companies […] who go from town
45 to town […] When the pantomimes begin, the Acrobats find a new field for employment. […] They do not, however, always have the good fortune to appear as principals. […] It is not until the stage-manager at rehearsal wants some daring spirit to tumble from the sky-borders on to the stage; to go round on the sails of a windmill amidst fireworks; or to be knocked through a
50 door, or out of a window, or down a trap, that a pale man, in an old coat that you have seen before, steps forward from the crowd at the wings, and says that he will undertake it, and that he can do any tumbling business required, for he is an Acrobat.

4.3

Q4 For this question, you need to refer to the **whole of Source 8A**, together with the **whole of Source 8B**.

Compare how the writers convey their different thoughts and feelings about their journeys.

In your answer, you could:

- compare their different thoughts and feelings about their journeys
- compare the methods they use to convey their thoughts and feelings
- support your response with references to both texts.

[16 marks]

LINK

This question refers to the whole text of Source 8A: *The Cruelest Journey*, and the whole text of Source 8B: *On Sledge and Horseback to Outcast Siberian Lepers*. These sources can also be found on pages 196–199.

Source 8A: *The Cruelest Journey* by Kira Salak

This extract is about writer and adventurer Kira Salak, at the beginning of her 600-mile journey travelling solo in a kayak from Old Segou in Mali to Timbuktu. She follows the same route taken along the River Niger by the 19th century explorer, Mungo Park.

Torrential rains. Waves higher than my kayak, trying to capsize me. But my boat is self-bailing and I stay afloat. The wind drives the current in reverse, tearing and ripping at the shores, sending spray into my face. I paddle madly, crashing and driving forward. I travel inch by inch, or so it seems, arm
5 muscles smarting and rebelling against this journey.

A popping feeling now and a screech of pain. My right arm lurches from a ripped muscle. But this is no time and place for such an injury, and I won't tolerate it, stuck as I am in a storm. I try to get used to the metronome*-like pulses of pain as I fight the river. There is only one direction to go: forward.

10   I wonder what we look for when we embark on these kinds of trips. There is the pat answer that you tell the people you don't know: that you're interested in seeing a place, learning about its people. But then the trip begins and the hardship comes, and hardship is more honest: it tells us that we don't have enough patience yet, nor humility, nor gratitude. And
15   we thought that we had. Hardship brings us closer to truth, and thus is more difficult to bear, but from it alone comes compassion. And so I already discover one important reason why I'm here on this river, and I've told the world that it can do what it wants with me if only, by the end, I have learned something further. A bargain, then. The journey, my teacher.

20   And where is the river of just this morning, with its whitecaps that would have liked to drown me, with its current flowing backwards against the wind? Gone to this: a river of smoothest glass, a placidity unbroken by wave or eddy, with islands of lush greenery awaiting me like distant Xanadus*.

I know there is no turning back now. The journey to Timbuktu binds me. It
25   deceives me with images of the end, reached at long last. The late afternoon sun settles complacently over the hills to the west. Paddling becomes a sort of meditation now, a gentle trespassing over a river that slumbers. The Niger gives me its beauty almost in apology for the violence of the earlier storms, and I'm treated to the peace and silence of this wide river, the sun on me, a
30   breeze licking my toes when I lay back to rest, the current as negligible as a faint breath.

Somono fishermen, casting out their nets, puzzle over me as I float by.

"*Ça va, madame*?" they yell.

Each fisherman carries a young son perched in the back of his pointed canoe
35   to do the paddling. The boys stare at me, transfixed; they have never seen such a thing. A white woman. Alone. In a red, inflatable boat. Using a two-sided paddle.

I'm an even greater novelty because Malian women don't paddle here, not ever. It is a man's job. So there is no good explanation for me, and the people
40   want to understand. They gather on the shore in front of their villages to watch me pass, the kids screaming and jumping in excitement, the adults yelling out questions in Bambarra which by now I know to mean: "Where did you come from? Where's your husband?" And of course they will always ask: "Where are you going?" "Timbuktu!" I yell out to the last question and
45   paddle on.

---

metronome: *a device that measures time with regular ticks*
Xanadus: *a beautiful and magnificent place*

Source 8B: *On Sledge and Horseback to Outcast Siberian Lepers*
by Kate Marsden

> Kate Marsden was a British missionary and explorer in the 19th century,
> who set out on an expedition to Siberia to try to find a cure for leprosy. This
> extract is about her journey through mosquito-infested marshes and forests.

On again for a few more miles; but I began to feel the effects of this sort of travelling – in a word, I felt utterly worn out. It was as much as I could do to hold on to the horse, and I nearly tumbled off several times in the effort. The cramp in my body and lower limbs was indescribable, and I had to discard
5 the cushion under me, because it became soaked through and through with the rain, and rode on the broad, bare, wooden saddle. What feelings of relief arose when the time of rest came, and the pitching of tents, and the brewing of tea! Often I slept quite soundly till morning, awaking to find that the mosquitoes had been hard at work in my slumbers, in spite of veil and
10 gloves, leaving great itching lumps, that turned me sick. Once we saw two calves that had died from exhaustion from the bites of these pests, and the white hair of our poor horses was generally covered with clots of blood, due partly to mosquitoes and partly to prodigious horse-flies. But those lepers – they suffered far more than I suffered, and that was the one thought, added
15 to the strength that God supplied, that kept me from collapsing entirely ...

My second thunderstorm was far worse than the first. The forest seemed on fire, and the rain dashed in our faces with almost blinding force. My horse plunged and reared, flew first to one side, and then to the other, dragging me amongst bushes and trees, so that I was in danger of being caught by
20 the branches and hurled to the ground. After this storm one of the horses, carrying stores and other things, sank into a bog nearly to its neck; and the help of all the men was required to get it out ...

Soon after the storm we were camping and drinking tea, when I noticed that all the men were eagerly talking together and gesticulating*. I asked
25 what it all meant, and was told that a large bear was supposed to be in the neighbourhood, according to a report from a post-station close at hand. There was a general priming of firearms, except in my case, for I did not know how to use my revolver, so thought I had better pass it on to someone else, lest I might shoot a man in mistake for a bear. We mounted again and went
30 on. The usual chattering was exchanged for a dead silence, this being our first bear experience; but we grew wiser as we proceeded, and substituted noise for silence. We hurried on, as fast as possible, to get through the miles of forests and bogs. I found it best not to look about me, because, when I did so, every large stump of a fallen tree took the shape of a bear. When my
35 horse stumbled over the roots of a tree, or shied at some object unseen by me, my heart began to gallop.

gesticulating: *using gestures to communicate*

Paper 2: Question 5

Question 5: Overview

? Focus	✓ Marks	🕐 Time	✳ AO
Present a viewpoint	40 marks	45 minutes	AO5, AO6

Question 5 tests both creative skills and technical skills.

In Paper 1 Question 5, the focus is on using language creatively. In Paper 2, you are still writing creatively but in a rhetorical style – you are arguing, persuading, or expressing a point of view.

You are provided with a statement about a topic that is explored in the sources in Section A and are invited to give your view on that statement.

From the 40 marks available, up to 24 marks are awarded for the quality and organisation of your ideas and up to 16 marks are awarded for the accuracy and variety of your technical skills – word choice, spelling, punctuation, and sentence types.

LINK

The knowledge section on pages 18–25 and 56–63 will remind you of key concepts, including rhetorical language and argument structural devices that will help you answer this type of question.

Question 5: Strategy

Follow the steps below to respond to a Question 5 task.

Step 1: Plan your argument. Decide on the view you will take to present your points and the **tone** and **voice** you will write in.

⬇

Step 2: Plan the **structure** of your response.

- Work out what you will write about in each paragraph.
- Decide how you will end your writing.

⬇

Step 3: Write your response, taking care with communication. Make sure everything you write makes clear sense, engages your reader, and uses language accurately.

- Present a strong argument. You could use **rhetorical devices**, emotive or figurative language where appropriate.
- Vary word, punctuation, and sentence structure to show off your range of vocabulary and technical skills.
- Organise your ideas to build a compelling argument, considering the requirements of the **form** stated in the question.

⬇

Step 4: Proof-read your work to make sure that spelling and punctuation are accurate and everything makes clear sense.

TIP

Make sure you allow yourself 45 minutes to write a detailed answer to Question 5. It is worth half of the Paper 2 marks.

Question 5: Key skills

Just like your Paper 1 Question 5 response, several key skills are assessed in Paper 2 Question 5. They are detailed below.

Skill	What this means you need to do	Assessment objective
Clear communication	Make sure everything you write makes clear sense.	AO5
Quality of ideas	Engage your reader with interesting ideas. Spend time planning how you will build an argument and choose a tone and voice that makes your response engaging.	AO5
Quality of vocabulary	Show that you can phrase your response in interesting ways. Take time to craft what you are writing. Use a broad vocabulary as well as rhetorical and emotive devices.	AO5
Structure and sequence	Plan the sequence of your response – what will happen in what order. Show that you can 'shape' a response by giving it an interesting structure.	AO5
Technical accuracy	Make sure that spelling, punctuation, and expression are as accurate as possible.	AO6
Technical variety	Show that you can use a range of punctuation and sentence types.	AO6

Here is a sample question. You will use it throughout this section to remind yourself of how to plan and write a Question 5 response.

Q5 'Schools are great places to be. They are places where close friendships are made, memorable events happen, and young people learn how to become successful adults.'

Write an article for a magazine in which you argue your point of view on this statement.

[40 marks]

This statement prompts you to think about ideas around a topic, in this case, school. There are several 'strands' to this statement. You don't need to write about them all in your response, but they are there to generally inspire your response.

You will be asked to write in one of four forms: letter, speech, article, or essay. The first three of these forms have been used most frequently, but the essay form is not very common.

The question specifically tests your ability to write an argument – a carefully structured point of view.

Here is a list of some examples:

Intriguing start: open with an interesting phrase, image, or question.

Anecdote: use a real or imagined short tale to humanise your argument.

Climax: have a 'high point' in your argument – your most compelling point, usually placed towards the end.

Rhetorical question: pose a question as a way of provoking thought.

Repetition: use a repeated image or phrase at certain points in your response.

Direct address: appeal directly to your reader, perhaps using the pronoun 'we' to create the sense of shared agreement.

Paper 2: Question 5

Question 5: Planning a response

Start by planning your argument. This is an essential part of the Question 5 task and should not be skipped.

The best responses are written as a coherent argument rather than just a series of points. Here is one possible plan:

> Overall argument: agree largely — schooldays are the best days of your life and help to prepare people for later life.
>
> Points:
> - the friendships you make at school are really close ones
> - you learn how to get along with people — children and adults
> - it's a carefree time in your life where you can make mistakes and learn from them
> - many of the skills you learn at school are very useful for being an adult
> - some of the adults are often inspiring, kind, and memorable figures.

TIP
Planning means thinking about the 'angle' you will take – the view and attitude you want to put forward and the points you will make. Make sure you have a logical, firm argument that runs throughout your response.

These ideas could lead to a successful response. The points are potentially good, but will need to be brought to life, perhaps by (real or imagined) memories and examples. You will need to make sure there is a convincing core argument that holds all of these points together.

Structure your argument

Plan the sequence of what you'll write about – carefully shape and sequence it. This is often more natural to do when you are writing a story, but it is also essential in argumentative writing. This means:

- thinking about how to open your response
- the order of your points
- how you will bring your argument to a close.

You can add notes or numbers to your plan which will remind you of the sequence you have chosen to follow when writing.

Remember the content of your argument is most important. The most important thing is *what* you write.

LINK
You can see some of these structural elements used in sample answers on pages 172–173.

TIP
Rhetorical devices can be very powerful in persuading the reader to agree with your point of view. If you do choose to use rhetorical devices, don't overdo it. It is better to use one rhetorical question rather than lots.

Choose a voice

Choose which voice you will write in. 'Voice' refers to the character or persona of the writer. It means things like their attitude and manner. The selection of a voice informs the tone and **register** you write in.

Although you can write a very good answer in your own voice, you are perfectly entitled to write in any voice you choose. Often, adopting a different voice leads to engaging responses and can, in some ways, be easier and more fun to write.

Below are two potential voices that might be adopted to answer the sample question on page 169.

1. A student who is at the end of their school career. They are stressed about exams, feel unsupported, and see no joy in school. Their friends feel the same. They see little point in what they learn at school and don't believe that anything they are being made to learn will help them once they've left school.

2. An adult looking back at their schooldays. They have many happy memories of people and places. They are still in touch with a couple of schoolfriends. They have fond memories of a teacher who inspired them. Looking back, they can see how school inspired them to learn and take chances in life.

> **TIP**
>
> Some students find it easier to start their planning by choosing a voice as this often leads more naturally to an argument. Try this method as you revise and prepare.

Write in an appropriate form

Write your response in the form given in the question, which will be either a letter, a speech, an article, or an essay. This means that you will need to show the basic conventions of these forms.

Some questions might also give a suggested **audience**, such as fellow students or a local council. Always write in a suitable tone of voice for your audience where one is specified. Where no audience is specified, you have more freedom to choose the tone of your writing.

> **TIP**
>
> Remember that the important thing is to engage your audience, so a lively tone often works better than a more formal one.

> **LINK**
>
> Look back to the Style section of Paper 1 Question 5 on page 109 as a reminder of how to ensure technical accuracy in your writing. It is relevant for this question as well.

Paper 2: Question 5

Question 5: Sample answer

Now read the following sample answer to the example Question 5 on page 169, alongside examiner's comments. It scores high marks.

❶ This opens the response in an engaging way. It signals the voice is that of a parent which adds a slight touch of humour.

❸ Here a type of counter argument is introduced which is used effectively to introduce another strand to the argument. Metaphorical language helps to engage the reader and convey the ideas presented. Accurate and varied punctuation is used.

The best days of your life? Not if you ask my kids. **❶** And yet some of my best memories belong to those carefree schooldays when mortgage and middle age were not part of the landscape. You've got to be careful not to wallow in sentimentality, of course, but in my immediate memory, the sun was always shining at school, the laughter was genuine, and you lived in the present. And the present was a great place to be. **❷** But if I think a bit harder, other less joyful memories rise up like spectres to spoil the feast: the dull homework; the hectoring headmaster; the misery of the changing room bullies. And yet, in a way, these are to be celebrated too. As I've said to my own children, life isn't always a pleasant stroll through a peaceful forest. There are times when the forest throws up hidden dangers — and it's how you handle those dangers that makes you an adult. So, in that way, school offers you a relatively safe space to enjoy success and confront problems. And there's always someone there to act as a guide. **❸** My own guide was Mr Charnley, our hairy and hilarious form tutor. The other staff called him Greasy Bob behind his back — it was an accurate nickname — but he was cool, too. He rode a motorbike. He played guitar in a band at weekends. He could make sixth formers laugh. Not an easy task for a teacher. And he was always willing to give genuine advice. The best advice he gave me was to follow my dreams. It sounds terribly cheesy put like that, but when I asked whether it would be better to do fine art or accountancy at university, he looked at me and said that I already knew the answer. I did. **❹** It might sound very dramatic to say that

❷ The paragraph sets up the initial strand of the argument. It's well-phrased and uses different types of sentences. The use of 'And' to open the first and last sentence helps to give a shape.

❹ The use of this anecdote adds a human, emotional element to the argument. There is light humour too and plenty of sentence variety.

5 This paragraph acts as a type of climax, bringing together an emotional element and logical reasoning.

school changed my life, but it did. I went on to do fine art and now have a rewarding career in design. I'd have been bored as an accountant. I don't remember much about the lessons, but I'll always remember Mr Charnley. He passed away not long after we left school but lives on in the memories of me and my friends. **5** My children often tell me school is boring. They hate PE. They hate school dinners. They hate exams. They might well be right, but in the years ahead, they'll come to realise that it's a golden age where the memories live long and the choices you make shape your life in ways you can't yet see. And if they're lucky, they'll find their own Mr Charnley. **6** The best days of your life? Definitely. **7**

6 This concludes the argument by clearly stating a position that has been built up in preceding paragraphs.

7 This final line echoes the opening line and the minor sentence concludes the argument in a definite manner.

Examiner's comments

This sample answer is very effective in the choice of voice. It is shaped well and there is a sense of an argument being built to a convincing conclusion. Emotional moments enrich and humanise the argument for readers. A variety of interesting vocabulary, punctuation, and sentence types are used. Carefully chosen rhetorical and figurative language is used.

TIP

The best way to improve your writing is to improve the content. More than other devices, focus on engaging your reader with a clear, thought-provoking argument.

REMEMBER

- Planning is essential. Work out the stages of your response before you begin writing.
- Aim to engage your reader by presenting a strong, coherent argument.
- Structure your response in a clear and engaging way.
- Use language and techniques in appropriate and engaging ways.
- Always proof-read your work – accuracy is important.

Key terms

Make sure you can write a definition for each of these key terms.

audience   form   register
rhetorical devices   structure
tone   voice

Paper 2: Question 5

Use the following questions to check your understanding of the knowledge covered in this section. Then cover the answers column with a piece of paper and write down as many as you can. Check and repeat.

Questions	Answers
1 How long should you spend on Question 5?	45 minutes.
2 How many total marks are available for Question 5?	40 marks.
3 How many marks are available for the quality of your ideas; and how many marks are available for your technical skills?	24 marks; 16 marks.
4 Structuring your work in an interesting way is less important in descriptive writing. True or false?	False.
5 Clear communication is important for good marks. True or false?	True.
6 Using a range of sentence types accurately can help to improve your mark. True or false?	True.
7 The best way to get a high mark is to use lots of rhetorical devices. True or false?	False.
8 The best answers always agree with the statement in the question. True or false?	False.
9 You must use an impressive word in every sentence. True or false?	False.
10 Summarise the four steps of the Question 5 strategy.	**Step 1:** plan your argument. **Step 2:** plan the structure of your response. **Step 3:** write your response. **Step 4:** proof-read your work.

Put paper here

Previous questions

Now go back and use these questions to check your knowledge of previous topics.

Questions	Answers
1 Planning a response takes up valuable time that would be better spent on writing that response. True or false?	False. It is important to plan to organise your ideas and build a cohesive argument.
2 What is a counter-argument?	A viewpoint that is different to your own.

Put paper here

Exam-style questions

Answer the exam-style questions below.

5.1

> **Q5** 'These days, young people have the chance to really enjoy life. They have great opportunities, amazing technology to use, and their opinions are valued.'
>
> Write a speech for a school meeting in which you argue your point of view on this statement.
>
> **[40 marks]**

5.2

> **Q5** 'It is essential that people show kindness towards others and try to understand their experiences and points of view. Too many people are only interested in themselves.'
>
> Write a letter to a newspaper in which you argue your point of view on this statement.
>
> **[40 marks]**

5.3

> **Q5** 'Visiting new places, even local ones, is exciting. You learn a lot about the places themselves and the people who live there. It also helps you develop as a person.'
>
> Write a magazine article in which you argue your point of view on this statement.
>
> **[40 marks]**

Paper 1: Sources

Source 1

***Dawn at Woolacombe Sands* by Jez Neumann**

This extract from a short story features Amir and Jane, a young married couple. They are visiting Woolacombe Sands, a beach in England.

As Amir and Jane walked along the narrow sandy path, Amir began to feel vague anticipation somewhere inside him. The sea was obscured for now though, and all that they could see were tall dune grasses, a seabird pecking at something on the path, and the open grey sky. A faint sun drifted high
5 above them, lonely in the emptiness.

Soon though, the path opened out and they emerged from the dunes. Amir realised he was finally there – standing on the beach at Woolacombe Sands at dawn alongside Jane, who had paused to take a single photo and then stood still, her eyes shut as if she was lost in some other unknown place.

10 Woolacombe Sands is, as the cliché goes, a feast for the senses. When you see it in the early morning light, the wide beach gapes, smiling emptily; it opens out in front of you, introducing you to the quiet mystery of the sea that lies behind it. There's a loud silence that lures you in. A brisk air embraces you like a reluctant friend. The scene reveals itself to you on
15 its own terms and asks you to witness its empty magic. But Amir didn't feel this. Not a bit. To him, it was quite literally nothing. A huge, gigantic, overwhelming nothing. Nothing at all.

"Don't talk. You'll only spoil the moment," Jane said, abruptly. She wasn't looking at Amir, but was instead staring out to sea, as if it – *somehow* -
20 understood her spiritually. The morning light was on her face. She seemed both present and elsewhere.

Amir began to open his mouth but closed it again. He wanted to speak but felt that Jane had already decided that he was not allowed to be part of the scene. His words and deeds were irrelevant. His thoughts were irrelevant too
25 apparently. Yet here they were, together and not together on a silent beach with last night's row hovering between them.

The beach was not really that interesting to Amir. It seemed point-free. Car parks had a purpose. Shops had a purpose. Sport did, too. But this was just some sand and salty water. It was nothing really. Amir decided it would be
30 better if he kept this to himself though, because Jane was currently adopting one of her many yoga poses and he knew from bitter experience that she didn't like being interrupted in such spiritual moments. There was a ship on the horizon and so Amir focused on this, wondering what was happening on board and where they were heading.

35 Moments passed. He still hadn't spoken, but wanted to find the right words, the right combination of words to make Jane happy again. Or at least one that didn't spark her anger. They ought to be trying to make their marriage work properly again. He wanted that, but now it seemed like they were in different spheres.

40 "Well, what do you feel?" Jane asked eventually, much to Amir's surprise. She wasn't looking at him and he couldn't tell if this was a trick question or not. It felt like there was a dam somewhere, just about holding things back.

"It's quite big," Amir said, which seemed to him to be the form of words which could do the least harm to the dam. A moment settled.

45 "Is that really the best thing you can find to say? It's quite big?" Amir still couldn't see Jane's eyes but realised the magical repairing incantation had eluded him.

He tried again. "I wonder where that ship is going," he said. A bit more of the dam broke.

50 "We come to place of serenity and all you can tell me is it's big and there's a ship?" Jane hissed.

"Well, what do you see?" Amir asked meekly.

"I don't see anything," Jane said eventually. "I feel it. I feel the inner language of nature, the certainty of time and the feeling that humanity is 55 ultimately powerless." She seemed less angry now, but whether this was a good thing, Amir didn't know.

"I understand that," Amir said, his hopes pinned to this bland statement.

When dams break, it's often a release.

"Amir. I want out. I can't live with you anymore."

LINK

Source 1 is used for the questions on pages 66–103.

Paper 1: Sources

Source 2

Millie **by Katherine Mansfield**

This extract from a short story is set on a farm in New Zealand in 1913. There has been a murder on a neighbouring farm and the murderer is still at large. Millie's husband has gone out to help find the murderer, leaving Millie alone.

Millie went back into the kitchen. She put some ashes on the stove and sprinkled them with water. Languidly, the sweat pouring down her face, and dropping off her nose and chin, she cleared away the dinner, and going into the bedroom, stared at herself in the fly-specked mirror […]. She didn't know
5 what was the matter with herself that afternoon.

[…] *Tick-tick* went the kitchen clock, the ashes clinked in the grate, and the venetian blind knocked against the kitchen window. Quite suddenly Millie felt frightened. A queer trembling started inside her—in her stomach—and then spread all over to her knees and hands. "There's somebody about."
10 She tiptoed to the door and peered into the kitchen. Nobody there; the verandah* doors were closed, the blinds were down, and in the dusky light the white face of the clock shone, and the furniture seemed to bulge and breathe … and listen, too. The clock—the ashes—and the venetian—and then again—something else, like steps in the back yard. […] She darted to
15 the back door, opened it, and at the same moment some one ducked behind the wood pile. "Who's that?" she cried, in a loud, bold voice. "Come out o' that! I seen yer. I know where y'are. [...] Come out from behind of that wood stack!" She was not frightened any more. She was furiously angry. Her heart banged like a drum.

20 "I'll teach you to play tricks with a woman," she yelled, [...] and dashed down the verandah* steps, across the glaring yard to the other side of the wood stack. A young man lay there, on his stomach, one arm across his face. "Get up! You're shamming*!" [...] [S]he kicked him in the shoulders. He gave no sign. "Oh, my God, I believe he's dead." She knelt down, seized hold of
25 him, and turned him over on his back. He rolled like a sack. She crouched back on her haunches, staring; her lips and nostrils fluttered with horror.

He was not much more than a boy, with fair hair, and a growth of fair down on his lips and chin. His eyes were open, rolled up, showing the whites, and his face was patched with dust caked with sweat. He wore a cotton shirt and
30 trousers, with sandshoes on his feet. One of the trousers was stuck to his leg with a patch of dark blood.

[…] She bent over and felt his heart. "Wait a minute," she stammered, "wait a minute," and she ran into the house for [...] a pail of water. [...] She dipped a corner of her apron in the water and wiped his face and his hair

35 and his throat, with fingers that trembled. Under the dust and sweat his face gleamed, white as her apron, and thin, and puckered in little lines.

A strange dreadful feeling gripped Millie Evans' [chest]—some seed that had never flourished there, unfolded and struck deep roots and burst into painful leaf. The boy breathed sharply, half choked, his eyelids quivered, and he
40 moved his head from side to side.

[…] "You're better," said Millie, smoothing his hair. "Feeling fine now again, ain't you?" The pain in her [chest] half suffocated her. "It's no good you crying, Millie Evans. You got to keep your head." Quite suddenly he sat up and leaned against the wood pile, away from her, staring on the ground.

45 "There now!" cried Millie Evans, in a strange, shaking voice. The boy turned and looked at her, still not speaking, but his eyes were so full of pain and terror that she had to shut her teeth and clench her hands to stop from crying. After a long pause he said in the little voice of a child talking in his sleep, "I'm hungry." His lips quivered.

50 She scrambled to her feet and stood over him. "You come right into the house and have a sit down meal," she said. "Can you walk?"

"Yes," he whispered, and swaying he followed her across the glaring yard.

---

verandah: *an open-aired porch with a roof*

shamming: *pretending*

LINK

Source 2 is used for the questions on pages 66–103.

Source 3

Facing the Light by Adele Geras

This is an extract from the beginning of a novel. Seven-year-old Rilla is visiting Willow Court, a grand old country house belonging to her family.

She is standing at the window. There's not even a breath of wind to move the white curtains and the grass outside lies dry and flat under the last of the sun. Summertime, and early evening, and she isn't in bed yet. She's nearly eight and it's too soon for sleeping. Everyone is doing something somewhere
5 else and no one is looking. The shadows of trees are black on the lawn and the late roses are edged with gold. There's a piece of silvery water glittering through the weeping willow leaves. That's the lake. Swans swim on the lake and she could go down to the water to see the white birds. No one would know and what you don't know can't hurt you.

10 She has to go, to flee, across the carpet woven with flowers and twisted trees, and then the door opens and she's in the corridor and it's dark there, always, even when the sun is shining outside, and a thick stillness takes up all the space and spreads down the staircase and she moves from step to step on tiptoe so as not to disturb it. Paintings on the walls stare at her as
15 she passes. Still life and landscapes spill strange colours and their own light into the silence and the portraits scream after her and she can't hear them. The marble floor in the hall is like a chess board of black and white and she makes sure to jump the black squares because if you don't, something bad is sure to happen, and maybe she just touched one black square on her way to
20 the garden but that wouldn't count, would it?

Then she's on the grass and the air is soft, and she runs as fast as she can down the steps of the terrace and over the lawn and past all the flowers and between high hedges clipped into cones and balls and spirals until she reaches the wild garden where the plants brush her skirt, and she's running
25 and running to where the swans always are and they've gone. They have floated over to the far bank. She can see them. It's not too far away so she starts walking.

Something catches her eye. It's in the reeds and it's like a dark stain in the water and when she gets a little nearer it looks like a sheet or a cloth and
30 there are waterplants and grey-green willow branches with skinny-finger leaves hiding some of it. If only she can get nearer to where the water meets the bank she can reach in and pull it and see what it is. The water is cool on her hand and there's something that looks like a foot poking out from under the material. Could it be someone swimming? No one swims
35 without moving.

Suddenly there's cold all around her and what she doesn't know won't hurt her but she knows this is wrong. This is bad. She should run and fetch someone but she can't stop her hand from reaching out to the dark cloth that lies on the surface of the lake. She pulls at it and something heavy

40 comes towards her and the time is stretched so long that the moment goes on for ever and ever and there's a face with glassy open eyes and pale greenish skin, and she feels herself starting to scream but no sound comes out and she turns and runs back to the house. Someone must come. Someone must help, and she runs to call them to bring them and she's

45 screaming and no one can hear her. Wet drowned fingers rise up from the lake and stretch out over the grass and up into the house to touch her and she will always feel them, even when she's very old. Now she knows and she can't ever stop knowing.

LINK

Source 3 is used for the questions on pages 66–103.

Paper 1: Sources

Source 4

The Bees by Laline Paull

This story set in a beehive and all the characters are bees. In this extract, the writer describes Flora 717, a worker bee, being born. After a struggle, Flora emerges from her cell and starts to learn about life inside a beehive.

The cell squeezed her and the air was hot [...]. All the joints of her body burned from her frantic twisting against the walls, her head was pressed into her chest and her legs shot with cramp, but her struggles had worked–one wall felt weaker. She kicked out with all her strength and felt something
5   crack and break. She forced and tore and bit until there was a jagged hole into fresher air beyond.

She dragged her body through and fell out onto the floor of an alien world. Static roared through her brain, thunderous vibration shook the ground and a thousand scents dazed her. All she could do was breathe until gradually the
10 vibration and static subsided and the scent evaporated into the air. Her rigid body unlocked and she calmed as knowledge filled her mind.

This was the Arrivals Hall and she was a worker. Her kin was Flora and her number was 717. Certain of her first task, she set about cleaning out her cell. In her violent struggle to hatch she had broken the whole front wall, unlike
15 her neater neighbours. She looked, then followed their example, piling her debris neatly by the ruins. The activity cleared her senses and she felt the vastness of the Arrivals Hall, and how the vibrations in the air changed in different areas.

Row upon row of cells like hers stretched into the distance, and there the
20 cells were quiet but resonant as if the occupants still slept. Immediately around her was great activity with many recently broken and cleared-out chambers, and many more cracking and falling as new bees arrived. The differing scents of her neighbours also came into focus, some sweeter, some sharper, all of them pleasant to absorb.

25 With a hard erratic pulse in the ground, a young female came running down the corridor between the cells, her face frantic.

'Halt!' Harsh voices reverberated from both ends of the corridor and a strong astringent* scent rose in the air. Every bee stopped moving but the young bee stumbled and fell across Flora's pile of debris. Then she clawed her way into the
30 remains of the broken cell and huddled in the corner, her little hands up.

Cloaked in a bitter scent which hid their faces and made them identical, the dark figures strode down the corridor towards Flora. Pushing her aside, they dragged out the weeping young bee. At the sight of their spiked gauntlets, a spasm of fear in Flora's brain released more knowledge.

35 They were police.

'You fled inspection.' One of them pulled at the girl's wings, while another examined the four still-wet membranes. The edge of one was shrivelled.

'Spare me,' she cried. 'I will not fly, I will serve in any other way—' [...]

Before the bee could speak the two officers pressed her head down until
40 there was a sharp crack. She hung limp between them and they dropped her body in the corridor.

'You.' A peculiar rasping voice addressed Flora and she did not know which one spoke, but stared at the black hooks on the backs of their legs. 'Hold still.' Long black callipers* […] measured her height. 'Excessive variation.
45 Abnormal.'

'That will be all, officers.' At the kind voice and fragrant smell, the police released Flora. They bowed to a tall and well-groomed bee with a beautiful face.

'Sister Sage, this one is obscenely ugly.'

50 'And excessively large.'

'It would appear so. Thank you, officers, you may go.'

Sister Sage waited for them to leave. She smiled at Flora.

'To fear them is good. Be still while I read your kin—'

'I am Flora 717.'

55 Sister Sage raised her antennae. 'A sanitation worker who speaks. Most notable …'

Flora stared at her tawny and gold face with its huge dark eyes. 'Am I to be killed?'

---

astringent: *dry and bitter*
callipers: *measuring instrument*

LINK

Source 4 is used for the questions on pages 66–103.

Source 5A

Endings by Petra Swift

> Source 5A is an extract from *Endings* in which Petra Swift describes taking her son to music college in London where he will begin a new stage in his life.

Yet another car steamed past us in the outside lane, throwing rainwater up the sides of our van. It was going to be a long journey from Berwick to London and although it was one we'd done a few times before, we'd usually go by train. But this time was different.

5 We left home at 6.30am with the intention of being in London by midday and so far, all was going well. We'd stopped once for coffee and so far, had encountered no traffic jams. I wished we had, just to put off the moment that lay ahead. In essence, this was a mum-and-son trip with a difference: at the end of the road, I'd drop Robbie, my teenage son, off at the music college

10 that would be his place of study – and home – for the next three years. I'd be returning home without him. I can't say I was thrilled.

We'd visited the college the previous spring before he'd applied. The place itself was little more than ten years old and still looked state-of-the-art. I remember thinking how my amazingly talented no-longer-little boy would

15 thrive there. I pictured him in one of the practice rooms, its lush carpet dampening the sound of the voices and instruments as fresh-faced students found their way through songs, initiating friendships that would hopefully last a lifetime – or at least three years. For that was the whole point of this place; its aim was to bring like-minded kids together and help them find a

20 career in music. Along the way, fun was guaranteed.

The college itself nestles in a busy part of the capital city, a lively, bustling building where a variety of students push confidently through the glass doors and spill out in the nearby high street in search of food, drink and fun. The sober redbrick buildings of my college experience are nowhere to be

25 seen. Instead, a comfortable newness is exuded.

When we visited last year, we met one of the tutors, a laid-back guy who told us his job was to inspire and facilitate the success of the students in his care. The tutors looked less like teachers and more like the kindly, slightly scruffy musicians Robbie spends most of his time with. I knew he'd love this college.

30 It seemed to exude freedom and commitment at the same time. The bright neon college sign promised a world of joy and an excitement that couldn't be had at home.

And yet now, more than a year later as we finally pulled up outside the college and looked around for the accommodation block, it felt less
35 welcoming, as if it was waiting to take away my boy. It was, I knew, a ridiculous and selfish feeling on my part but it was true that this was a bittersweet day. If Robbie was to have a future in music, he needed to be here in the capital at the heart of the country's music scene. It was a big achievement for him to get here and one that made me glow. It was a new
40 beginning. But it was also an ending. The end of childhood and a loosening of the child-parent ties.

It didn't take too long to unload the van, much less to place his few belongings into his new room. Underneath Robbie's teenage bravado there was uncertainty though. We both knew the significance of the day but didn't
45 need to voice it. We'd always had a tacit understanding of such things. A final cup of coffee in a nearby café put off the departure by half an hour. I resisted any foolish shows of emotion. He needed to focus on how exciting things were going to be, not feel guilt or worry for a tearful parent.

Anyway, the much-dreaded moment was over quickly. A quick hug and a
50 few words and then he was off into a new world. As I drove away, a host of memories from years past played through the screen in my head: his first steps, a holiday in Dorset, the time we nearly lost him to pneumonia.

A different road now lay ahead.

LINK

Source 5A is used for the questions on pages 120–167.

Source 5B

A Gentleman's Journal by Finlay Graham

> Source 5B is an extract from *A Gentleman's Journal*, written in 1872 by the Scottish writer Finlay Graham. In it, he describes his old college and the departure of his son, also called Finlay, to study there.

Another unremarkable day, notable only for the departure of Finlay, my youngest and my namesake, to his new place of study in the highlands. Like his four brothers before him, he was always destined to study at my old college, a forbidding stone stepmother that would make him a man. I recall
5   the day I left home as if it were yesterday, like him, a wet-behind-the-ears boy of eight, lugging my leathery old suitcase and heading off to live in that same strange world with strange rules.

The college itself is a sight to behold. It sits in gallant loneliness amongst the cold highlands, as if waiting patiently for those few weeks of the year
10   when the sun shines. Its isolation is part of its charm. Until the real snows come, you can rely on a train once a day to take you to the little station at the end of the line, from which the college is a short journey on foot. As you arrive, the first thing you see is a long, gravelled driveway, invariably wet with rain, that leads you to an imposing but slightly dilapidated
15   entrance way. There was always something frightfully gothic about that view, and the mild terror I felt as entered the building for the first time remains with me even now.

Finlay's new life will challenge him; he is a dear boy, but he has never been what you might call engaging. Of the five brothers, he is the most
20   introverted, keeping his own company and often spending hours in his room, avoiding sport and much preferring reading, which in itself is a fine pursuit, but not one which easily endears you to others. His brothers are more outgoing and – I hesitate to say – more academic. I do fear he will struggle a little against the notable reputations of his brothers, but as a father, you have
25   to accept these things and find joy where you can.

I imagine Finlay will experience the same things as I did at the college: the draughty windows, the meagre* food and the occasional bouts of homesickness. Yet he will also experience the joy of boyish company, the rigour of lessons and the feeling of belonging to a tradition. The college did
30   become a thing of beauty to me over time; it seemed enormous in my first year, but six years later it had become my dominion*, one I was desperately sad to leave behind. Finlay will, like me, learn to resent the summers spent at home, those long days away from his college friends and the busy rooms where true friendships are made.

35 Finlay will be lucky if he experiences the schoolmasters of my youth. [My] teachers were heroic, if that doesn't sound too sentimental. Mr Brownlow was the finest of them. A whirlwind of a man, one for whom life held no fear. But *he* did inspire fear, at least at first. It's true to say that I dreaded his lessons in my first year, his deep, gruff voice echoing across the room as he

40 insisted on publicly humiliating those whose work was less than acceptable.

To look at, old Brownlow seemed insubstantial. Slight, balding and with a face as red as a post box, he would stand at the door as you entered his room. There was no familiar greeting, little warmth and certainly a feeling that you had entered his territory. The start of each lesson was always a

45 quiet affair, until he warmed to his theme. Typically, we would sit silent in our rows, and he'd parade up and down, winding himself up like a Catherine wheel*, sparks beginning to fly as his passion for his subject took hold. He was very much the boss, the expert, the sergeant major and interruptions were not welcome. As I grew older, my fear for him gave way to respect. The

50 fearsome energy was merely an act; he was playing a part and once you'd earned his respect, he allowed you to see his gentle side, which manifested itself in a fascination for insects and a deep love of the highlands.

Heaven knows what old Brownlow would make of Finlay if he taught him. Perhaps he would do the boy good. Although I missed Finlay's departure

55 earlier, I do know that he'll be in safe hands and hope to see a more assured young man when he returns at Christmas.

---

meagre: *not very much*

dominion: *a place where someone has control*

Catherine wheel: *a fast spinning firework*

LINK

Source 5B is used for the questions on pages 120–167.

Paper 2: Sources

Source 6A

Cruellest reality TV show ever by Tanith Carey

The following newspaper article was written by Tanith Carey, a parenting expert, in response to the Channel 4 programme, *Child Genius*.

At the tender age of eight, Tudor has been picked to play soccer for no fewer than three Premier League junior teams: QPR, Tottenham and Chelsea. This achievement alone would be enough to make most fathers' hearts burst with pride. But, unfortunately for Tudor, he appears to have a very long way to go
5 before he meets the sky-high expectations of his demanding dad, Tolu.

So far, the most heart-rending scenes on Channel 4's reality series *Child Genius* – in which 20 children are subjected to a terrifying barrage of tests – have been the sight of this small boy hiding his face in his hands as he weeps. The reason? He has not scored as well as his father tells him he
10 should have done. […] Yet rather than commiserate with his son after a disappointing performance, it is Tolu, who declares that he finds the contest 'emotionally draining'. He then tells Tudor: 'Maybe you're not as good as we thought.' […]

Even for a nation well used to the mercenary* exploitation of spy-on-the-wall
15 television, this has raised concern. As one worried viewer pointed out, the series would more aptly be named 'Pushy Parents'. For it is really all about the Eagle Dads and Tiger Mums, who want to show off how much work they have invested in their youngsters.

The show first aired in its current format last year, and – as the author of
20 a book looking at the damage caused by competitive parenting – I had thought we would not see a return of this toxic* mix of reality TV and hot-housing*. I had expected the sight of children as young as eight crying to prick the conscience of the commissioning editors.

A vain hope, of course. […]

25 *Child Genius* has tapped into an increasingly dangerous trend in parenting; the misguided belief that your offspring is a blank slate and if you hot-house them enough, you can be solely responsible for their success. Parenting is turning into a form of product development. Increasingly, we are falling for the notion that if we cram enough facts into their little brains we can make
30 sure they come out on top. The end result is a rise in depression and anxiety among a generation who believe they are losers if they fail, or could always do better if they win.

Like all offspring of pushy parents, who feel their family's affection is conditional on their success, children like Tudor are not just weeping
35 because they didn't score well. When he tries to cover his tears with his hands, saying 'What I achieved was absolutely terrible', he is facing a much darker fear: That he will lose his father's love if he does not come up to scratch. […]

Of course, the goal of reality TV is to entertain — but should dramatic story-
40 lines really come ahead of a child's emotional well-being?

Perhaps it's a measure of their state of mind that some parents, such as psychologists Shoshana and Sacha, who featured in the first two episodes, saw nothing harmful in describing their approach to bringing up their daughter Aliyah, nine, as though she is 'a well-bred race-horse'. Shoshana
45 openly pities parents left to bring up children without her skill set. She was blissfully oblivious to the fact that the rest of us were watching, slack-jawed in disbelief at how hard she pushes her child. Far from rushing to adopt such techniques, parents have reacted in horror. The internet has been buzzing with viewers saying they found the series 'upsetting to watch',
50 'heartbreaking' and expressing concern […]

No doubt the reality is that Tolu is also a loving father, who sincerely believes he is doing the best for his son, and the producers have edited the programme to make him look like the ultimate caricature of an overbearing father.

55 But for me, one question remains: How much longer are we going to allow Channel 4 to encourage extreme parents to push their helpless children to breaking point in the name of entertainment?

---

mercenary: *money-grabbing*

toxic: *poisonous*

hot-housing: *intensely educating a child*

LINK

Source 6A is used for the questions on pages 120–167.

Source 6B

Children

> The following newspaper article was written in the 19th century. It offers views on how to raise children.

It is a mistake to think that children love the parents less who maintain a proper authority over them. On the contrary, they respect them more. It is a cruel and unnatural selfishness that indulges children in a foolish and hurtful way. Parents are guides and counsellors to their children. As a guide

5 in a foreign land, they undertake to pilot them safely through the shoals and quicksands of inexperience. If the guide allows his followers all the freedom they please; if, because they dislike the constraint of the narrow path of safety, he allows them to stray into holes and precipices* that destroy them, to quench their thirst in brooks that poison them, to loiter in woods full of

10 wild beasts or deadly herbs, can he be called a sure guide?

And is it not the same with our children? They are as yet only in the preface, or as it were, in the first chapter of the book of life. We have nearly finished it, or are far advanced. We must open the pages for these younger minds.

If children see that their parents act from principle – that they do not find

15 fault without reason – that they do not punish because personal offence is taken, but because the thing in itself is wrong – if they see that while they are resolutely but affectionately refused what is not good for them, there is a willingness to oblige them in all innocent matters – they will soon appreciate such conduct. If no attention is paid to the rational wishes – if no

20 allowance is made for youthful spirits – if they are dealt with in a hard and unsympathising manner – the proud spirit will rebel, and the meek spirit be broken. […]

A pert or improper way of speaking ought never to be allowed. Clever children are very apt to be pert, and if too much admired for it, and laughed

25 at, become eccentric and disagreeable. It is often very difficult to check our own amusement, but their future welfare should be regarded more than our present entertainment. It should never be forgotten that they are tender plants committed to our fostering care, that every thoughtless word or careless neglect may destroy a germ of immortality*.

---

precipices: *steep, dangerous places*
immortality: *living forever*

LINK

Source 6B is used for the questions on pages 120–167.

Source 7A

The future is here by Hannah Hussein

This extract is about how children use technology for entertainment.

In 1972 we didn't have computers. Well, they had them in London probably, but we certainly never had them when I was a kid in Bradford. A bike? Yes. A football? Yes. A computer? Definitely not. I love all things technological now, but I'm not sure I would have liked to grow up surrounded by phones, tablets
5 and laptops. And definitely not social media. I'm never off it these days, but I think it's a difficult world for teenagers to negotiate. That's why I was initially reluctant for my daughter to get a phone.

Gradually, of course, Basma wore me down. Kids are good at that. If you could see our house right now, you'd see a plethora* of technology. Phones
10 plugged in to chargers, an expensive computer sitting on my antique desk, a tablet lying on the floor just waiting to be stood on. Very much like the houses of our friends, no doubt – technologically and materially rich but time-poor. We've got a doorbell that means I can see who's outside, even when I'm miles from home. I've got the ability to make a Hollywood
15 quality movie on my phone. I've got a state-of-the-art recording studio on my computer. I can switch the heating on from work. And as is typical, my daughter can work all of these tools much faster and better than me.

Basma is currently in that funny teen phase now, but when I look back at her childhood, I view it with a mixture of fondness *and* horror. Nappies
20 and CBeebies I could do without, but the anarchy, creativity and general stupidity of having a toddler in the house is brilliant. Well, to a point.

The magic of snow delighted Basma. Making snowdogs, sledging, snow angels … I'm not sure how I kept up to be honest. It was always her play that fascinated me. She was always creative, making robots out of toilet rolls,
25 building a plasticine house for the hamster, and trying to dig a well in the back garden. She did it with a knowing smirk, reserving her most energy-sapping efforts until I'd just sat down after a hard day at work.

Somewhere along the line though, plasticine gave way to gaming and drawing became Tiktok. Basma still plays, but the games she plays are not
30 in the family home, they're somewhere in the digital ether. It's a world I'm no longer required to be part of, the messaging and memes out of reach. The screen of her phone is also out of my reach, often tilted away from my view, and hidden behind a passcode. I'm still not sure what I think about children, parents and privacy.

35 Everyone thinks their childhood was better than their own kids. Less technologically advanced, but more creative. Outdoors rather than indoors. Yet when I really think about it, I reckon the children of this generation have got much to celebrate. Technology has made them communicate, albeit in a different way. Social media is primarily about feelings. And Basma
40 is fantastic at reading people. She knows how to challenge, comfort and entertain.

My daughter's digital teen years are mainly good ones. At the swipe of a screen, she finds a recipe for the occasional family meals she makes, she learns how to do CPR* (let's hope I'm not the first recipient of her new-found
45 skills) and also engages with the issues I want her to know about: global poverty, justice and equality. Most profoundly, the thing her childhood has taught her most is to love. Basma is a carer. She cares for people, animals and anything that exists.

A friend of mine has recently become an older mother. She loves it, but I can
50 see the tell-tale weariness in her eyes. The lack of sleep, the nappies, the sheer graft of parenthood. Part of me would like to be building snowdogs again in a carefree past, but would I really swap the precocious, maddening, self-absorbed, yet deeply caring fourteen-year-old daughter of now for the four-year-old of the past? No chance.

---

plethora: *a very large amount of something*

CPR: *cardiopulmonary resuscitation (a lifesaving technique)*

LINK

Source 7A is used for the questions on pages 120–167.

Source 7B

***Acrobats* by Albert Smith**

> This extract was written in the 19th century and is about children playing in the streets of Victorian London.

As you pass through one of those […] narrow dirty streets […] you will be struck, above all things, by the swarms of children everywhere collected. They scuffle about, and run across your path, and disappear, like rabbits in a warren, in obscure holes. They wait on the kerb until a cab approaches,

5 and run under the very knees of the horse. They collect round the open water plug, and spend the entire day there, all returning wet through to the skin. […]

[…] You occasionally see a girl of seven or eight years staggering under the weight of a baby whose sole nurse she is; but seldom find them with

10 brothers and sisters. They are only acquaintances. Their parents live huddled up in dirty single rooms, […] they turn their children out to find means of amusement and subsistence, at the same time, in the streets.

Of all their favourite haunts, there is not one more popular than the bit of open ground where a mass of houses have been pulled down to make room

15 for a new street or building. If they find an old beam of timber, so much the better. They turn it into a see-saw, and, this accomplished, a policeman is the only power that can drive them from the spot. They build forts […]. They scuffle the mounds of rubbish perfectly smooth by running, or being dragged up and down them; they make huts; and know of nothing in the world

20 capable of affording such delight, except it be the laying down, or taking up, of some wooden pavement.

Picture such a bit of ground, on a fine afternoon, alive with children. Amongst the revellers there is a boy, who for the last five minutes has been hanging by his legs to a bit of temporary railing, with his hair sweeping the

25 ground. Others would have had a fit long before, but this appears to be his natural position. On quitting it, without caring for the empty applause of the crowd, he goes to a retired corner of the plot, and, gravely putting his head and hands upon the ground, at a short distance from the wall, turns his heels up in the air, until he touches the house with his feet. This accomplished,

30 he […] claps his shoeless soles together […] and then calmly resumes his normal position, and walks away, not caring whether anybody regards him or not.

This boy is destined to become an Acrobat – at a more advanced period of his life to perform feats of suppleness and agility in the mud of the streets,

35 the sawdust of the circus, or the turf of a race-course. His life will pass in a marvellous series of positions, and its ordinary level course will be unknown to him. He will look upon chairs as articles of furniture only used to support people with the crown of their heads on the top back rail, or their legs on the seats of two stretched out to the utmost extent allowed by their length.

40 Ladders, with him, will in future only be ascended by twisting in and out the rounds like a serpent. […]

The Acrobats are generally seen in London after the racing season, or when the metropolis lies in their way from one course to another. Some go to the sea-side […] Others join travelling companies […] who go from town

45 to town […] When the pantomimes begin, the Acrobats find a new field for employment. […] They do not, however, always have the good fortune to appear as principals. […] It is not until the stage-manager at rehearsal wants some daring spirit to tumble from the sky-borders on to the stage; to go round on the sails of a windmill amidst fireworks; or to be knocked through a

50 door, or out of a window, or down a trap, that a pale man, in an old coat that you have seen before, steps forward from the crowd at the wings, and says that he will undertake it, and that he can do any tumbling business required, for he is an Acrobat.

LINK

Source 7B is used for the questions on pages 120–167.

Source 8A

The Cruelest Journey by Kira Salak

This extract is about writer and adventurer Kira Salak, at the beginning of her 600-mile journey travelling solo in a kayak from Old Segou in Mali to Timbuktu. She follows the same route taken along the River Niger by the 19th century explorer, Mungo Park.

Torrential rains. Waves higher than my kayak, trying to capsize me. But my boat is self-bailing and I stay afloat. The wind drives the current in reverse, tearing and ripping at the shores, sending spray into my face. I paddle madly, crashing and driving forward. I travel inch by inch, or so it seems, arm
5 muscles smarting and rebelling against this journey.

A popping feeling now and a screech of pain. My right arm lurches from a ripped muscle. But this is no time and place for such an injury, and I won't tolerate it, stuck as I am in a storm. I try to get used to the metronome*-like pulses of pain as I fight the river. There is only one direction to go: forward.

10 I wonder what we look for when we embark on these kinds of trips. There is the pat answer that you tell the people you don't know: that you're interested in seeing a place, learning about its people. But then the trip begins and the hardship comes, and hardship is more honest: it tells us that we don't have enough patience yet, nor humility, nor gratitude. And
15 we thought that we had. Hardship brings us closer to truth, and thus is more difficult to bear, but from it alone comes compassion. And so I already discover one important reason why I'm here on this river, and I've told the world that it can do what it wants with me if only, by the end, I have learned something further. A bargain, then. The journey, my teacher.

20 And where is the river of just this morning, with its whitecaps that would have liked to drown me, with its current flowing backwards against the wind? Gone to this: a river of smoothest glass, a placidity unbroken by wave or eddy, with islands of lush greenery awaiting me like distant Xanadus*.

I know there is no turning back now. The journey to Timbuktu binds me. It
25 deceives me with images of the end, reached at long last. The late afternoon sun settles complacently over the hills to the west. Paddling becomes a sort of meditation now, a gentle trespassing over a river that slumbers. The Niger gives me its beauty almost in apology for the violence of the earlier storms, and I'm treated to the peace and silence of this wide river, the sun on me, a
30 breeze licking my toes when I lay back to rest, the current as negligible as a faint breath.

Somono fishermen, casting out their nets, puzzle over me as I float by.

"*Ça va, madame?*" they yell.

Each fisherman carries a young son perched in the back of his pointed canoe
35 to do the paddling. The boys stare at me, transfixed; they have never seen
such a thing. A white woman. Alone. In a red, inflatable boat. Using a two-
sided paddle.

I'm an even greater novelty because Malian women don't paddle here, not
ever. It is a man's job. So there is no good explanation for me, and the people
40 want to understand. They gather on the shore in front of their villages to
watch me pass, the kids screaming and jumping in excitement, the adults
yelling out questions in Bambarra which by now I know to mean: "Where
did you come from? Where's your husband?" And of course they will always
ask: "Where are you going?" "Timbuktu!" I yell out to the last question and
45 paddle on.

---

metronome: *a device that measures time with regular ticks*

Xanadus: *a beautiful and magnificent place*

LINK

Source 8A is used for the
questions on pages 120–167.

Paper 2: Sources

Source 8B

On Sledge and Horseback to Outcast Siberian Lepers
by Kate Marsden

Kate Marsden was a British missionary and explorer in the 19th century, who set out on an expedition to Siberia to try to find a cure for leprosy. This extract is about her journey through mosquito-infested marshes and forests.

On again for a few more miles; but I began to feel the effects of this sort of travelling – in a word, I felt utterly worn out. It was as much as I could do to hold on to the horse, and I nearly tumbled off several times in the effort. The cramp in my body and lower limbs was indescribable, and I had to discard
5   the cushion under me, because it became soaked through and through with the rain, and rode on the broad, bare, wooden saddle. What feelings of relief arose when the time of rest came, and the pitching of tents, and the brewing of tea! Often I slept quite soundly till morning, awaking to find that the mosquitoes had been hard at work in my slumbers, in spite of veil and
10 gloves, leaving great itching lumps, that turned me sick. Once we saw two calves that had died from exhaustion from the bites of these pests, and the white hair of our poor horses was generally covered with clots of blood, due partly to mosquitoes and partly to prodigious horse-flies. But those lepers – they suffered far more than I suffered, and that was the one thought, added
15 to the strength that God supplied, that kept me from collapsing entirely …

My second thunderstorm was far worse than the first. The forest seemed on fire, and the rain dashed in our faces with almost blinding force. My horse plunged and reared, flew first to one side, and then to the other, dragging me amongst bushes and trees, so that I was in danger of being caught by
20 the branches and hurled to the ground. After this storm one of the horses, carrying stores and other things, sank into a bog nearly to its neck; and the help of all the men was required to get it out …

Soon after the storm we were camping and drinking tea, when I noticed that all the men were eagerly talking together and gesticulating*. I asked
25 what it all meant, and was told that a large bear was supposed to be in the neighbourhood, according to a report from a post-station close at hand. There was a general priming of firearms, except in my case, for I did not know how to use my revolver, so thought I had better pass it on to someone else, lest I might shoot a man in mistake for a bear. We mounted again and went
30 on. The usual chattering was exchanged for a dead silence, this being our first bear experience; but we grew wiser as we proceeded, and substituted noise for silence. We hurried on, as fast as possible, to get through the miles of forests and bogs. I found it best not to look about me, because, when I

did so, every large stump of a fallen tree took the shape of a bear. When my
35 horse stumbled over the roots of a tree, or shied at some object unseen by
me, my heart began to gallop.

---

gesticulating: *using gestures to communicate*

LINK

Source 8B is used for the
questions on pages 120–167.

Assessment Objectives

The Assessment Objectives are the skills that underpin all qualifications. The AQA GCSE English Language written exam papers are testing six assessment objectives (AOs), as follows:

Assessment Objectives	
AO1	• Identify and interpret explicit and implicit information and ideas • Select and synthesise evidence from different texts
AO2	Explain, comment on and analyse how writers use language and structure to achieve effects and influence readers, using relevant subject terminology to support their views
AO3	Compare writers' ideas and perspectives, as well as how these are conveyed, across two or more texts
AO4	Evaluate texts critically and support this with appropriate textual references
AO5	Communicate clearly, effectively and imaginatively, selecting and adapting tone, style and register for different forms, purposes and audiences. Organise information and ideas, using structural and grammatical features to support coherence and cohesion of texts
AO6	Use a range of vocabulary and sentence structures for clarity, purpose and effect, with accurate spelling and punctuation.

OXFORD
UNIVERSITY PRESS

Great Clarendon Street, Oxford, OX2 6DP, United Kingdom

Oxford University Press is a department of the University of Oxford. It furthers the University's objective of excellence in research, scholarship, and education by publishing worldwide. Oxford is a registered trade mark of Oxford University Press in the UK and in certain other countries.

© Oxford University Press 2024

Written by Steve Eddy, Graham Elsdon, and Jennifer Webb

Series Editor: Jennifer Webb

The moral rights of the authors have been asserted

First published in 2024

British Library Cataloguing in Publication Data
Data available

978-1-382-03980-2

10 9 8 7 6 5 4 3 2 1

The manufacturing process conforms to the environmental regulations of the country of origin.

Printed in the UK by Bell and Bain Ltd, Glasgow.

Acknowledgements
The publisher would like to thank the following for permissions to use copyright material:

Monica Ali: Brick Lane (Doubleday, 2003), copyright © Monica Ali 2003, reprinted by permission of The Random House Group Ltd, Penguin Random House UK.

Gavin Bell: 'Through the Pyrenees on the Little Yellow Train', Daily Telegraph, 28 March 2016, copyright © Telegraph Media Group Ltd 2016, used by permission of TMG.

Charlie Brooker: 'Apple's software updates are like changing water in a fish tank: I'd rather let the fish die', The Guardian, 22 Sept 2014, copyright © Guardian News & Media Ltd 2014, reprinted by permission of GNM Ltd.

Tanith Carey: 'Cruellest reality TV show ever', Daily Mail, 3 Aug 2014, copyright © Daily Mail 2014, reprinted by permission of the author and Solo Syndication for the Daily Mail.

Rose George: 'The hunter who killed Cecil the lion doesn't deserve our empathy', The Guardian, 29 July 2015, copyright © Guardian News & Media Ltd 2015, reprinted by permission of GNM Ltd.

Adèle Geras: Facing the Light (Orion, 2013), copyright © Adèle Geras 2003, used by permission of Peters Fraser & Dunlop (www.petersfraserdunlop.com) on behalf of Adèle Geras (Loose Ships Ltd).

Patricia Highsmith: 'The Snail Watcher' from Eleven (Bloomsbury, 2007), copyright © Patricia Highsmith 1970, reprinted by permission of Diogenes Verlag AG.

Rachel Joyce: The Unlikely Pilgrimage of Harold Fry (Black Swan, 2013), copyright © Rachel Joyce 2012, reprinted by permission of The Random House Group Ltd, Penguin Random House UK.

Hari Kunzru: Transmission (Hamish Hamilton, 2004), copyright © Hari Kunzru 2004, reprinted by permission of Penguin Books Ltd, Penguin Random House UK.

Alan Paton: Alan Paton: 'The Waste Land' in Tales from a Troubled Land (Scribners, 1961, 2003), copyright © Alan Paton 1961, reprinted by permission of the Ewing Trust Company

Laline Paull: The Bees (Fourth Estate 2015), copyright © Laline Paull 2014, used by permission of HarperCollins Publishers Ltd.

John Steinbeck: Grapes of Wrath (Penguin, 1976), copyright © John Steinbeck 1939, copyright renewed 1976 by Elaine Steinbeck, Thom Steinbeck and John Steinbeck IV reprinted by permission of Penguin Books Ltd, Penguin Random House UK

Photos: p106: Parikh Mahendra N / Shutterstock; **p108**: Marco Rubino / Shutterstock; **p110**: Shelli Jensen / Shutterstock; **p115**: ESB Professional / Shutterstock; **p116**: Prostock-studio / Shutterstock; **p117**: m.mphoto / Shutterstock.

The publisher would also like to thank Helen Backhouse and Adam Robbins for sharing their expertise and feedback in the development of this resource.

Although we have made every effort to trace and contact all copyright holders before publication, this has not been possible in all cases. If notified, the publisher will rectify any errors or omissions at the earliest opportunity.

Links to third party websites are provided by Oxford in good faith and for information only. Oxford disclaims any responsibility for the materials contained in any third party website referenced in this work.